GUARDIAN OF
THE PRESIDENCY

GUARDIAN OF THE PRESIDENCY

THE LEGACY OF RICHARD E. NEUSTADT

MATTHEW J. DICKINSON

ELIZABETH A. NEUSTADT

EDITORS

BROOKINGS INSTITUTION PRESS
Washington, D.C.

Copyright © 2007
THE BROOKINGS INSTITUTION
1775 Massachusetts Avenue, N.W., Washington, D.C. 20036
www.brookings.edu

Library of Congress Cataloging-in-Publication data

Guardian of the presidency : the legacy of Richard E. Neustadt / Matthew J. Dickinson and Elizabeth A. Neustadt, editors.
   p.   cm.
   Summary: "Richard Neustadt's former colleagues and students celebrate the rich and diverse contributions he made to political and academic life in the United States and beyond"—Provided by publisher.
   Includes bibliographical references and index.
   ISBN-13: 978-0-8157-1842-0 (cloth : alk. paper)
   ISBN-10: 0-8157-1842-X (cloth : alk. paper)
  1. Neustadt, Richard E. 2. Political scientists—United States—Biography. 3. Harvard University—Faculty—Biography. 4. Political consultants—United States—Biography. I. Dickinson, Matthew J. II. Neustadt, Elizabeth A. III. Title.
   JC251.N48G83 2007
   320.092—dc22
                                       2007023888

9 8 7 6 5 4 3 2 1

The paper used in this publication meets minimum requirements of the American National Standard for Information Sciences—Permanence of Paper for Printed Library Materials: ANSI Z39.48-1992.

Jacket photograph: Richard Neustadt, Boston, July 15, 1993
Photograph Richard Avedon
© 1993 The Richard Avedon Foundation

Typeset in Adobe Caslon

Composition by Cynthia Stock
Silver Spring, Maryland

Printed by R. R. Donnelley
Harrisonburg, Virginia

For those who strive to keep alive
the nobility and fun of politics

Contents

FOREWORD

DORIS KEARNS GOODWIN

WHEN I WAS asked to write a foreword to this book, which brings to life a truly remarkable man, I was thrilled. For nearly forty years, from the spring of 1965, when he came to Harvard University while I was in my first year of graduate study, until his untimely death in 2003, Richard E. Neustadt played a central role in my life—as my teacher, mentor, and finally my friend. His friendship remains one of the most cherished memories of my life.

Each of these chapters reveals a different aspect of the work of this gifted man who reached the top in an unusually wide range of fields—as a public servant, a professor, an institution builder, and a writer whose scholarship will last for generations. These pages also show, however, the astonishing range of close relationships that Neustadt developed with his colleagues and his students, winning our lasting affection through his generosity of spirit, his contagious laughter, his unquenchable interest in our work, and his exceptional faculty for bringing out the best in all of us.

Harvey Fineberg writes of Neustadt's "abiding respect for the views of others regardless of their status or station." Graham Allison recalls his mentor's uncanny ability to let his colleagues take credit for his achievements.

"Never before had any reader been so helpful" in critiquing a manuscript, Charles Jones writes, "and only one since: him." Jonathan Alter remembers the lavish time and colorful stories his former teacher willingly shared with him when he embarked on his recent book about Franklin Roosevelt. Matt Dickinson suggests that the integrity of Neustadt's character and his ability to walk between the two worlds of politics and academia "enriched everyone, from President to student, who had the great fortune to know Dick."

As I read Ernest May's analysis of the "molding events" in Neustadt's "many-sided" life—the flu epidemic in 1918, the Great Depression, Pearl Harbor, his role on Truman's White House staff, his work with John Kennedy—I realized more than I had before the extent of Neustadt's involvement in a number of the "molding experiences" that have shaped my own journey through the worlds of academia, government, and writing.

As a teaching assistant in Neustadt's celebrated course on the Presidency in 1966, I caught an invaluable firsthand glimpse of the qualities that make a great teacher: the careful preparation that went into each one of his lectures, his subtle blend of penetrating analysis with spirited human anecdotes, his infectious enthusiasm for his subject, and, above all, his ability to weave his own experience into his scholarly points so that the figures he described became flesh and blood to his enraptured students.

I can still see him as he stood on the stage of Harvard Hall delivering his lectures. As Anthony King so vividly describes, "He spoke very . . . very . . . very slowly," with long pauses between his sentences, which gave the impression that he was still thinking about what he was saying, allowing us to believe that if we listened carefully enough we would not simply be passive recipients of his knowledge; we might magically enter his mind and begin to replicate his manner of thinking!

Nor will I forget the many evenings at the Neustadt house on Traill Street where his wife, Bert, fed us better than we could possibly eat anywhere else as graduate students. The give and take of the dinner discussions never ceased to amaze me. One moment, we were listening to Neustadt's stories about President Truman. The next moment, he was listening to our stories of the classroom discussions that followed his lectures. Sometimes he would start the conversation with a question. "Do the times make the man or does the man make the times?" He was the star but he made us feel that we were educating him. And always there were lively arguments about present-day politics. These dinners, occasionally followed by games of charades in the living room, mitigated the loneliness that graduate students commonly feel and gave us a feeling that we had found a second home.

While I was Neustadt's teaching assistant, he encouraged me to take a White House Fellowship, even though it meant postponing my dissertation. Knowing how much his own service in the Truman White House had contributed to his scholarship, he was anxious for his graduate students to have an opportunity to experience the practice of governing firsthand. I ended up working directly for President Johnson and then accompanied him to his ranch to help him on his memoirs during the last years of his life. In the vulnerable state in which the President found himself during his retirement, he opened up to me in ways he never would have had I known him only at the height of his power, sharing his fears, his sorrows, and his worries about how history would remember him. Indeed, the older I've become, the more I realize what a privilege it was to have spent so many hours with this aging lion of a man—a privilege that fired within me the drive to penetrate the inner persons beneath the public figures that I have tried to bring to each of my books since then.

When I returned to Harvard in 1969 after my White House Fellowship, Neustadt proposed that I take over his Presidency course while he was in the process of creating the Kennedy School of Government. It was a terrifying prospect to follow in his footsteps, knowing how legendary his course had become, but he shared his notes, his insights, and, most important, his confidence that I could do it. Under his guidance, the course became for me a labor of love. The case studies he had devised—Truman's attempted steel seizure and his firing of General MacArthur, Kennedy and the Bay of Pigs and the Cuban missile crisis, Johnson and the passage of the Voting Rights Act—gave the students a firsthand look at the decision-making process inside the White House, offering such rich portraits of the Presidents and their cabinet officials that it seemed as if the events were taking place at that very moment.

After I had taught the Presidency course for several years, Neustadt loved to tell the story of walking behind two undergraduates crossing Harvard Yard. They were comparing notes about their classes. "I'm taking Doris Kearns's course on the Presidency," he heard the first student say. "Didn't that used to be taught by Richard Neustadt?" his companion asked. "Yeah, I think so," replied the first. "Whatever happened to him?" The other student shrugged and said, "I dunno. I think he died!" It was so typical of this great-hearted man that he relished telling this tale that put his protégée in the spotlight at his own lighthearted expense.

His self-deprecatory humor was part of his charm. I can still hear his laughter when he told of attending a White House reception with Bert during Johnson's Presidency. As all of us who knew Bert can testify, she was a stunning woman—a Katherine Hepburn look-alike with high cheekbones and a perfect figure. Standing just in front of Dick on the receiving line, Bert reached the President first. Not surprisingly, Johnson was so smitten by her looks and her easy smile that he engaged her in conversation for a full five minutes before he noticed that the line had come to a dead halt. When Dick's turn finally came to shake the President's hand, Johnson smiled, looked back at Bert and over to Lady Bird, and said: "I see that we both married above our station."

While I was writing my first book on Lyndon Johnson, my father died of a sudden heart attack. My mother had died when I was fifteen. Bert and Dick insisted that I spend a good part of that summer with them on Cape Cod. What better place not only to heal but to watch a master craftsman at work as he played with every sentence and every paragraph, seeking, as Beth Neustadt writes, "a particular rhythm for each sentence," probing for "just the right phrase." Under his guidance, I came to understand that the key to reaching a larger audience lay in developing a narrative style, complete with rich details and colorful anecdotes. I dedicated that first book to my parents and to Bert and Dick Neustadt.

Neustadt's classic work, *Presidential Power*, became a bible for me as I set out to become a presidential biographer. As Graham Allison observes, this original study established Neustadt as "the most penetrating analyst of power since Machiavelli," and profoundly influenced the way generations of scholars would write and think about the Presidency. With each new subject, I returned to the book, each time gaining fresh insights that I had missed in my earlier readings.

Of even greater value, however, were the long conversations with Dick as I followed my study of Lyndon Johnson with studies of Franklin Roosevelt and Abraham Lincoln. How he loved to talk about Franklin Roosevelt, who was, as Jonathan Alter correctly observes, "the gold standard for him," a natural politician blessed with profound self-confidence and a remarkable capacity to transmit his cheerful strength to others.

Labor Secretary Francis Perkins claimed that Roosevelt's "capacity to inspire and encourage those who had to do tough, confused and practically impossible jobs was beyond dispute." Like everyone else, she said, she "came away from an interview with the President feeling better, not because he had solved my problem . . . but because he had made me feel more cheerful, stronger, more determined."[1]

The same could be said of Richard E. Neustadt. I can still recall the enthusiasm with which he greeted my decision to study Franklin and Eleanor Roosevelt and the home front during World War II. To my worry that so many books had been written about the Roosevelts, he countered with the observation that this was because they were worthy of so many books. Besides, he said, "This project will consume several years of your life. Who would you rather wake up with in the morning and think about when you go to bed at night? Franklin Roosevelt or Millard Fillmore?" A terrific question, for as it turned out, my study of the Roosevelts and the war years took longer to write than the war took to be fought. A similar discussion preceded my decision to study Abraham Lincoln. Once again Neustadt encouraged me to think big, expressing confidence that somehow I would find my own way into this historic figure.

To this day, I still experience occasional nightmares in which I am heading into a final examination totally unprepared. For some unknown reason, I have failed to attend any of the classes and have done none of the reading. I know many others share some variant of this dream. Beyond this familiar dream, however, I am periodically visited by another, more peculiar, dream in which I am seated in a chair faced by a panel of all the Presidents I have studied. A large audience has gathered. Each President takes his turn, outlining everything I got wrong in my understanding of him, his inner circle, and his era. But when I wake I take comfort in the thought that if such a panel were to be assembled, the moderator would be none other than Richard E. Neustadt, "the guardian of the Presidency." And while he would acknowledge where my interpretations had gone wrong, he would, given his sympathetic and generous spirit, be sure to tell the panel and the audience everything I had gotten right. And that would be the only message I would need to hear!

PREFACE

THE IDEA FOR *Guardian of the Presidency: The Legacy of Richard E. Neustadt* first emerged in conversation among members of an informal advisory group that Dick Neustadt's daughter, Beth, convened shortly after his death on October 31, 2003. He had been candid with her concerning his plans for his estate, but his sudden death left her feeling less than wholly prepared for decisions that might arise regarding matters that they had not yet discussed. In particular, Beth learned only after her father's death that she was now his literary executor. (This meant, among other tasks, finding a home for the extensive library Neustadt had collected at his Cape Cod house. It is now part of the Scripps Library and Multimedia Archive at the University of Virginia's Miller Center of Public Affairs.)

In addition to her stepmother, the British politician Shirley Williams, Beth approached two of Dick and Shirley's longtime friends, both of whom had also been her father's colleagues: Professor Anthony King, of the University of Essex, and Professor Ernest May, of Harvard University's Kennedy School of Government. Beth also approached Charles O. Jones of the University of Wisconsin–Madison and a nonresident senior fellow at Brookings, with whom her father had more recently become acquainted.

Beth had never met Chuck Jones, but his piece "Richard E. Neustadt: Public Servant as Scholar," published in 2003 in the *Annual Review of Political Science,* had made an indelible impression on her, particularly because of the response it elicited in her father: Dick had sat her down to read it at the first opportunity, while—entirely uncharacteristically—he crowed with pleasure about feeling so well understood. Beth was seeking advisers who could help her to determine what her father would have wanted done about whatever matters might now arise. Given her father's response to this piece, it felt natural to include its author as one of these advisers. All generously agreed to help.

Over the next several months, among the issues that emerged was whether—and how—to commemorate Dick's legacy. Shirley was the first to moot the idea of a biography. The notion of capturing memories of Dick Neustadt while they were still relatively fresh and while contemporaries of his were still accessible was, of course, appealing. However, Beth found the prospect of a biography of her father daunting. It struck her that her mother or brother would have been better suited to pursuing such a project than she (the family rebel), since both had been more attentive to the specifics of her father's career. But they had both predeceased him; the thought of trying to do justice to a book about him without their input made Beth feel all the more bereft. Then Tony King offered a characteristically incisive observation. The challenge of such a book, in his view, was that, whereas biographies normally track an individual's ascent up a mountain peak, Dick Neustadt's career was more accurately characterized as a small mountain range, with numerous peaks representing different roles, some climbed sequentially and others simultaneously. Tony's assessment made the biographical task conceptually manageable and provided the framework for the present volume, which focuses on Dick Neustadt as an adult, at work, in a variety of professional roles.

Matt Dickinson and Beth had met only briefly during her father's lifetime. While a Ph.D. candidate in Harvard's Government Department, Matt was serving in 1986 as the head teaching fellow the final time Dick taught his celebrated lecture course on the American Presidency. Subsequently, Dick agreed to chair Matt's doctoral dissertation committee, and, when Matt, as a newly minted Ph.D., returned as a professor in the Harvard Government Department in 1993, Dick agreed to come out of retirement to co-teach with him a graduate-level seminar on the Presidency. As with so many of Dick's students and colleagues, these experiences left an indelible imprint on Matt both professionally and personally.

After Dick's death, Matt sent a condolence note to Beth at her home in London, in which he offered a moving account of a visit the two men had had just three weeks earlier at her father's cottage on Cape Cod—a hideaway overlooking one of Wellfleet's large freshwater ponds. There, on Gull Pond, the two men had met to discuss Matt's proposal for a book that would examine Dick Neustadt's impact on the study of the Presidency. Matt wanted Dick to write the book's final chapter, which would serve, in effect, as a retrospective on his life's work. Although excited by the prospect, Dick, ever the realist (and by now eighty-four), refrained from committing himself to producing such a chapter until he had walked Matt through the likely writing and production schedule in careful detail. As Dick explained, because this final chapter could only be crafted in response to the others, he—although currently healthy—just might not be around to accomplish that task. Five days after their meeting, Dick boarded a long-haul flight to London for what proved to be the last time.

The following summer, by arrangement, Matt, his wife, Alison, and their two sons, Seth and Ethan, traveled to Wellfleet to meet Beth and her daughter, Rachel, at the cottage. Supervised by Alison, the three children made their way across the three-quarter-mile expanse of Gull Pond and through the sluiceway to Higgins Pond in Dick's red canoe—a journey that canoe practically knew by heart. In the cottage, Beth and Matt settled into two of the four rocking chairs that encircled the fireplace, and talked and talked. Rooted in a shared loss, a cross-family friendship began to take hold; later, when the prospect of a book about Dick Neustadt emerged, this friendship expanded to include an editorial partnership.

Because Beth lives in London and Matt in Vermont, they conducted joint editorial efforts almost entirely via transatlantic e-mail. Matt thinks their perspectives and styles are complementary and meshed together fortuitously well. Beth thinks his patience and innate kindness, at times when her angst over deadlines got the better of her, also were key, and were all the more impressive, given that, during this period of collaboration, Matt's own father, Henry Dickinson, died, and along with mourning that loss, Matt was left shouldering the brunt of the task of sorting out his father's estate.

In addition to coediting this volume, Matt wrote one of the chapters. He used this double contribution as leverage in his gentle but persistent and eventually successful campaign to persuade Beth to offer a personal contribution of her own. The primary task of this book is to examine Dick Neustadt in his professional roles; Beth's Afterword offers a personal perspective, aimed at shedding some light on what went on backstage as her father carried out these roles.

Richard E. Neustadt died at home in the picturesque village of Furneux Pelham, in Hertfordshire, in the early afternoon of Friday, October 31, 2003. On the previous Sunday, while rearranging boxes of books, he slipped and became immobilized with severe back pain. He was assisted to bed, where, over the next several days, first a locum and then the local general practitioner attended him. They confirmed recurrence of sciatica and prescribed medication for the pain. As Dick drifted into unconsciousness, the local GP decided to call a consultant physician to the patient's bedside for a second opinion. The consultant physician arrived twenty minutes after Dick had succumbed. The cause of death was recorded as pneumonia. Dick himself would have thought this a better way to go than most.

Having passed his eighty-fourth birthday, he had lived almost twenty-five years longer than he expected; more than once he'd observed that none of the men in his direct line had lived beyond sixty, and he regarded these extra years as "gravy" (though he made less light of this family statistic after his only son, Rick, died at forty-seven). Dick did not survive to receive an honorary degree from Harvard, but did live long enough to learn that he'd been chosen to receive it, a surprise and particular delight to him, since he understood well how unusual it was for the university to bestow this honor on one of its own. And, thanks to Larry Summers's willingness to break with Harvard convention—a predilection for which that Harvard president has more often been criticized than praised—by giving voice to unorthodox views or, in this case, by releasing traditionally embargoed information, he made the university's intention to recognize and honor Dick Neustadt known to the public at the Harvard memorial service for him in April 2004.

Our contributors offer portrayals of Dick Neustadt at different times of his life and from different professional perspectives. Inevitably, each chapter reflects its writer as well as the subject—in each instance, Richard E. Neustadt refracted through the lens of the respective viewer. As these authors can attest, this book was not conceived as a festschrift; we enjoined them to eschew creating the halo effect that often surrounds such accounts of individuals by those who knew them personally. Rather, our hope, as editors, is that these glimpses through the writers' lenses of Dick Neustadt's various professional roles will, collectively, provide insights about how this purposeful and intellectually ambitious yet personally unassuming man went about his work. These insights are intended to be of use particularly to those who seek to carry on with this work.

The first editorial task was to determine, with input from the advisory group, what roles the volume would treat, and then to invite and secure chapter authors. The contributors to this volume include three members of the original advisory group—Ernest R. May, Charles O. Jones, and Anthony S. King. Shirley Williams decided that despite her professional association with Dick, their relationship was ultimately too personal for her to write about it here. Her decision may well have been influenced by discussions between the two of them, particularly in what proved to be the final year of their marriage, in which Dick urged her to get on with writing her memoirs. Nonetheless, she has been an advocate of this project throughout and was instrumental in obtaining the contributions of Theodore C. Sorensen and Arthur Schlesinger Jr. We are particularly grateful for and touched by Arthur Schlesinger Jr.'s contribution—it proved to be the last piece that he wrote for publication; he sent it to us less than a month before he died, early in 2007.

Our other contributors also all knew Dick Neustadt; most were his students, and most interacted with him in the role about which they have written. Although all undoubtedly had very substantial competing demands on their time, when approached each readily agreed to contribute to this book. We know—although there was something of a generational as well as, perhaps, a cultural divide between those who explicitly commented about it and those who did not—that for all of them, the task of remembering, as well as the crafting of their contributions, was a labor of love. Dick would, we feel, have been rather embarrassed, but deeply touched, by their willingness to invest in this work. Moreover, numerous additional colleagues and sometime students provided anecdotes and background material to those listed here as authors. No doubt, a great many more voices could have been included; the editors take full responsibility for the choices reflected in *Guardian of the Presidency*, which we regard as providing an early assessment rather than the final word on Dick Neustadt's life, achievements, and influence.

On our own behalf, and on behalf of our authors, we would like to extend thanks to the following people who offered substantive contributions to one or more chapters: Helena Kerr do Amaral, Michael Barzelay, Francis Bator, Xandra Bingley, Phil Bennet, Derek Bok, David Broder, Heather Campion, Al Carnesale, Daniel I. Davidson, David Ellwood, Christopher Honey, Howard Husock, Ira Jackson, Michael Janeway, Vernon Jordan, Minh Ly, Cathy McLaughlin, Jonathan Moore, Mark Moore, Tom Schelling, Edith Stokey, Richard J. Tofel, Robert Shapiro, and Pete Zimmerman.

Thanks are also due to the following individuals and organizations: for their administrative support, Josh Cherwin, Joan Goodman-Williamson, Sally Makacynas, and Amy Thompson; for his encouragement and counsel in the early stages of conceptualizing this book, Michael Aronson; for their assistance with identification, selection, and handling of photographs, Larry Converse, the Pucker Gallery, Katherine Scott, and Diane Sibley; and for securing copies of Neustadt's correspondence with Lyndon Johnson and related documents, Allen Fisher, an archivist at the Lyndon Baines Johnson Library. The Avedon Foundation merits a special word of thanks for not only permitting us to use Richard Avedon's wonderful portrait of Dick, which appears on the cover of this volume, but also waiving their usual fee.

We are especially grateful to Pietro Nivola, director of the Governance Studies program at Brookings Institution, and Robert Faherty, director of Brookings Institution Press, for taking on this venture; to Janet Walker, for shepherding it through and taking the additional complication of transatlantic coeditors and last-minute editorial corrections in her stride; and to Katherine Scott, for recurrently finding twenty-seven hours in every day and nine days in every week; she did it all with grace and skill.

Beth wishes to thank Rochelle Friedman, David Jones, and Sam Passow for their encouragement and support throughout this project; Doris Kearns Goodwin and Emily Neustadt for their honest, constructive critiques of early drafts of the Afterword; and Rachel E. Neustadt for her later contributions to it.

We both wish to express our appreciation to Shirley Williams, for reading and commenting on every chapter.

Finally, our thanks to Alison Joseph Dickinson for editorial assistance on Matt's chapter and for her support throughout this endeavor. To her and to our children: one way or another, we hope there's another opportunity for a reunion on Gull Pond before too long.

M.J.D., Ripton, Vermont, and E.A.N., London
June 2007

CHAPTER ONE

"Placing" Richard E. Neustadt

ERNEST R. MAY

FOR MORE THAN a quarter-century, from the 1960s almost to the 1990s, Dick Neustadt and I taught a course called The Uses of History at Harvard's John F. Kennedy School of Government. In 1986 we distilled from it the book *Thinking in Time: Uses of History for Decision Makers.*[1]

The subject of the course and the book was how decisionmakers and those who work for them could analyze and take account of what had happened in the past without being trapped into seeing history as a source of legible "lessons." We commenced and continued the course and wrote the book partly because of a deeply shared belief that examination of supposed historical precedents had led decisionmakers astray more often than it had helped them. Appeasement in the 1930s was, after all, an attempt to avoid the supposed rigidities of statecraft prior to 1914. Some of the rigidity in the West during the cold war came from seeing appeasement as the great mistake now to be avoided.

Dick and I offered our students and readers a few easily remembered techniques. Dick labeled them "mini-methods," lest economists and earnest social scientists suppose that we were competing in manufacture of capital-M Methods. One of these mini-methods we called placement. In essence, we argued that people could correct or at least sophisticate their stereotypes of other people by "placing" men and women in their own individual histories. To what generation did they belong? What were their roots? Above all, what public events of the past had helped to mold their perceptions of the present? To what experiences were their minds likely to fly if they faced circumstances even remotely similar? To what supposed lessons of history, in other words, were they likely to be especially prey? In *Thinking in Time* we supply many examples.[2] I will not repeat them here. What I hope to do is simply help readers of this book "place" Neustadt himself.

As other essays here document in detail, Dick's career was many-sided. Most people who did not know him well would, however, bracket him in one of four stereotypes. The first is "presidential scholar," the usual choice made by academics. The second is "presidential adviser," the journalists' most common shorthand label. The third is "founding father" of the Kennedy School of Government, a characterization routinely used by Kennedy School veterans. The fourth is "consort," to those who saw him chiefly in the company of the British political leader Shirley Williams, whom he married in 1987. Of course, other stereotypes attached to him— sage, teacher, Democrat, and so forth. But these four are the ones Dick himself would probably have lighted on had he been asked to use himself as subject for a "placement" exercise.

None of the four stereotypes is wholly amiss but each is limited. The result of "placing" a person should be to see that person as more than one-dimensional. The reason for seeking this result, as Dick tirelessly explained to students, is to achieve better understanding of the individual's proclivities. One of Dick's key findings as a presidential scholar had taken form in the proposition that achievements by Presidents were products of persuasion, not legal authority. He had seen Presidents and effective presidential aides exercise the power of persuasion partly by instinctively "placing" those whose cooperation or consent they needed. Robert Caro can title a volume of his biography of Lyndon Johnson *Master of the Senate* because Johnson so carefully studied the full biographies of all his fellow senators. He knew just which buttons to press, his last resort sometimes being the question, "What would your mother want you to do?"

But "placement" was for Dick more than an aid to persuasion or possibly manipulation. It was in his view an essential part of good staff work. A staffer, he argued, needed a deep understanding of his or her boss and of the people with whom the boss interacted so as to anticipate and guard against possible misjudgments.

Dick remembered President-elect Kennedy's saying during the 1960–61 transition that he knew no one at the CIA except Richard Bissell, then head of the Agency's clandestine operations. Bissell had once taught economics at Yale and had been a teacher or colleague of some of Kennedy's close-in aides. He also had played an important role in carrying out economic details of the Marshall Plan. An unexamined stereotype based on this knowledge of Bissell's background helped to make Kennedy less skeptical than he should have been when Bissell came to the Oval Office in early 1961 as chief advocate for a plan to land a brigade of Cuban exiles at the Bay of Pigs. Dick believed that Kennedy would have been better served if members of his staff had given him more information about Bissell's recent role as chief salesman for covert operations and had also helped Kennedy "place" the CIA as an organization and Bissell's operations wing in particular. He might have learned that the CIA's intelligence directorate was forbidden to surface its own view that there would be little or no support in Cuba for the Bay of Pigs brigade and that Bissell's own number two, Richard Helms, had strong but muffled misgivings about the operation.

"Placement" was a technique that Dick employed as "presidential adviser," as "founding father," and perhaps in other roles. Alas, it is past our power to apply it now either to persuade Dick of something or to help him in one or another of his undertakings. Yet "placing" Dick may be useful to readers so that they better understand some of his choices as described in other chapters of this book.

Born in the early summer of 1919, Dick was part of what, in their taxonomy of generations, the social historians William Strauss and Neil Howe call the G.I. Generation—renamed by Tom Brokaw "the Greatest Generation."[3] The year of Dick's birth saw the Paris Peace Conference, the Senate's rejection of the League of Nations, and ratification of the constitutional amendment outlawing alcoholic beverages. None of these coincidental events left—or could have left—much mark on the infant Neustadt. Largely from sampling students in our classes, we concluded that events in the few years preceding and following an individual's birth were likely to be those with least influence on that individual's historical consciousness.

By the time the person was old enough to attend to conversations at home, these events would still be memorable enough to be referenced, if at all, in cryptic shorthand—"the League" or "that damned amendment." They would also be too recent to be taught in school. Dick told me that, for him, high school U.S. history had not even reached Theodore Roosevelt, let alone Wilson. (For me, a decade younger, it reached Wilson but went no further.)

In Dick's case, however, one event took place in his infancy that would rank as what he called a "molding" event: the worldwide Spanish influenza epidemic, which occurred during and after the Great War and did not spare the United States. It passed its peak a few months before Dick's birth, but it continued to claim a scattering of victims. One, in 1923, was Dick's mother. He never mentioned her to me. Nor did I ever tell him that my own mother had died when I was approaching four, in an automobile accident. It was left to Dick's daughter, Beth, to tell me, after Dick's death, of this potentially bonding experience.

For Dick, the family tragedy was part of a national, indeed world, tragedy. The 1918–19 influenza epidemic killed more people worldwide than the war itself. Dick grew up hearing friend after friend speak of flu victims in their own families. At some point, these memories came together as a double molding event for Dick, for they crystallized in his mind the very concept of the molding event. And he made direct use of this insight when, as consultant to then Secretary of Health, Education, and Welfare Joseph Califano, he and Harvey Fineberg (now of the National Academies) wrote their report on the swine flu scare of 1976 and President Ford's eventually aborted effort at universal vaccination. The report became public as their book, *The Epidemic That Never Was.*[4] It made the point that the swine flu scare became acute because so many citizens who were members of the then-dominant "G.I. Generation" carried memories of the post–Great War influenza epidemic. It also made the point that, although epidemiologists recognized that swine flu was not the same as the Spanish flu of 1918–19, they had their own memories of the 1968 Hong Kong flu pandemic, which could have been made less deadly by an ambitious vaccination program. The analogy in the experts' minds inclined them to take advantage of the spurious analogy in the popular mind. And no one made the President any the wiser.

For Neustadt, a second molding event was the Great Depression. His father had gone back and forth between public and private employment. When the stock market crash of 1929 developed into a worldwide Great Depression, Dick's father was managing a welfare program in Philadelphia partly funded by the state of Pennsylvania and partly by the Rockefeller Foundation. As Pennsylvania's tax receipts shrank, the state withdrew support. So did the foundation. Dick's father moved to the District of Columbia, where he became manager of one of the programs of the National Recovery Administration. When the Supreme Court ruled the NRA to be unconstitutional, Dick's father became a regional manager for the Social Security Administration and moved the family to San Francisco. So it was that Dick attended Western High School in D.C. and then the University of California at Berkeley.

Just as Dick and I never talked about our mothers, so we said little to each other about other aspects of our family histories. The information in the preceding paragraph is drawn (almost verbatim) from Martha Joynt Kumar's invaluable tribute to Neustadt in the March 2004 issue of *Presidential Studies Quarterly*.[5] From my joint teaching with Dick, I infer that the Great Depression was a molding event for him, as it was for most people who witnessed its misery at first hand. Dick was a third of the way into his eleventh year when the stock market started its crazy fall. He was three months short of being fourteen when FDR was inaugurated. He lived in Washington during the frenetic experimentation of what historians sometimes distinguish as the first and second New Deals.

Dick carried throughout his life memories of how the Depression had exposed the frailty and cruelty of free market capitalism. These memories influenced his lasting skepticism regarding the science of economics. In the 1960s he would favor requiring instruction in micro- and macroeconomics for the degree in public policy at the new Kennedy School. At the time, economics seemed the reigning methodology for designing solutions to public-policy problems. Dick admired the minds and talents of economists, particularly ones such as John Dunlop and Thomas Schelling, who had grappled with practical as well as theoretical problems. But Dick reasoned that, as he often put it, the course requirements would equip Kennedy School graduates to "spit in the eyes" of economists, not to imitate them.

While Dick was grudgingly accepting of the proposition that the science of economics had improved since 1929, he was convinced only that economists had learned how to prevent that "last war," not to anticipate the next. He viewed the 1930s as a warning against trusting the forecasts of any experts. In our classes and our book, we used the Great Depression, along with the American Civil War, as examples of events for whose character or magnitude precedents provided no adequate guidance.

The 1930s also served Dick as a molding experience because the New Deal (or New Deals) provided him with so many examples of creative presidential entrepreneurship. When outlining for John F. Kennedy the perils and opportunities before him, Dick cited FDR as the model of a President who kept everyone guessing about the state of his own mind; encouraged conflict among advisers—even to the extent of giving two or more the same assignment; kept his own options open; saw to it, as a rule, that hope for the best never prevented his doing the good; and, more often than not, took a long view of what presidential power could accomplish.

In Washington in the 1930s, Dick had met at the family home in Cleveland Park prominent members of FDR's circle, including Harry Hopkins, the ex–social worker who conceived and ran several programs to relieve unemployment, and Frances Perkins, another former social worker whom FDR had brought from Albany to be secretary of labor. Perkins fascinated Dick. In 1913 she had married Paul Caldwell Wilson, but she kept her maiden name, defending in court her right to do so. A Boston Brahmin do-gooder with practical skills resembling those of a Tammany Hall precinct leader, she was the ringmaster behind the Social Security Act of 1935. Dick liked to tell students how she effected the final compromises by bringing together the key disputants, locking them in her dining room with a bottle of bourbon on the table, and telling them they could come out when they had reached agreement.

Another part of the Social Security story that Dick often cited concerned Luther Gulick, an expert on government efficiency. Once in existence, the Social Security Administration had developed not only regional offices but a central facility where records were kept of the individual accounts of every holder of a Social Security card. Gulick pointed out to FDR the large savings that could come from shutting down this central facility and, indeed, ending all pretense that a Social Security account resembled an individual insurance policy.

FDR replied, "Luther, your logic is correct, your facts are correct, but your conclusion's wrong. . . . That account is not to determine how much should be paid out and to control what should be paid out. That account is there so those sons-of-bitches up on the Hill can't ever abandon this system after I'm gone."[6]

For Dick, Social Security symbolized the way, in the United States, that politicians—and only politicians—could figure out how actually to serve the public's interests. In the 1980s, when number counters were writing off Social Security as bankrupt, Dick used his many friendships in Washington to work for the creation and success of a bipartisan commission headed by Alan Greenspan. Envisioned by Dick as an updated version of the gathering in Frances Perkins's dining room, this commission included representation of every group with a big stake. The commission did in fact produce recommendations that rescued Old Age and Survivors Insurance for at least a couple of decades. The history of the Greenspan commission became a stock item in our course and is one of the "success stories" in the opening part of *Thinking in Time*.

Dick graduated from Berkeley in 1939, just about the time when public attention began to gravitate toward foreign rather than domestic affairs. In California, Japan's war in China had been in the headlines since 1937. The crisis of September 1938 over Czechoslovakia had drawn nationwide attention to the danger of a new war in Europe. Neville Chamberlain's overoptimistic report that the Munich Conference in late September and the ensuing agreement meant "peace for our time . . . peace with honour" was broadcast in elementary schools including my own in Fort Worth, Texas. Hitler had sworn at Munich that his demand for Czechoslovakia's German-speaking Sudetenland would be his last territorial demand. Dick received his B.A. just a few months after Hitler broke this promise and seized what remained of the Czech state, and the British and French responded by giving an unconditional guarantee to Poland. In September 1939, within less than three months of Dick's commencement, Hitler, with the Soviet Union in his camp via the nonagression pact with Stalin, attacked and dismembered Poland, and Britain and France declared war against Germany.

Being Jewish, Dick's family had from the beginning been horrified by Hitler. At the time, however, most Americans assumed that the wars on distant continents would not involve the United States. Dick's own goal was to prepare for a career comparable to his father's. It would be in government, would not be based on elective office, but would not be simply bureaucratic. In 1961 he would spend a year at Nuffield College, Oxford, where he saw at first hand models that in 1939 could have existed only in his imagination. He saw, at Oxford high tables, senior British civil servants ("officials") mixing with politicians ("ministers") up from Westminster. He had married Bertha Frances Cummings in 1945, and he liked to tell of Bert's coming away from an evening with an especially elegant British "official," saying, "He's not the least like X"—X being the then most exalted person in the U.S. civil service.

To pursue his career goal, Dick enrolled in 1939 in a two-year master's program in Harvard's Littauer Center for Public Administration. After receiving the degree, he became a candidate for a doctorate in political economy and government. His student days at Harvard coincided with the sea change that would soon lead FDR to declare that "Dr. New Deal" was being replaced by "Dr. Win-the-War." In early 1941 the United States had begun to supply Britain with massive aid styled as "lend-lease." In June, Hitler attacked his erstwhile ally, the Soviet Union, and Roosevelt coaxed the Congress into authorizing lend-lease aid for the Communist Soviet Union. In the autumn FDR ordered the U.S. Navy to "shoot on sight" any German submarine spotted in the western Atlantic. The December Pearl Harbor attack, followed by Hitler's spontaneous declaration of war, made the United States an active belligerent in both the Atlantic and the Pacific.

Pearl Harbor was in its way a molding event for Dick. It helped shape his understanding of the politics of foreign policy. What stayed with him was recollection of how the shock of the Japanese surprise attack transformed the public mind. On December 6, 1941, a substantial percentage of vocal Americans still expressed doubt that U.S. vital interests would be at risk if Nazi Germany and Imperial Japan came to dominate their regions of the globe. On December 8, hardly a trace of this doubt persisted. Americans became more or less united around a shared premise that would guide U.S. behavior in the postwar era. As Dick would put it to our students, Americans concluded that, if they let dictators take over places like Prague, Czechoslovakia, and Harbin, China, Pearl Harbor would be bombed again.

Dick had left Cambridge for Washington in mid-1941, taking a civilian job in the Office of Price Administration. In 1942 he joined the Navy and became a commissioned officer serving in the Pacific theater with one of the construction battalions ("Seabees") that built bases for the fleet. Though I was in the Navy later, during the Korean War, Dick and I seldom swapped sea stories. Characteristically, what Dick took away from his time in uniform was political rather than personal. It stayed with him that, when the Seabees went to work on a new base, their first priority was to put up an officers' club. He found this an amusingly instructive example of the logic of organizational routines. On the one hand, it reflected the fact that the Navy was less democratic than the other services. The Army and Army Air Corps would have been deterred by worry about bad public relations. On the other hand, it made perfect sense, given that understanding and cooperation among the officers would be the key to quick and successful completion of the construction project. In our course, we sometimes made the U.S. Navy a subject for institutional "placement."

The grand events in Dick's life came in the 1950s and later. They were his service, under Truman, in the Bureau of the Budget and then as a special assistant to the president, the publication of *Presidential Power*, his time with JFK, and his subsequent involvement in creating the memorial to JFK that commenced as the Institute of Politics and that eventually welded the Institute and the Littauer Center together as the new Kennedy School.

Since many other essays in this volume deal with these events, little needs to be added here, especially since Dick and I inclined to argue to students that the molding events deserving their attention are ones that occur in an individual's formative years. But recollection of the earlier events in Dick's life may aid appreciation of how his mind used these later, better-known experiences.

Dick brought to his opportunity to observe the Truman presidency what he had read about FDR and what he had gleaned from insider gossip not known to the larger public. While it is not too much to say that Dick loved Truman, it is nevertheless clear from any reading of *Presidential Power* or of Dick's transition memorandums for Kennedy that FDR remained for Dick the gold standard of presidential performance. This held true even in the warning passages in his writings. In *Presidential Power*, he uses Truman's takeover of the steel industry as a vivid example of presidential overreach.[7] (He held himself partly to blame for not having foreseen the backlash.) But the model to which he refers (and would refer when writing later of Eisenhower, LBJ, Nixon, Reagan, and Clinton) was the second-term hubris of FDR evident in the "Court packing" debacle and the budget retrenchment that reversed the indications of recovery from the Great Depression.

Association with President Kennedy and his brother Robert caused Dick in some respects to reshape the ideal presidential type he had modeled on FDR. The Kennedy brothers showed a quality that was not equally visible in FDR: fearless intellectual curiosity about the processes of governance. Oliver Wendell Holmes was not entirely wrong when he said that FDR had a first-class temperament but not a first-class mind. There is no record of Roosevelt's acknowledging a blunder and trying to learn from it, as JFK did after the Bay of Pigs. Kennedy asked, "How could I have been so stupid?" He then created a secret commission to answer that question; his brother was one of its four members.

Kennedy reacted similarly when cancellation of the Skybolt missile created a minor but startling crisis with the United Kingdom. He asked Dick to find the explanation of why it had happened. The result was the now-famous Skybolt study, which Dick delivered to the White House just before Kennedy's murder in November 1963.

That ghastly event led in time to Dick's leaving Columbia for Harvard, where he became "founding father" as well as "presidential scholar" and "presidential adviser." In the Institute of Politics he brought together on the one hand Washington luminaries such as Jacqueline Kennedy and Averell Harriman and on the other an eclectic mixture of professors and students from Harvard's varied faculties. At Columbia, Bert Neustadt had presided over a famous informal salon where students and faculty mingled with their friends from Washington and the United Kingdom. On one occasion Dick's students were able to question, face to face, former President Truman, and now Bert and Dick continued the tradition in a comfortable frame house on Traill Street, about a mile from Harvard Yard.

I first met Dick soon after he came to Cambridge. We had a long lunch at the Faculty Club, where, as I could see in retrospect, Dick was exercising the mini-method we would later label "placement." Very little of the conversation that ensued—indeed, of the hundreds of our conversations—was personal, about family or pastimes or such. Neither were Dick's questions political in the ordinary sense of the term. I don't think he went away knowing anything new about how I voted or even how I felt about the unfolding war in Vietnam. Instead, he probed for understanding of how public events might have influenced my becoming a professor, writing on certain topics, teaching certain courses, and the like.

We hit it off at once, recognizing a shared conviction that history was probably the most powerful influence on "ministers" and "officials" alike. Before long, we began to design and offer the course that led to *Thinking in Time*. Its first tryout was a half-semester module that met evenings in the house on Traill Street, with Bert providing catering and charming one and all.

Over time, I saw Dick "place" many people. I came to understand better what he had been looking for in his long series of lunch meetings with faculty members. From an early point, if not from the very beginning, he thought that the fitting memorial for President Kennedy would be something larger and more traditional than the Institute of Politics. Lucius N. Littauer, a Harvard graduate and entrepreneur who had endowed the Littauer Center back in 1938, intended it to be the base for an independent professional school comparable to the Harvard Business School. In practice, the Faculty of Arts and Sciences' Economics and Government (political science) departments milked Littauer's gift, leaving the Littauer Center as little more than a place offering seminars for civil servants sent to Harvard at their agencies' expense. Dick hoped that the new endowment for the Institute of Politics could be used to make Littauer's vision a reality. His wish was shared, perhaps even fostered, by Don Price, the shrewd, modest dean superintending the Littauer Center. Neustadt was a professor in the Department of Government as well as director of the Institute of Politics. Price made him his associate dean as well.

Dick was scouting for faculty members who could be recruited to this new enterprise. He wanted a cadre that could weigh in as equals of the heavy hitters in the Economics and Government departments. I was a good example of what he sought—a chair-holding tenured professor well regarded within his own department but not entirely comfortable there. I pulled my oar in the History Department, and I admired colleagues whose only interest was recovery of the past, but I felt closer to the small number of Harvard historians who went back and forth between the university and the public sector. I particularly respected William L. Langer, a great historian of European diplomacy who had taken leaves of absence to run research and analysis in the World War II Office of Strategic Services and later to create the Office of National Estimates in the new postwar CIA. Dick and Price found a dozen or so professors with similar potential for being drawn into a separate faculty providing education for public service.

One of these was John Dunlop. A labor economist who commuted to Washington as a mediator and adviser to unions, he was thrust by the turmoil surrounding the Vietnam War into the deanship of Harvard's Faculty of Arts and Sciences. He was thus in a position to provide major help to Dick and Price. Another ally was Derek Bok, then dean of the Harvard Law School. Himself having some training as an economist, Bok had collaborated with Dunlop in a seminar that was a stellar component of the Littauer Center program. Bok moreover believed that the existing third-year program in the Law School lacked substance and that a separate faculty in the university could be of great service to law students interested in going in and out of the public sector.

All this Dick found out through patient conversation after conversation with scores of individuals. He "placed" them well enough to understand their likely preferences and wishes. He also "placed" members of the Economics and Government departments likely to look askance at the projected new faculty. He and Price, with Dunlop and Bok, devised a minimalist strategy that began with a proposal that the Faculty of Arts and Sciences authorize a new Ph.D. program in public policy. Once this proposal was passed, it was much less difficult to proceed to the creation of a separate faculty to administer the degree. An alliance between Dick and Robert Kennedy meanwhile subdued opposition within the Kennedy family and their circle (grounded in fear that *their* endowment would go the way of Littauer's).

To understand Dick's success as "founding father," one needs to see him not only acting on the presumption that, in any sphere, power depended on persuasion but also on developing and practicing the art he would later teach as "placement." He drew this idea partly from reflecting on the molding events in his own life. And he exemplified magnificently for colleagues and students how that art could be used.

I did not see Dick with Shirley in the U.K. often enough to be able to contribute to "placing" him as "consort," but Beth Neustadt has shared with me some correspondence from her English brother-in-law, who captures Dick's spirit as Shirley's consort "and so much more."

"Beth," Chris Honey wrote, "it was heartwarming to see our little village's memorial service for Dick go so well, the parish church so full, the mood so warm. I'd no idea how many people knew him around here, and yet equally so many of them seemed genuinely bowled over to discover that he was not merely Shirley's husband, 'the American professor' or (as one friend put it) 'the man of exquisite manners,' but a scholar of world renown and an adviser of Presidents and governments. But that surprise is merely another reflection of his extraordinary modesty, and how happily and readily he stood out of the limelight here, while loving the fact that Shirley was—and is still—in it. Indeed, some of my happiest memories of him are of evenings at our supper table, when he would listen and challenge and persuade and cajole her about some coming speech or meeting or event. Ever the supportive consort, he was so much more than that: he was expert coach, devoted supporter, dispenser of wisdom and good-humoured sparring partner."

I can end this sketch with a reminiscence of how Dick used Shirley to teach "placement" to our American students. He would recite the basic details of her career: thirty-five years in the Labour Party; minister in Labour governments; member of the "gang of four" that seceded from Labour to form the new Social Democratic Party (later renamed Liberal Democrats); onetime secretary general of the Fabian Society; and so forth. Dick would then ask students to surmise Shirley's views on a range of controversial public issues. Invariably, the students would presume her views to be those common to the feminist Left, including a commitment to "choice"—the right of women to elect abortion. Dick would then disclose that Shirley is a devout Roman Catholic and is deeply conflicted regarding abortion. As recently as this year, I heard a former student cite this example as one that came frequently to mind, prompting him never to take for granted the views of fellow politicians.

Dick was a teacher who had the rare gift of giving students lasting insights. "Placement" is an illustration, but only one of many.

CHAPTER TWO

PRACTICUM ON THE PRESIDENCY, 1946 TO 1953

MATTHEW DICKINSON

It's a little-known historic event that Dick and I were sent on a secret mission to the Middle East by President Kennedy. Our plane was shot down. We were seized by terrorists. We were set up against the post to be executed. They said, "Each one of you has one wish before you are killed." Dick said, "I'd like to give a little speech about Harry Truman," and I said, "I'd like to be shot first."—Remarks by Theodore S. Sorensen on the twenty-fifth anniversary of the founding of the Institute of Politics.

DICK NEUSTADT HAD a deep affection and abiding respect for the Presidency. Those feelings were nurtured by sixty years of public life in a succession of Presidency-related roles, from White House staffer to scholar to adviser-consultant to institution builder. Somewhere in this occupational progression, he assumed what became his defining role: guardian of the Presidency. In this capacity he exhibited grace, wisdom, and fidelity to the office that came to define his legacy.

Sorensen's death wish notwithstanding, this essay examines the roots of Neustadt's leading role: his almost seven years, from 1946 to 1953, as a staff member in the Truman administration. This period takes precedence, I shall argue, not just chronologically but also in terms of its importance to his life's work. As Sorensen's bon mot suggests, Neustadt derived life-long lessons regarding the American presidency from his Truman experience—lessons most famously distilled in his pathbreaking book *Presidential Power*. But Neustadt's four years in the Bureau of the Budget (now the Office of Management and Budget) and three in the White House did more than serve as a teaching tool—they ignited a passion for the Presidency that burned brightly for the rest of his life, and that continues to serve as a source of illumination after his death.

The impact of the Truman years is evident in even a cursory overview of Neustadt's career path. He earned his doctorate from Harvard University in 1951 while working in the BoB; his dissertation analyzing the evolution of legislative clearance in the executive office drew on BoB archives he accessed while employed there and on material gathered by the Hoover Commission, a study group appointed by Truman to examine the organization of the Presidency. The dissertation in turn became the basis of perhaps his two most influential scholarly articles, published in 1954 and 1955, which documented the rise of legislative clearance and the development of the President's program.[1] These established his bona fides as a political scientist and helped him earn tenure at Columbia University. There he published *Presidential Power*, a book whose most prominent case studies—the steel seizure, Douglas MacArthur's firing, the Marshall Plan—are drawn from Truman's presidency. Not only did the book establish Neustadt as the nation's foremost Presidency scholar, it also brought him to President-elect John F. Kennedy's notice. Kennedy prevailed on Neustadt to serve as a transition adviser in 1960–61, and subsequently employed him as a consultant and troubleshooter, perhaps most famously to investigate the Skybolt controversy.[2] Neustadt's success as both presidential adviser and scholar in turn helped stamp him as that rare individual able to move seamlessly between the somewhat distinct worlds of academe and presidential politics, making Neustadt an invaluable resource to scholars and political practitioners alike. It also made him Robert Kennedy's choice in 1965 to establish the Institute of Politics (IOP) at what became, under Neustadt's guidance, Harvard's John F. Kennedy School of Government. Neustadt spent the last four decades of his life there, teaching and mentoring successive generations of students, advising Presidents and their aides, and confirming his reputation as the nation's foremost Presidency scholar.

The origins of Neustadt's legacy as guardian of the Presidency, then, can be traced to the seven years he spent cutting his political teeth in the Truman administration. But to view this period only as a professional apprenticeship, noteworthy primarily for laying the foundation for Neustadt's life's work, misses an important component of the Truman experience. Of all his many roles, his years as a Truman staffer were the most fulfilling,

professionally speaking. Forever after, through the succession of occupa-
tions, Neustadt continued to identify himself in terms of that first professional experience: he was a "political bureaucrat." He did so, I suspect, for
at least two reasons. First, he was always more interested in the practice,
rather than the study, of governing. And the Presidency—Teddy Roosevelt's
"bully pulpit"—stands at the vital center of governing institutions in the
United States. Second, working for Truman, in the White House, was a
once-in-a-lifetime opportunity. Neustadt's White House colleague Ken
Hechler described it this way: "It was a beautiful, wonderful experience,
working hard along with highly competent people. You really had a sense
of history about it, too, at the end of every day, working for a really great
president of the United States."[3] Neustadt's perspective, given to me years
later when I served as head teaching fellow for his Presidency course at
Harvard University, was more succinct but no less revealing: "It was great
fun!" That fun owed much to Truman's personal characteristics and his
relations with his staff. "We loved the man," Neustadt remembered—a
view universally echoed in every Truman staff memoir, oral history, or
interview I have read.

The rest of this essay delves more deeply into the "great fun." The goal
is to both chronicle Neustadt's activities as a junior staffer under Truman
and to show how those activities helped inspire and prepare him for a lifetime devoted to guarding the Presidency. That legacy no doubt owes much
to Neustadt's extraordinary personal characteristics. But it also benefited
from a remarkable formative experience that provided an unsurpassed perspective into the American presidency—one not likely to be matched any-
time soon.

*Entering the Golden Age: Neustadt and the Bureau of the Budget,
1946 to 1950*

"Dick Neustadt was headed for a career in government." So writes Charles
O. (Chuck) Jones in his wonderful biographical study "Richard E.
Neustadt: Public Servant as Scholar."[4] In Jones's piece, Neustadt describes
his father as a Progressive-era Democrat, but one who worshipped the
Republican President Teddy Roosevelt. Neustadt evidently absorbed his
father's Democratic partisan leanings and his strong belief in public service,

an ethos that was strengthened during Neustadt's high school years spent in Washington, watching Franklin Roosevelt and his New Dealers transform the nation. It was a heady time, one that not only significantly reshaped governmental policies and institutions but also permanently elevated the President's public stature. Neustadt recalled, "People do not believe me when I say that no one walked on the sidewalk in Washington in 1934; they floated six inches above it. At night . . . you could . . . look over at the White House and see that halo."[5]

After graduating from high school Neustadt left Washington to attend the University of California at Berkeley, receiving his B.A. in history in 1939. He then came back east to pursue a joint degree in political economy and government at Harvard University. But Pearl Harbor intervened, and Neustadt joined the Navy in 1942. After his discharge, four years later, he found the prospect of returning to Harvard to write his doctoral dissertation "intolerable." Instead, having already taken the civil service examination, he joined the Bureau of the Budget as a civil servant working in the Estimates Division, where he was responsible for reviewing the budget requests of the presidential staff agencies located in the Executive Office of the President. He served as a budget examiner for two years, during which he acquired a deep knowledge of the operations of the major presidential staff agencies. He also honed the participant-observer skills that would characterize his later research.

It was an auspicious time to work in the BoB. Under the leadership of its director, James Webb, the agency was poised to enter its "golden age" as the preeminent presidential staff agency. The BoB had been created in 1921, to assist the President with putting together an executive budget. For most of its history it had been dominated by a "green eyeshade" mentality focused on economizing on government spending and maintaining efficiency in operations.[6] With the rapid expansion of government under FDR, however, these virtues became less appreciated; Roosevelt sought an agency that focused more on helping him manage the rapidly growing executive branch than in pinching pennies. Toward that end, in 1939— operating under reorganization authority granted him by Congress— FDR relocated the BoB from the Treasury Department into the newly created Executive Office of the President (EOP), part of the modernization of the institutional Presidency. Together, the EOP agencies would assist the President with budgeting, policy planning, administrative management, and personnel control. The goal was to provide FDR with administrative authority commensurate with his burgeoning responsibilities.

From 1939 through 1945, under the able leadership of Harold Smith, the BoB began to fulfill these hopes. It grew from a little under fifty employees to more than four hundred, and took on new responsibilities for fiscal analysis and administrative management in addition to its traditional budgeting, statistical analysis, and legislative clearance functions. Nonetheless, when Webb assumed the BoB's helm in July 1946, the agency faced several challenges as it struggled to adapt to a peacetime era.

One challenge came in the guise of new presidential staff agencies that threatened to encroach on the BoB's turf and complicate its organizational routines. In 1946, Congress, concerned that the rapid demobilization of the armed forces would overwhelm labor markets and contribute to renewed levels of high unemployment, passed the Employment Act. Among its provisions, it established a three-member Council of Economic Advisers (CEA), charged with advising the President on macroeconomic issues. The President was expected, with the CEA's assistance, to submit an annual Economic Report to Congress describing the nation's employment policies. By creating the CEA and mandating the annual report, Congress explicitly recognized that the federal government in general, and the President in particular, was responsible for maintaining economic prosperity.

The CEA's creation affected the BoB in several ways. First, the BoB's budgetary clearance and fiscal policy analysis roles now had to be meshed with the CEA's macroeconomic policy recommendations. This meant, among other adjustments, coordinating the process of writing two annual reports to Congress: the Budget Message and the Economic Report. Second, in its administrative management role, the BoB was charged with helping the CEA work out its own organizational routines.[7]

Archives at the Harry S. Truman Presidential Library reveal that in his capacity as budget examiner with responsibility for the EOP agencies, Neustadt was centrally involved in helping the BoB make these adjustments. For example, his memo titled "Basic Questions and Assumptions" stipulates ten detailed questions "which require answers in the course of consideration of basic Bureau-Council relations and Council operations."[8] This is an early example of Neustadt doing what he did best: posing a series of questions as a "forward thinking" exercise designed to illuminate both choices and potential outcomes. It is precisely the strategy he recommends that Presidents undertake to guard their own power prospects.

Neustadt did more than ask questions regarding the CEA—he was actively involved in finding answers. One way he did so was by helping the BoB devise administrative routines to stay abreast of the CEA's policy recommendations, as contained in the Economic Report, in order to fit them into the BoB's budgetary picture. In February 1947, for example, Neustadt notified his supervisor, Elmer Staats, that "Hirst Sutton [a fellow BoB employee] has asked Fiscal [the BoB's fiscal division] to check through the [CEA] Council's breakdown for accuracy and completeness and then to develop some kind of inventory on where responsibilities for actions lie, to whom assignments have been made, and what can be done to develop status reports for the Budget Director." The goal was "to get an inflow of information on progress whereby the Budget Director may be kept informed of developments."[9]

The information flow also ran in the other direction; Neustadt briefed Bertram Gross, the assistant to the CEA chair, on the BoB's organization and procedures: "As you know, the Bureau includes five principal divisions," he wrote Gross, and then proceeded to describe each of them in great detail. Ever cautious not to mislead, Neustadt concludes, "The foregoing summary should be handled with care, since it will not provide a complete picture without elaboration. 'Half truths' are as dangerous where the Bureau is concerned as anywhere I know."[10] Again, this presages Neustadt's later admonitions to political practitioners regarding the necessity to understand different organizational vantage points—and the dangers in failing to do so.

And it meant discussing with CEA members how they proposed to interact with other governmental actors, including the President. After one such meeting with Leon Keyserling, one of the three CEA members appointed by Truman, Neustadt summarized Keyserling's preferences for meeting with the President—"It boils down to the following. . . . With the President, the full Council should meet with him once monthly at least. . . . Agendas should be prepared in advance. . . . He sees this as vital"—before moving on to Keyserling's views regarding relations with the cabinet, departmental staff, and other governmental agencies.[11]

More generally, Neustadt performed a number of what he described as "housekeeping services" for the CEA: assigning it an account number for appropriations, advising on the use of consultants, discussing procedures for hiring secretaries, and so forth.[12] Of course, the CEA was but one of the EOP agencies for which Neustadt did budget examinations. Extrapolating from his dealings with the CEA, one sees that Neustadt capitalized on his role as budget examiner to place budget estimates in their larger policy and institutional context; he viewed agencies' requests as one part of a larger institutional mosaic in which all the pieces were located by reference to the President's position. This proved invaluable to his development as a historical-institutionalist specializing in Presidency-related operations. Not incidentally, it also brought him to Webb's attention. "[T]hey decided to promote me . . . to make me staff assistant to the Budget Director," Neustadt recalled.[13] Hechler remembered that several BoB employees vied for this plum position: "Webb sent out word that he would like to have a personal assistant, and a number of us competed for that job, including myself. Dick Neustadt . . . won out."[14] In his new role, Neustadt served as Webb's "water boy." This meant, among other functions, serving as an informational conduit between Webb and the rest of the BoB. Webb remembers, "I was talking to political people every day. Senators would call me up—when Dick came into my office to handle the in-basket . . . I wouldn't let him listen in on the conversation but he could hear my end of the conversation. So he got information that he could pass on to the Bureau of the political problems and pressures that come from the U.S. Senate."[15] It is not hard to imagine that in the process of listening in, Neustadt received an unparalleled education regarding "high politics" of the time.

At the end of 1947, Neustadt moved to the BoB's Legislative Reference Division (LRD) as a special assistant and self-described "general handyman" to Staats, who had been appointed assistant director of the budget in charge of the legislative and executive clearance functions. Working out of his second-floor office (which he shared with two other assistants) in the Old Executive Office Building across the street from the White House, Neustadt reported directly to the LRD's director, Roger Jones, who became an important mentor in Neustadt's professional development.[16]

The promotion to the LRD took place at a fortuitous time for Neustadt's education. A year earlier, in the 1946 midterm elections, the Republican Party had won majorities in both houses of Congress. Although divided government, in which different parties control the Presidency and Congress, has become quite frequent in the post–World War II era, 1946 was the first time it had occurred since Hoover's last two years as president in 1931–32, and only the second time in the BoB's entire history. No one was really sure how it would affect agency operations or influence—particularly under a President who had not yet been elected in his own right.

Despite the Republican takeover, Truman intended to resubmit his "Fair Deal" domestic program for congressional consideration. To help facilitate passage of his legislative agenda he ordered the BoB to develop communication channels with leading members of both parties in Congress. "President Truman decided to have the BoB conduct . . . an institutionalized process of liaison with all the committees in both Houses," Roger Jones, Staats's assistant, recalls. The President "felt it was important—particularly when Congress was controlled by the opposition—for committees to have information available about the relationship of pending legislation to the president's program." That presumed there was a presidential program, of course. To create one, the BoB under Webb's direction began to use more systematically the State of the Union, the Budget Message, and other special messages (now including the Economic Report) as vehicles for transmitting Truman's legislative program.[17] The LRD took primary responsibility for this task.

Historically, the LRD exercised two primary functions within the BoB: it analyzed and cleared department-proposed legislation and testimony to ensure that these were in accord with the President's preferences (going so far as to help draft bills, executive orders, and proclamations when necessary), and it advised Presidents on whether to sign or veto enrolled bills (legislation that had passed Congress and awaited presidential action). However, under Smith's leadership these functions had been performed only sporadically, in large part because the LRD remained understaffed. With the Republican takeover in 1946, however, Truman's interest in developing a legislative program to send to Congress dovetailed neatly with Webb's desire to expand the BoB's influence.

"[W]e took it very seriously," Neustadt's LRD colleague Milton Kayle recalled. "We were the agency of last resort. We were the last place in the clearance process before something went across the street."[18] By the time Neustadt came aboard, the clearance process was undergoing further refinement, with an eye to the 1948 presidential election. Truman sought to use the clearance process to contrast his full legislative agenda with the lack of legislation coming out of the Republican-controlled "do-nothing" 80th Congress. Archives show that Neustadt became centrally involved in tweaking clearance procedures to implement this strategy. For example, in August 1948 he suggested improving the "selection and routing procedure" by which bills were tracked. "It need not be pretty," he wrote Roger Jones, "as long as it is complete."[19] Neustadt also reviewed Truman's legislative agenda, looking for potential stumbling blocks prior to sending items on to Congress. His memos in this regard are replete with advice regarding what action to take: "intensive development staff work" needed, or "problem requiring review to insure that we know where agencies are going."[20]

After Truman's stunning upset win over Dewey in the 1948 presidential election, and with Democrats also retaking control of Congress, the development of the President's legislative clearance process, in Roger Jones's words, "took on a more positive and definite history. For the first time . . . [t]he president set forth his entire legislative program, along with estimates of cost."[21] Neustadt was again in the thick of these developments. A sampling of the relevant archives suggests the range of his activities. That November he recommended bypassing the executive-branch departments when developing language for the President's annual messages to Congress, since "most of the material last year was of little use in writing."[22] The BoB, working with the White House, could take on this task. In the fall of 1949, he recommended that the LRD exercise an enhanced role in evaluating agency proposals for the White House, in part by preparing the supplementary material on legislative proposals sent to the President.[23] By 1950, Neustadt was working more directly with the White House staff, urging the LRD to expand its monitoring as legislation wended its way through Congress, in order to discover where presidential items were hitting roadblocks and, "having identified the problems, inventory possibilities for repairs and mobilize spot salvage operations."[24]

In reviewing Neustadt's legislative clearance-related memos, one is struck by his perspicacity in linking Truman's immediate political interests to broader institutional concerns; he is as much a partisan for the Presidency as he is for the President. For example, an October 1948 memo warns Staats that clearing legislation with multimember commissions, such as the National Security Resources Board (NSRB), was a sticky issue.[25] "[The] NSRB's functions, as a body advisory to the President, are vested by statute in its agency members *collectively*," Neustadt summarized.

"This means that a recommendation to the President from the Board can be expected to report the view of the members meeting as the Board. But it doesn't automatically follow that the views of the Board are necessarily the same as those of its individual members in their capacities as heads of single departments. The members must wear two hats, psychologically as well as legally, if the Board is to have any identity and cohesion." In order to protect Truman's interest in properly clearing legislation with the NSRB, then, Neustadt recommended that the BoB solicit individual board members' views as well as those of the board as a collective entity.[26]

In carrying out his BoB functions, Neustadt exemplified what Hugh Heclo describes as "neutral competence": nonpartisanship, historical memory, continuity, and—not least—administrative competence. Although Neustadt was a Democrat who supported Truman's Fair Deal, he was acutely aware of the necessity for the BoB to avoid appearing to advocate for any particular policy. A memo Neustadt wrote to Staats discussing an apparent gap between Truman's legislative preferences and his budgetary priorities illustrates this well. Truman had advised his cabinet to read "his campaign speeches thoroughly and work up draft legislation to implement his commitments." As Neustadt noted, however, the very next day Truman met with his budget staff to preview the 1950 budget. Here Truman pressed agency officials to hold down spending on the present programs, "at least until new revenues were assured by increased taxations." The problem, as Neustadt noted, is that "between these statements of the President's is a great conceptual gap." After discussing the different ways to bridge this gap, Neustadt identifies the danger to the BoB's institutional interests, if it should come out strongly for a more limited legislative program in order to balance the budget. "In this event, the Bureau as such will be hard put to play the role of a neutral Presidential staff concerned with presenting all aspects of the problem so that the President can make a sound and informed decision. Yet that is preeminently the role which the Legislative Reference Division must play in exercising our coordination and clearance functions. . . . I am unable to see how we can perform these functions if . . . we . . . are tagged as contenders rather than as neutrals in so basic a struggle within the Administration."[27]

It is not possible in a chapter of this length to capture the full range of Neustadt's activities during his four years in the BoB. But even this brief overview is enough to reveal how his time there helped him hone his skills as a "President watcher." By virtue of his duties as budget examiner, and his subsequent role in clearing legislation, Neustadt absorbed intimate knowledge of the institutions on which Presidents depend for advice and expertise. Similarly, he gained keen insight regarding the policy process, particularly as it pertained to the President's needs as a legislative leader. And he gained an appreciation for the importance to Presidents of supplementing the more political White House staff with a separate, career-based staff oriented toward the needs of the Presidency as an institution as much as to the partisan interests of the individual President. All of these would become staples of his later teachings.

But Neustadt's BoB experience also paid dividends in a more immediate and practical sense. At Roger Jones's insistence, Neustadt took time off from his BoB duties in 1948 to research and write a thesis on the evolution of the legislative clearance process. "I have been most interested in coming to grips with this idea," he wrote Payson Wild, the dean of Harvard's Graduate School of Arts and Sciences, "particularly since virtually nothing has been done on it anywhere and since it is so intensely illuminating on the problems of policy formulation, coordination and control at the Presidential level."[28] His decision to tackle the thesis was influenced, as he told his adviser Merle Fainsod, "by great luck and a couple of fortuitous circumstances." One of those circumstances, of course, was his access to BoB files. But he also benefited from the activities of the first Hoover Commission, which was then conducting its study of the executive branch. Neustadt, by virtue of his BoB connections, gained access to the commission's source material, and this, together with the BoB archives, allowed him to reconstruct the history of the legislative clearance process.

In May 1948, Neustadt felt comfortable enough with his project to make it "announceable to Harvard, especially since nobody down here has the least doubts about the gleam in my eye about it."[29] After working through the archival material, Neustadt took time off from his BoB functions, beginning in late December 1949, to write the dissertation. By the time he submitted the completed dissertation to Harvard six months later, however, the "gleam" was long gone, replaced with a strong desire to be finished with the project: "I have finally managed to complete a revision of the preface and the concluding chapter for the damned dissertation," he wrote Fainsod that summer.[30] Although acknowledging "it could undoubtedly be greatly improved if I had the time . . . I simply do not and feel now that this has got to be it."[31] His plans to turn the dissertation into a book after leaving government service, "if we are still at peace," never reached fruition, but he did carve the two very influential articles cited earlier in this chapter out of it.

Neustadt's time crunch likely had something to do with circumstances in his personal life at this time: "Number two has arrived!" he proudly proclaimed to his friend Herman Somers in August 1949. "Seven pound girl named Elizabeth Ann. Everybody is fine. They are both home and all very happy about it, except Ricky who doesn't know what has hit him yet."[32] As it turned out, neither Ricky nor young Betsy would see very much of their father for the next three years. The White House was calling.

In Truman's White House, 1950 to 1953

One way in which Webb demonstrated the BoB's value to Truman in this period was by encouraging his staffers to work on detail for the White House. In several cases this served as a prelude to a permanent shift by BoB staffers to the White House employment rolls. Eventually fully a third of the civilian staffers in Truman's White House were former BoB employees. Neustadt was one who made the move. Philleo Nash, a former Truman White House aide, recalls that Neustadt "was one of those bright young budgeters who was given the annual chore of writing the presidential portion of the budget message—the narrative portion. Because they have to get material from everybody from all over the Government and work with all members of the White House staff . . . they get to be known to them, and quite frequently to the President too. . . . My recollection is that this is the way Neustadt came into [the White House]."[33]

According to Stephen Spingarn, a White House aide for whom Neustadt originally worked, for more than two years Neustadt "had been the Budget's liaison man with the White House staff on matters relating to presidential legislative recommendations."[34] In the area of legislative clearance, of course, the BoB worked hand in glove with Truman's special counsel, who was in charge of policy development. Initially this was Clark Clifford, but in January 1950, Charles Murphy replaced him. Murphy recalls that Neustadt "rather badly wanted to join us on the White House staff. . . . I thought it was true then, that if a man wants to work with you there's a better chance of him turning out well than if otherwise."[35] Murphy's foresight proved accurate.

In May 1950, Neustadt officially joined the White House staff, on Murphy's recommendation, as Spingarn's assistant.[36] "Charlie suggested to me, Dick Neustadt, and I realized . . . that this was a wonderful choice because . . . Neustadt already knew the whole picture and would start in high gear. . . . And of course he was tremendously able—the last thing I did when I left the White House was to write the strongest kind of memorandum to Don Dawson, who was personnel chief . . . urging that Neustadt be promoted from grade fourteen to fifteen, although he had only been there five months I think at the time."[37]

Neustadt, as he reported to his professors at Harvard, was "tremendously pleased by this development." For one thing, it meant he no longer had "time to fool around any further with the thesis."[38] When Spingarn left Truman's staff, Neustadt began working directly as one of Murphy's assistants, one of five aides working for the special counsel's office at this time.[39] Because existing statute only authorized a limited number of White House aides to bear the title "administrative assistant," Neustadt received a newly created title: "special assistant to the President."[40] Although his office remained in the Old Executive Office Building (along with most of Murphy's staff), he spent much of his time working directly with Murphy.[41]

The White House staff under Truman operated under a different code of conduct than does its contemporary counterpart. Staffers were then expected to work out of the limelight, in the cloak of anonymity famously prescribed by the 1937 Brownlow Committee Report.[42] As Harold Enarson, an assistant to the senior White House aide John Steelman, observed, "This was a time in the management of the office of the Presidency when it was unheard of by anybody from the White House staff to appear on "Face the Nation" or "Meet the Press" or to issue statements of any kind. . . . It was so well understood that you didn't have to articulate it."[43] Most observers remembered that Truman's aides lived up to this ideal. "They really seemed to have the 'passion for anonymity' which had been recommend by the Brownlow report . . . for presidential staff assistants," recalls Lincoln Gordon, who worked for Truman's White House military representative Averell Harriman. "They had no desire to become major operators themselves. They were remarkably effective and absolutely selfless."[44]

Truman, as George Elsey, another White House aide, remembers, would have it no other way: "The White House staff in the Truman days was a very personal staff to President Truman. White House staff members did not seek publicity for themselves. . . . In those days there was only one man in the White House who had any authority and that was the President himself."[45]

Truman's White House staff was also much smaller than its modern counterpart. Neustadt estimates that during the 1951–52 period, when it reached its maximum size, the White House numbered no more than twenty-two aides with substantive policy roles, compared to more than four times that number today. This meant, by necessity, that Truman's aides were generalists whose roles were tied to the President's daily activities as dictated by recurring cycles of governing—the budgetary and legislative clearance process, appointments and cabinet meetings, annual speeches, press conferences, as well as the requisite ad hoc troubleshooting of problems as they arose. Elsey recalls, "We were generalists who came from different areas of experience and brought . . . a bit of extra perspective or depth of knowledge from our special area but generalists we readily became, and generalists we stayed."[46]

Although composed of generalists, Truman's White House staff did divide into two somewhat distinct functional orbits that revolved around Steelman and Murphy, respectively. At the risk of oversimplification, Steelman's group dealt with "operational" problems, such as mediating labor disputes. Murphy's shop, in addition to putting together Truman's legislative program, wrote speeches and was generally involved on the policy side. As one of Murphy's assistants, Neustadt performed a variety of roles. In a 1951 memo, Neustadt summarized his job as "handling matters involving presidential programs and policies, with special reference to the legislative program." He elaborated on this overview by breaking his job into nine subcategories, including identifying and reviewing "problem areas" related to the development of the President's legislative program; coordinating the development of presentations of these programs to Congress; helping Murphy maintain contact with congressional leaders and committee chairs, and representatives of private organizations; reviewing BoB recommendations regarding enrolled bills and other legislative proposals; undertaking ad hoc assignments from Murphy or other senior White House staff aides; and "receiv[ing] callers in the Executive Office, referred to him, for discussion of particular problems."[47] Years later he was somewhat more self-effacing in an interview with Chuck Jones: "I did all kinds of things . . . policy things, some political things. I had a large hand in screwing up the steel seizure. I remember that well."[48] Not everyone shares Neustadt's evaluation of his performance in this celebrated case; Nash recalls that Neustadt's outstanding contribution "was the work he did on the steel strike. He was the staff man on that. . . . It was here that he gained his intimate knowledge of the Presidency which was the basis of this book on presidential power that brought him to the attention of JFK."[49]

Neustadt, along with David Bell, David Lloyd, and Elsey, served also as one of Truman's speechwriters. There was no set pattern to writing speeches in the Truman White House, but major speeches generally began with Murphy sitting down with the President to discuss the themes Truman wanted to touch on.[50] A committee of two to three aides, of which Neustadt often was a part, would then work up a first draft, which Murphy would review, bringing in additional writers as he felt necessary. After going through several more drafts, Murphy would deliver the revised draft to Truman, where it would be reworked again. After that it might be circulated to related departments for additional input before achieving final form.[51] In this manner a major speech might go through five to ten drafts before the President finally gave a mock reading at a speech conference, which would be attended by all the speechwriters involved.

Neustadt later recalled, "Truman's speeches . . . were written not by writers, but by lawyers and economists and public administration specialists. . . . This did not bring the highest literary quality . . . but it certainly meant a sensitive awareness of their potential as vehicles for making or influencing policy."[52] In discussing his speechwriting role, Neustadt remembered that it took him some time to understand Truman's particular style and cadence of speaking. As Elsey put it, "Truman was no FDR, He was no Jack Kennedy. He didn't pretend to be, and he was the first to know that the speech style written for an FDR would have sounded false coming from him"[53]

By virtue of working on Truman's speeches, Neustadt was part of an "action-forcing process" that could have wide policy repercussions. A classic illustration is Truman's public statement announcing the firing of Douglas MacArthur in April 1951. Initially Truman had intended to announce the firing the day after telling MacArthur in private. But plans changed when MacArthur got wind of the announcement, and Truman decided to issue an immediate press statement. Murphy, working with Bell, Neustadt, and Theodore Tannenwald, was charged with drafting the statement. "So we worked on a press statement from about five in the afternoon until about ten at night," Tannenwald recalled.[54] The decision proved highly controversial, and serves as one of the principal illustrations in Neustadt's *Presidential Power* regarding a President's failure to protect his sources of bargaining power. Neustadt's participation in these events lends his account, and the lessons he draws from them, a level of authenticity and power that conventionally trained academics rarely if ever achieve.

Much of what Neustadt did as a White House aide involved collecting and disseminating intelligence and serving as a conduit for information. In this capacity he helped bridge the gap between the two White House power centers that were often viewed as competing for Truman's support across a range of policies. Enarson, who worked in Steelman's shop, remembers "vividly that from time to time I would meet Dick Neustadt in the hall or see him at the White House mess and he would ask me, 'What about this?'"[55] Neustadt was "a very aggressive person and eager to operate at the highest levels. . . . To the extent that there was rivalry, it was a muted rivalry."[56]

One of the important methods by which Truman's senior White House aides stayed abreast of each other's work was through the daily staff meeting chaired by the President. Neustadt did not regularly attend this meeting—only the senior staff did—but archives suggest that he did occasionally participate if his particular task required his attendance.[57] However, as a junior staffer, he was intimately involved with coordinating Murphy's activities with the other senior staff members, including Steelman and, beginning with the Korean War, Harriman. Much of this took place informally, through Neustadt's interactions with the other principals' junior staff in hallways and through other informal get-togethers.[58]

Although Neustadt did not report directly to Truman on a daily basis, his job brought him into frequent contact with the President. For instance, Neustadt traveled with the President when he flew to San Francisco to address the opening session of the Japanese Peace Treaty conference, in

September 1951. He also participated in several of the eleven trips Truman made to his Key West holiday spot, where the President often took working vacations of up to a month.

In one respect, working in Truman's White House did not differ substantially from working there today; as Neustadt recalled, "Everybody worked hard, and the hours [were] long. . . . When we were involved with a message or speech . . . you barely got home to sleep. Then there would be a breather of . . . a day or two, which did not coincide with weekends. . . . You could tell the results in terms of the families—wives and small children suffered." Murphy remembered that "we had a limousine and along about 11 or 12 o'clock at night, we would load everybody in the car and the driver would take us home. When we passed each fellow's house, we would wake him up and let him out, and we all got back in the morning."[59]

And yet, despite the long hours and the separation from families, Truman's staffers looked back on the experience with great fondness, in large part because of their respect and admiration for Truman. "President Truman was an exceptionally kindly man, [a] humble human being in all of his relations with subordinates," Neustadt remembered.[60] That humility made the working experience more pleasurable for all the staff members. But they were also, for the most part, very fond of one another. In Murphy's words, "We did have a lot of fun. You could hear Dick Neustadt laughing across the hall, and then the rest of us laughed too."[61]

In 1952, however, the fun was coming to an end. Truman announced that he would not seek reelection. That July, the Democratic Party held its national convention to formally nominate Adlai Stevenson as the party standard bearer. Murphy asked Neustadt to write the first draft of the Democratic Party platform—it was traditional for the incumbent President to make a draft available as a starting point for the party's nominee. Neustadt, according to Murphy, "did an excellent job" clarifying "the policy of the President at that time. . . . I think it was a far better document from a literary standpoint, and probably from the standpoint of content, than the one that came out eventually."[62]

As the 1952 campaign unfolded, Truman agreed to make a 26,000-mile campaign swing by rail on Stevenson's behalf. Neustadt joined a coterie of speechwriters who accompanied him, specializing in the shorter remarks that Truman made from the back of the train during the many whistle-stops. "I wrote all the 'extemporaneous' whistle-stop speeches," Neustadt remembered. "There were 300-odd speeches. I could never write speeches again."[63] James Sundquist remembered that Neustadt's "outlines were so complete that if the President decided only to read the outline, it still came out as a speech and toward the end, that's about what happened. Dick had these speeches numbered and would rotate them somewhat so that if there wasn't anything special to say at a particular place, he'd pull out number five which hadn't been given yet that day."[64]

Neustadt, according to Sundquist, also wrote the first draft of Truman's "Farewell Speech," an effort that took over a month to complete. "This was a labor of love," Sundquist recalled. "Everybody agreed this had to be a masterpiece in which we would express in a sensitive way our feeling about the seven years of the Truman administration."[65] The speech was broadcast from the White House on January 15, 1953.[66]

When Truman announced that he would not run for reelection, Neustadt and other administration members began plotting their next step. Several decided to hitch their wagon to Stevenson's star. David Bell recalled that most of the "Murphy Group," including Neustadt, Ken Hechler, and David Lloyd, transferred their support to Stevenson while still working in the White House. Bell recalled that he used Neustadt, among others, as his liaison to the Truman White House in order to clear and coordinate Stevenson's campaign statements with Truman's position, and familiarize their candidate with the legislative and policy histories of the various campaign issues.[67]

Despite their efforts, however, Eisenhower handily defeated Stevenson. Neustadt—not yet thirty-five, married, and with two young children—faced an uncertain future. In the interim after the election, while waiting for Eisenhower to be sworn in, Neustadt kept busy by considering ways to reorganize the Democratic National Committee. But the precariousness of his position was brought home when Emmet Hughes, one of Eisenhower's assistants, met with some of Truman's staff, including Bell and Neustadt, to discuss transition issues. Bell remembers, "This was the subject of a joke between Neustadt and myself . . . because we were in our early thirties, but Hughes was even younger, and we ruefully remarked to each other that this was the first time we had ever been replaced in our jobs by a younger man."[68] Neustadt later summarized, in his typical fashion, his feelings at having to leave government service after seven years: "You can't have fun all your life."[69]

Conclusion

If someone set out to design a practical curriculum for learning about the Presidency, it is hard to see how he or she could improve on Neustadt's seven years working for Truman. This is not to suggest that just anyone who took this "course" would have benefited to quite the degree that Neustadt did; he had the instincts, intelligence, and temperament to fully capitalize on these experiences to a far greater degree than most people. As a budget examiner, assistant to the Bureau of the Budget director, and member of the Legislative Reference Division, Neustadt became intimately acquainted with the key presidential staff agencies and the process of legislative development. His four years in the BoB coincided with its maturation as the primary presidential staff agency in the Executive Office of the President. By the time he moved officially to the White House, in 1950, he had already served as a de facto staff member there for many months. As a junior White House aide, he was involved in a range of activities, from policy development to speechwriting to political liaison and general troubleshooting. In contrast to his years as a civil servant in the BoB, Neustadt's White House service exposed him to the more partisan side of the Presidency, including party and congressional relations.

By all accounts he was effective in these roles. In his letter recommending Neustadt for promotion, Spingarn writes, "His mind is quick, alert and imaginative. . . . He has those superior qualities of good sense and good judgment. . . . His approach to problems is down-to-earth and practical. His knowledge of government is exceptional." Murphy, in forwarding Spingarn's recommendation for Neustadt's promotion, added that he "agree[d] fully with what Steve has to say concerning Dick's outstanding ability."[70] David Bell, Neustadt's White House colleague, recalled, "I learned a lot from argument and conversation with Dick Neustadt. . . . We developed together . . . the process of recording what the President's legislative program was, and what progress was being made on it through the various stages of congressional consideration." There was no blueprint for this task—it was something that Neustadt and others puzzled through, with huge implications for the President's role as legislative leader.[71]

Unlike White House staff members today, Neustadt joined Truman's personal staff possessing extensive governmental experience. So did most of his White House colleagues. "Almost all the members of the presidential staff had government work histories far antedating their White House service," Neustadt remembered. More important, the "largest single group of aides came not only from government, but from a single agency, the Bureau of the Budget."[72] This reflected Webb's effort to make the BoB useful to the White House staff, and thus to Truman. But in progressing from the civil service–dominated BoB to the more politically oriented White House staff, Neustadt benefited by in effect viewing the Presidency from both the institutional and the political-partisan perspective; he understood the distinction between serving the President, and serving the Presidency. In later years he would lament that neither scholars nor presidential aides seemed to recognize the difference.

Of course, these seven years provided the raw material from which he fashioned his theories of the Presidency. Nash remembers that Neustadt "was a very bright, very capable, very attractive personality, and one who made clear that he was observing as he was operating, and he was a practicing political scientist, at the same time that he was a functionary. This was understood by everybody and objected to by none, as far as I know."[73] Although he earned his Ph.D. at Harvard University in the Government and Political Economy program, his understanding of the Presidency derived more from his actual service to Truman than to any observational skills honed through academic training. Likewise, his later research on the Presidency, unlike that of most contemporary Presidency scholars, was motivated more by a concern for governing than for abstract theorizing or puzzle solving. As he noted in *Presidential Power*, "I never had much interest in exposing problems, period. The point is to pursue at least the glimmerings of possible solutions. . . . Presidents and their staffs seek advice; they need it; they deserve the best the rest of us can offer."[74]

In seeking those solutions, Neustadt as scholar valued objectivity and dispassionate analysis—this extended even to his examination of the Truman Presidency. In an interview with Truman in 1955, one of two he conducted with the ex-President for *Presidential Power*, Neustadt quizzed Truman regarding his initial support for MacArthur's decision to push beyond the 38th parallel into North Korea, an action that precipitated a massive Chinese counterattack. Truman explained his support: "[MacArthur] was the commander in the field. You pick your man, you've got to back him up. That's the only way a military organization can work." But Neustadt pressed Truman: If State or the Pentagon had "showed some spine" in recommending that MacArthur stop before crossing the 38th parallel, would Truman have acted differently? "To this," Neustadt writes in his notes, "Truman makes no real reply; perhaps didn't grasp; perhaps didn't want to."[75]

Although Neustadt went on to write the best-selling study of the Presidency, he never considered himself a scholar first; he was, he told Chuck Jones, "a political-level bureaucrat who drifted back to academia, where I had never been except as a graduate student."[76] But neither in later years did he trumpet his presidential experience; visitors to his Kennedy School office saw few visible indicators of his White House service. He remained committed to that "anonymity" that was so much a part of the Truman-era ethos of service. It was an ethos that in so many ways steered him toward his life's role as guardian of the Presidency—a role that enriched everyone, from President to student, who had the great fortune to know Dick.

CHAPTER THREE

SCHOLAR-ACTIVIST AS GUARDIAN: DICK NEUSTADT'S PRESIDENCY

CHARLES O. JONES

JUST OVER A year before his death, Dick Neustadt wrote of his perspective in regard to the role of scholars in presidential research over time:

> I may not be a "new" institutionalist, but I certainly am an "old" institutionalist. . . . We old institutionalists were deeply interested in the fine detail of organizational and procedural behavior, especially with respect to moments of major alteration in either or both, that is, to "change-points." . . . I grant that it is hard to get the access I commanded from inside the Budget Bureau, free to roam its files and myself the "entrepreneur" of change in 1948 and 1949. But I did not think it impossible then. . . . Yet with respect to change-points in the institutional surroundings of the president, there remains so much we do not know, or do not know in comparably illuminating detail. Without it, all sorts of judgments on decision making, policies, and politics are suspect.[1]

Dick was worried that something was missing in contemporary study. Able young scholars test various research methods, many of which permit one to work far from Washington, at home in the academy. Acknowledging that his own experience was possibly sui generis, he believed there were other ways short of working in the White House to produce "fine detail of organizational and procedural behavior," notably by interviews and work in the presidential libraries.

And there was more still that bothered him. Old institutionalists cared. In an earlier address to scholars gathered at Columbia University in 1996 to discuss the state of the Presidency, he urged moving beyond findings to their effects. "The argument can be made that as scholars we are not obliged to care, one way or the other. Perhaps so, though as heirs to Tudor universities, which we all are, I wouldn't press the point. Even so, as citizens we're bound to care. In my time, that might have sufficed; I cannot speak for yours."[2]

He may not have been able to speak for later generations of scholars but he surely wanted them to pay attention to what he had to say. Why? Well, apart from any author's desire to be read and heard, there was in Dick Neustadt a strong custodial interest in the Presidency as an institution. Those who studied and wrote about the Presidency were entering a realm in which he had a proprietary stake. Such work might be paid some heed by the White House and elsewhere in Washington, an outcome he very much encouraged. But his strong preference was for the proper motivation and for an institution-building purpose.

I always had the feeling that Dick judged himself part of an enterprise devoted more to governing than to professional political science. In large part this orientation was an accident of how his career developed: first in governing, training in public policy as he went, then a transition to academia, and finally to building and helping to manage a school and institute designed to turn out those interested in governing. Yet he was not drifting along these pathways; Dick was himself directed by the values of public service that he learned from his father. He was in charge of his choices at each of the stages along the way. He was quite explicit in an interview in the fall of 2001 that he would not have gone into academia had Adlai Stevenson won the Presidency in 1952. And, truth be told, he never really wanted to be a political scientist as that role was developing during his career. Why? Much of the discipline's core was moving away from his cohort's concerns about governing. Here is some of what he said in that interview:[3]

So the question [in 1952] was: What to do? I'd been at the White House. I could have gone up on the Hill. I could have gone to the [Democratic] National Committee. I didn't want to do that. It just seemed like the fringes. I wanted to get out of there.

Two things have happened [since 1952]. People with White House experience today have all kinds of job opportunities that didn't exist in my time. Indeed, to get into academia then was real hard. I was almost grudgingly allowed to start at the bottom rung to see if I could satisfy my colleagues that I was serious. But the expectation was that he isn't serious. It was not a benefit to have had the practical experience.

Now [White House staff] have all kinds of openings in journalism or law and business. Nobody was offering [those jobs] to Truman's people. I might well have never gone to academia if I were contemporary.

This story of disillusionment or disconnect with the transition to the academy has been oft told by others who have served in government and schools of public administration or public policy. However, most of these others did not write the equivalent of *Presidential Power* (first published in 1960), an award-winning book that got the attention of political scientists, journalists, politicians, bureaucrats, and a President, John F. Kennedy. Dick had wanted to demonstrate that he was serious about academic work. To say the least, he successfully accomplished this goal.

Having achieved academic status by writing a transformative book on a major political institution, he could then take up serious custodial work as a guardian of what he had created. Further, there was the nurturing required of a living institution. Forevermore the name *Neustadt* would be associated with the American Presidency. He had taken possession of what would then be a life's work.

Guardianship

The common use of the word *guardian* to mean "keeper," "protector," or "custodian" is how it is used here. Legitimacy is strongly implied—indeed, there is a legal use of the term for those entitled to act for others judged not competent to act for themselves. Dick's authenticity in this role followed from his personal experiences in the White House, his close professional association with Presidents and their aides and advisers, the training of political bureaucrats provided by a school he helped to found and manage, and his possession of the correction he had made to existing scholarship with the publication of *Presidential Power*. I suspected at times he might also have felt a legal guardianship for those incapable still of comprehending his correction. More probably, however, what I observed was simply exasperation that certain folks (fellow academics, journalists, presidential aides, even Presidents) did not, or could not, understand either his formulations or their applications.

There are countless examples of his guardianship. I must stay with those I know personally, guessing that they are representative but warning that in volume they have to be a tiny fraction of what he accomplished throughout his career in this role.

My personal testimony begins with the Neustadt shelf in my bookcase. I can honestly say that I feel his presence, advising me to "get it right." I regularly consult his meticulous formulations, often applying them anew. My copy of the original book (alas, a second, not first, printing) looks tired from page turning and underlining. But it still has its jacket, if worn and taped to hold it together. Tucked inside are my notes from its use in a course I taught in 1960 at Wellesley College, my first teaching job. I have a strong memory of being totally absorbed as I read portions of *Presidential Power* on a beautiful fall day along the shores of Lake Waban, on the Wellesley campus. I couldn't wait to tell students about it. Imagine! I could start them off with the correction rather than with that in need of correction.

Another mind-altering experience for me as a young political scientist, then a graduate student at the University of Wisconsin-Madison, was reading *The Governmental Process*—also a second printing and even more time-worn—by David B. Truman. I do not recall registering then that Dick and David were together at Columbia University and did not learn until I interviewed Dick in 2001 how important the Trumans were in the publication of *Presidential Power*. David aided in getting Dick the time he needed to finish the book and read the manuscript; his wife, Elinor, typed the manuscript. Also, as revealed in Dick's obituary for David, he "even found a publisher for 'Presidential Power' when I'd failed after four tries."

David's obituary was the last writing that Dick asked me to read: "If you have any trouble with this, let me know."[4] As fate would have it, the obituaries of the two friends would appear in the same issue of *PS: Political Science and Politics*.[5]

My most direct and continuous contact with Dick began in 1993. In a letter to Tom Mann, then director of the Governmental Studies Program at the Brookings Institution, Dick wrote that "Brookings should review in depth, interviewing intensely, what went right and wrong during the eleven weeks between election and inaugural in the three most recent change-of-party presidential transitions . . . : 1976, 1980, and 1992."[6] As it happened, Mann had invited me to come to Brookings for a period of time as Douglas Dillon Visiting Fellow. Dick's proposal and my visit coincided nicely. The result was *Passages to the Presidency: From Campaigning to Governing*.[7]

The proposal itself is a fine example of Dick as guardian, one of many. His interest was not, indeed never, solely scholarly. The proposal was motivated in part by his having monitored the Clinton transition. In his letter to Mann, he observed that the Reagan team had learned from the mistakes made by Carter in the 1976 transition, "while Clinton's people . . . managed to reproduce them." He chose Brookings because of its reputation for doing work that was action oriented, including previous work on transitions. He even advised when such a study should be published: "Publicizing . . . this study, with emphasis on practical 'dos' and 'don'ts' should be deferred until the spring of the next election year [2000]."

The study was, in fact, published earlier than Dick recommended, as the first product of an extensive "Transition to Governing Project" funded by the Pew Charitable Trusts and administered by Brookings, the American Enterprise Institute, and the Hoover Institution. The rationale at Brookings was to begin attention-getting dialogues regarding the importance of the transition during the run-up to the election year.

What *was* published and publicized in 2000 to fit Dick's timetable was a handbook for presidential transitions entitled *Preparing to Be President*.[8] It was a collection of Dick's transition memos to presidents and advisers, from 1960 forward. The idea for the collection emanated from an early meeting devoted to the Transition to Governing Project. Donna Shalala, then secretary of health and human services in the Clinton administration, proposed a handbook for transitions; I suggested there was one—an unpublished version: Dick Neustadt's memos. Since I was at Nuffield College, University of Oxford, at the time, it was delegated to me to ask Dick—by then living in the U.K.—whether he might entertain the idea of publishing the memos. He consented, and an arrangement was worked out between him and the Transition to Governing Project directors.

I agreed to edit the collection and thus had a chance to work directly with Dick. We collaborated at every stage. I wrote the introduction and selected and edited the memos to be included. He reviewed what I had done and wrote what turned out to be a final memo: "Neustadt Advises the Advisers." Dick was informed later that the collection was, in fact, relied on as a handbook by the incoming George W. Bush administration. One of the most tentative elections in history featured one of the most effective transitions (due, of course, to many factors but surely aided by the memos).

Dick read and critiqued two of my book manuscripts: *The Presidency in a Separated System* and *Passages to the Presidency.*[9] The guardian role was evident in the critiques, to include a tutoring dimension. I confess to serious trepidation (is there any other kind?) when told by Tom Mann that Dick would be reading the *Separated System* manuscript. I had conflicting reactions: I very much wanted to find out what he thought but I was apprehensive about what he would say (actually, I was terrified). He was *the* man and I was writing about the institution he owned (my view even then). Would he spend much time reading and commenting? Would he read and reject? Would he read and object?

Had I known then what I learned in time, I would have been less anxious. A guardian is certain to take serious work seriously. He surely did read and comment—six single-spaced pages. The bottom line in his letter to Bruce K. MacLaury, president of Brookings, was in the first two sentences: "I think well of Chuck Jones's manuscript, very well indeed. By all means publish it."[10] Then the custodian took over. He had fully engaged the argument and the evidence. Proposed changes were consistently made to strengthen or clarify the main theme. He was direct, even firm, but on my side. Never before had any reader been so helpful, and only one since: him. For in addition to providing the critique, he took time to guide.

I was only slightly less apprehensive with the second book manuscript, *Passages to the Presidency,* on transitions. Yes, I knew what to expect: a thought-provoking critique with constructive suggestions for improving the manuscript. And I also had consulted Dick along the way, keeping him informed of my progress. After all, it had been his idea to do the book. Yet, he had taken possession of this topic, too, in 1960, the same year *Presidential Power* was published. For it was widely known in Washington and elsewhere that he had written the memos that shaped a model transition for Kennedy. And so I was presuming to write informatively for the keeper of knowledge on the subject.

The review was supportive but more critical than for the *Separated System* manuscript—again, six single-spaced pages of constructive comments sent to MacLaury's successor at Brookings, Michael Armacost. Dick was most helpful with the finding that I had the most trouble elucidating. Everyone I had interviewed for the book agreed that Clinton's transition was among the least effective in modern times. However, I concluded that it was a mistake to judge his transition by traditional criteria. Clinton's passage was not from campaigning to governing in the usual sense. Campaigning would not cease upon Bill Clinton's being elected. Rather it would be incorporated into governing. It is worth quoting Dick on this point because what he writes is illustrative of the wisdom of experience and his confidence in his role. First, he proposed substituting "conventional" for "traditional," a nice instance of his attention to the precise meaning of words. Second, he emphasized that the change was not merely in moving from campaigning to governing.

> Rather . . . the change consists in the character of governing itself, which henceforth need be acknowledged to include a large growing proportion of "policy campaigning." In short, it is the conventional definition of "governing" which changes. The standard for judging effectiveness in transition from electioneering to governance need be adapted accordingly, but not, as Jones suggests, superseded.[11]

These two letters reviewing my manuscripts are prime examples of the special standing of a guardian. In Dick's case he combined the training of a public service–oriented political scientist with the experience of a political bureaucrat at the highest level in government. He instinctively knew how to get the most out of both knowledge areas, tailoring his comments to be of utmost use to diverse audiences. I believed that he wanted more from the transition manuscript than I as a pretender to the first (the training) but lacking the second (practical experience) could provide. I will return to this point below.

Who was affected by Dick's guardianship? My personal examples identify one group: presidential scholars. Anecdotal evidence from other scholars confirms my experience and is consistent: its hallmarks were cooperation in reading manuscripts, detailed and helpful comments, attention to means for publicizing findings, and scanning always for what might be useful in governing. That last point needs special emphasis. Dick wanted presidential scholars to think beyond the "publish or perish" imperative to the potential effects of their findings. To do so requires a conceptual understanding of a working government, which was his strength.

It follows that White House residents were subjected to Dick's monitoring eye. After all, *Presidential Power* may have been written to correct what we were teaching about the presidency, but it also was written to serve the best interest of Presidents and other power holders. At one point in my interviews with Dick, I asked whether he could identify "a unity of purpose and direction" in the corpus of his work. Dick paused longer than normal (conversations with Dick were punctuated with pauses, breaks that were obviously busy times for his mind). Then he began slowly: "Well [pause], yes [pause], I think so." And then he began a somewhat rambling response, a portion of which went like this:

> It's all about decisionmaking at a high political level in a separation of powers system, and the interplay of the ostensible power holder and the institution around him, and the dilemma of how in a system in which everybody swears an oath of office and everybody's responsibility is different from everybody else's, the poor slob who's ostensibly on top of the whole thing helps himself to survive. I guess that [pause] and how he thinks about the survival problem and meeting the decisionmaking requirements, how he thinks ahead about it.[12]

He then began to talk about how several of his books and chapters added to *Presidential Power* in the revised edition contributed to this theme.

The question clearly interested Dick, and, as it turned out, he was not happy with his response during the interview. Shortly after he returned to England, he sent me a letter clarifying his thoughts:

> Chuck: You asked me how I'd characterize the central theme, if any, of my written work, over the years. I don't think I gave you an adequate answer. The true answer, I think, on reflection, is that I'm constantly

in pursuit of *Presidential Power*'s fundamental question: how should a person think about the possible effects of his own choices on his own prospects for influence within the institutional setting of his office?[13]

As before, he then discussed how various published works contributed to or elaborated on this central theme. He closed with "How about that? I'm glad I continued to address that question: nobody else does!" Later he edited the statement a bit more, as I had decided to include it in the profile I wrote for the *Annual Review of Political Science*.[14]

Dick's theme question requires the analyst to assume the role of the decisionmaker. How else can one evaluate whether the office holder is operating effectively? So the test for Presidents is the extent to which they are sensitive to the influence of future effects on the choices made. Included is the delicate matter of weighing the importance of making a choice versus anxiety regarding its future effects. One can imagine a President and his advisers "overgaming" the politics of a decision to such a degree that it interferes with acting on a critical issue. One is reminded of the observation that most decisions are made with too little time and poor information.

Dick certainly understood the need to act, whether or not a President could fully judge the effects of the action on the prospects for personal influence. But as a guardian of presidential power, he would still support prospective thinking. Presidential authority, essentially the institutional setting of which Dick speaks, is not typically self-executing. So Presidents have to persuade, all the while preserving their capacity to do so. That process makes *them* guardians, too.

Presidential guardianship is an attribute worth interpreting within the Neustadtian perspective. Dick expected Presidents to protect themselves by thinking politically and futuristically. It greatly troubled him when they did not do so. And though Dick was partisan in his personal politics, he was a nonpartisan preserver of the Presidency. Nixon and Watergate were, of course, the supreme example to show the detrimental effects of presidential decisions on institutional capacities. But Clinton's personal behavior also was judged to have risked *his* Presidency and diminished *the* Presidency. In both the Nixon and Clinton cases, Dick was anxious, too, that their having let down their guard influenced their subsequent motives. With power and status weakened, their attention turned to bolstering personal legacies rather than to repairing institutional damage. No true guardian could approve. Legacies should not, and ultimately will not, be contrived.[15]

The Case of Clinton's $85 Million Campaign Fund

One of the features of Dick's scholarship is the exquisite use of stories to illustrate the utility of his concepts. I have one such in our correspondence. The stimulus in this case was his having read a manuscript I wrote on permanent campaigning for an anthology edited by Norman Ornstein and Thomas Mann.[16] The paper focused on lessons to be learned from the Clinton presidency, for his successor. In the last paragraph I warned against automatically judging campaigning while governing to be bad. I encouraged analysts to focus on effects rather than simply expressing personal preferences, mostly expressed as opposition to campaigning as interfering with governing. Dick's reaction to the paper concentrated on that point and the specific issue during the Clinton presidency of raising $85 million to run television ads in 1995 and 1996. Use of the White House, notably the Lincoln Bedroom, for donors was generally criticized. Here was a perfect "Neustadt" case, that is, one encouraging a search for broader lessons about the Presidency. This story permitted him to wrestle with the intersection of governing, policy campaigns, and reelection campaigns.

Now I must turn it over to Dick. This matter was the subject of three letters. To me, it is a classic illustration of guardian behavior—curiosity, concern, irritation, and tenacity, with an overlay of rationality and sensitivity to what is best for the Presidency. First comes the need to understand the context and how it had changed. He wrote:

> I fear that in opposing the "permanent campaign" to "governing" we are in danger of creating what our . . . field will take as opposites, and screw the distinction up. . . . Governing for presidents used to consist, most concretely, of necessitous (and volunteered) dealings with Congress, Executive agencies, the Court, the national press corps, other governments, national interest groups and organized partisans, always in the context of elections and public relations, which were equally necessitous, this being a democracy. So what's changed?
>
> The context has changed. It has deepened, widened, grown more pervasive, more problematical, and in conjunction with those other

things more pertinent . . . especially participation, simultaneously, in the permanent campaign, of everybody in support of everything—that's all!

This is not to say that the permanent campaign is synonymous with the presidential election campaign, although Clinton may once have confused them, a distinction you don't make quite clear [in the paper].

Next, Dick moved to consider Dick Morris and the fundraising by the Clinton White House in 1995 and 1996 that invited criticism in the press and elsewhere and encouraged talk of the "permanent campaign." The change in context—deepened, widened, more pervasive—meant "the terms and conditions of the dealings must change." Dick believed these "terms and conditions" could, and did, change.

> But they can [change], the last year [1996] shows us that. And up to a point they will. The only question is whether, in a separated system and a private enterprise system, the "will" can come close enough to matching the "must," for the comfort of prudential types like you and me. [Here is a fine example of Neustadt writing: a seemingly throwaway sentence, upon third reading, reveals its profound message.—C.O.J.]
>
> To me, the single most interesting thing in Dick Morris's book [*Behind the Oval Office*] was the revelation that for a year and a half the White House had been putting paid ads out on local TV almost everywhere except Massachusetts (and England) where I was, and except New York, Washington, and parts of LA, where the national reporters were, ads explaining substance, that is to say, Clinton's stands on issues, and where he differed from Gingrich, and why.[17] From here [the U.K.], I'd been unable to understand, how he'd been able to win the [1995] budget fight in public opinion: Contrast poor Bush in 1990. Now I think I know.

Then comes the irritation, such that he would pursue the subject further and make it the subject of two subsequent letters.

> The other side of the coin is that this substantive TV is said to have cost $85 million. I think I know who raised that personally: Clinton and Gore. I used to worry that fund raising was forcing congressmen to put legislating third in their order of priorities (with fending off

staff second). Now, having seen Gore a year ago, after two weeks of it, perhaps I have to say the same for presidents and governing. And all because we let TV sell all the time, while, absent adequate party organizations, we tolerate the rise of a new, private profession, the campaign consultants. All in the name of free private enterprise. Makes me sick.[18]

Two months later a second letter arrived, bearing witness to the tenacity of the guardian. Dick continued to think about this issue, labeled a "puzzle" in this letter. He had decided that what went on in 1995 and early 1996 "was not campaigning in the narrow sense of directly contesting the election. Rather, it was governing, jousting with Congress in the year before the election, and no more (or less) mixed up with the impending electoral context than has usually been the case late in a President's third year."[19] What concerned him about this puzzle was why no one made this distinction: campaigning as governing for lawmaking purposes versus campaigning for electoral purposes. He continued:

> These weren't campaign funds in the traditional sense, they were governance funds, if you please. And the only reason they had to be raised is because in contrast to the days of radio, or newspapers for that matter, the President gets insufficient free air time, from an insufficiency of channels, to make his points reliably to audiences nationwide.
>
> That money is simply a form of tribute, exacted from the President of the United States by the people who already possess profitable licenses to exploit public resources, the airwaves. There's altered governance for you!

Notice how he moves from the practice of viewing fundraising in an electoral campaigning framework to the broader contextual issue of governing in an age of a communications revolution. New distinctions were required, yet "college-educated" journalists "with upper middle class egos"—"GooGoos, every one!"—missed the "tribute," concentrating instead on reforming campaign finance regulations. "GooGoos" are "Good government types"—a favorite Neustadt term.

The third letter on this issue, still on Dick's mind—came in early 1998. Dick had found evidence to support the distinction he had written about earlier. His sources (of which he had dozens at the highest levels) explained that the White House was in a battle with a campaign-oriented Speaker of the House, Newt Gingrich, who was willing to have the government shut down, believing that Clinton would lose should that happen. The TV ads were a means to win that battle; it was, in fact, won by Clinton. Dick explains:

> Yet the President was also being pressed by his political consultants and advisers to fund and launch issue ads for reasons to do wholly with the coming campaign: get his numbers up in advance of the primaries. When Clinton decided to get the money and do the ads, most people in the White House took it to be campaign [electoral] politics. A year later the President may have forgotten the other motive. So when the press says that is what it was, nobody there [in the White House] was alert to draw the distinction.[20]

It is unquestionably the case that winning a budget battle over an aggressive opposition party Speaker of the House had major implications for the 1996 presidential campaign—but no more or less than any other triumph for a President in the months before a reelection year. Governance has always had relevance for elections. Dick's point was that in a new communications era, Presidents had to win in the political and policy context in which they served. In Clinton's case, the 1994 election results had devastating effects on the President's reputation and prestige. He needed a governance win in 1995 and it was believed by most observers that the television campaign helped get him one.

It is worth noting that the restoration of Clinton's status in 1995 contributed to a productive year for major legislation in 1996. Remarkably, once the budget impasse was broken, a flood of bills was enacted into law, third most in the post–World War II period by my count and that of David R. Mayhew.[21] The partisan split in Congress had not changed. Republicans were still in the majority in each house. What had changed was precisely what Dick had recommended in *Presidential Power* for a President who had lost reputation: "Induce as much uncertainty as possible about the consequences of ignoring what he wants."[22] Speaker Gingrich went from certainty regarding Clinton's low status to uncertainty regarding the consequences Dick wrote about and finally to certainty of the bad effects of his (the Speaker's) miscalculations.

The Battles He Won—The Wisdom He Imparted

My final topic reviews the dangers for the guardian in being too diligent. We all wish we could have conversations with those whom we have lost. So much between friends doesn't get said. Tomorrow will be soon enough, until it isn't. Diligence is a subject I wish I had brought up with Dick. Why? Because I think he troubled himself unnecessarily about his role. I have thought about the matter enough to formulate two advisories (to neither of which he would have paid much heed!):

> Don't fight battles you have already won.
>
> New generations seldom acknowledge the derivation of accepted wisdom (and often get it wrong anyway).

In his own mind, Dick fought political science as a discipline and those who he believed misinterpreted or misused *Presidential Power*. In the first of two interviews I had with Dick, this one in London, in 2001, he said:

> I had to convince my academic colleagues that I was serious about their business. . . . *Presidential Power* was an effort to fill the gap between the academic literature that existed in the middle 50s on the Presidency and my experience with it. If one could fill that gap the political scientists would think that was a contribution. *I don't think the political scientists would think that was a contribution now.* [My emphasis][23]

Frequently, in the two interviews and in our correspondence, he was critical of the discipline of political science for not being more purposefully connected to the practice of governing. Clearly Dick wanted to "win" in political science scholarship on his terms. He won, even triumphed. He connected theory and practice, even as others did not. He wanted to guard the Presidency as an institution. He guarded, assiduously. He lived successfully and with impact in two worlds of politics—that of the scholars and that of the practitioners. He won the battles he engaged, if not necessarily conquering his adversaries. I regret not telling him these things for whatever reassurance doing so might have imparted. Would it have brought reassurance? Truth be told, probably not, although Dick, unfailingly courteous, would have expressed gratitude for my efforts.

Regarding my second advisory—that new generations seldom acknowledge the derivation of accepted wisdom—Dick's work has become accepted wisdom. In fact, he liked acknowledging that "separated institutions *sharing* powers" had become a cliché. He often spoke and wrote about "change-points." His book *Presidential Power* was one such in presidential studies, just as he intended. Research and writing about the Presidency would never again be the same. Sadly, professors and scholars never really know the full impact of their work. But what we do know about *Presidential Power* suggests that it has had greater effect than any other book about a political institution, as measured by sales, breadth of readership, referencing, and endurance. As noted earlier, his name came to be synonymous with his topic, and he received recognition in and out of academia. Conferences were held on the anniversaries of the publication of the book, countless panels held at professional meetings.

Yet when I asked him about the book's impact, his response evidenced a great deal of thought on his part, much of it expressing disappointment. "What have I done wrong?" he asked exasperatedly at one point. He pointed out that in filling the gap in the literature he was "leaning on an open door," that is, someone had to come along and correct what had been written. He was obviously aware that the book was successful by standard measures: "People are still arguing, kicking at it forty odd years later. Some courses still use it." He was proud of how it was written: "It was written to be read by journalists as well as academics and I think that succeeded. People did read it." He was "charmed" when the chancellor of UCLA wrote him: "It was eye opening. I learned so much about my job from it."[24] Yet Dick doubted its success by measures that meant something to him.

> My ambivalence comes out of the fact that the book essentially is a long windup, trying to change the way one looked at these institutions in order to address the problem of what does the nominal power holder think about, how does he anticipate if he wants to improve the chances that he is going to have the wherewithal to do things. . . . I was really trying to come to grips with what is the essence of political thinking, looking ahead, trying to anticipate how do you hold on to what you got and improve it. . . . But by and large, nobody noticed that that was what the book was about, and still hasn't. Nobody tried

to build on that, improve on it, certainly it can be improved on. . . . So in that respect, I don't feel that it was a great success.[25]

True enough, not everyone understood all of what he so meticulously set forth. I know I didn't fully appreciate the intricacy of argument. And he was properly sensitive to whether readers comprehended the contributions made by additional chapters in subsequent editions. In defense of readers, adding chapters to the original text did ask them to integrate the new into the original. I raised that with him at one point and he agreed. Most readers were likely to treat those chapters as discrete contributions; that is the way it typically happens with subsequent editions, if personal experience is any guide.

How might I have discussed my second advisory with him? I expect I would have begun by suggesting that he was setting too high a standard. From 1960 forward, presidential scholars began to make reference to Neustadt's ideas when they placed and justified their own work. A few sought to supplant his status, but no one ever did. For many, probably most, scholars *Presidential Power* acquired the status of accepted wisdom. It is likely that some understood it all but found the formulations too challenging for designing proofs or improvements. Others took portions only, as suited to their personal interests in the institution. Still others misunderstood purpose and concepts, yet wrote critiques or made applications that came to be cited by others as credible. Some in later generations were bound to test Dick's research by means of contemporary social science methods. All of that is in the nature of work that comes to be seen as "accepted wisdom." As Dick noted, it gets "kicked at." We lose control of what we write once it is in print. But, Dick, I will match *Presidential Power* against any book on political institutions you wish to name and declare you the winner.

Again, I think I can anticipate the well-mannered response. And so I would feel better. But Dick's motive was not only to *get* it right but, as well, to make those who count understand enough to *do* it right. Dick Neustadt's presidency was born of experience, nurtured by scholarship, and safeguarded by assiduous supervision. There was little time or space for self-congratulation. It follows, then, that what has subsequently gone wrong would be taken personally by the guardian. So be it. I still wish we had had the conversation.

I came to know Dick late in his life and mine. I cannot say that we knew each other well, but we were getting there. It was especially fulfilling to have worked with him on four projects bound to reveal more about his perspectives on the Presidency: two directly related to his work (editing his transition memos and writing a profile of his scholarly contributions); two related to mine (his reviews of two book manuscripts). Will there be another like Dick Neustadt? We discussed that in the interviews. Names came to mind, but none quite fit Dick's life experience. As it turned out, we haven't needed another, and perhaps do not even now. How rewarding it was to know him.

CHAPTER FOUR

Avoiding the Hazards of Transition: Neustadt's Lessons

HARRISON WELLFORD

ON INAUGURATION DAY at the United States Capitol, a new President is being sworn in by the Chief Justice of the Supreme Court, amid throngs of adoring supporters and the subdued rearguard of the outgoing administration. Change is in the air and for the moment, as President Reagan used to say, there is morning in America. Meanwhile down Pennsylvania Avenue in a large white house, there is an eerie calm. The halls are empty, doors to offices of the most powerful men and women in the world are left open, computers are unplugged and hard drives erased, papers are strewn on the dark blue carpets, and the few telephones that ring through from the nation's busiest switchboard go unanswered. The White House, the nerve center of the most powerful nation on earth, awaits its new occupiers and no one is really in charge. This is the scene I witnessed twenty-six years ago when I served as President Carter's aide in the Carter–Reagan transition in 1981. The scene was much the same when I participated as a member of the incoming President's team in 1976 and 1992.

A Transition unlike Any Other

Presidential transitions in America are unlike any others. When the election of a new President involves a change in party, the Constitution, statutory deadlines, and political custom subject the United States government to the most radical change of power of any democracy in the world. In eleven frantic weeks, from election to inauguration, the President-elect must abruptly shift gears from campaigning to governing and prepare to take over a government that has been almost entirely decapitated of its senior policy officials. The White House staff turns over completely and must be rebuilt from scratch. Because political appointees now layer executive agencies and departments five to six levels down, the turnover of leadership in the rest of the government is also severe, leaving little institutional memory to guide the country's new leaders. Over 1,100 senior policy officials, all personal appointees whom the President alone can appoint and dismiss, must be recruited, assigned, and confirmed, a process that may not be completed until the end of his first year, over twelve months after the election.

In parliamentary democracies, there is little transition shock. In Great Britain, the transition after a change in parties takes place in a day. Nonpartisan senior civil servants enjoy respect and control long vanished in the United States and the front benches from the new prime minister's parliamentary party move seamlessly into his cabinet.[1] This is not the case in the United States. Most of the outgoing President's senior appointees in the White House and departments and agencies are heading for the exits while he remains in power for eleven weeks after the election. Even when they linger in their offices, their minds are on their next career moves, not on running the country. The President-elect has no authority to decide anything until the inaugural, and the outgoing President's influence is like a large balloon with a slow leak. With each week that passes, his effective power deflates. The anticipation of the power shift by the winning transition team, the outgoing administration, and political leaders worldwide is intense and creates the threat of a power vacuum unless this period is carefully managed through teamwork by the incoming and outgoing Presidents.

There is also no guarantee that international crises will take a holiday while the new President assembles his team. The government must go on, especially in a time of war. Historians have speculated that a presidential transition might be an ideal time for an enemy to strike, but this has not occurred. The response to the death of Stalin in 1952, the run-up to the Bay of Pigs in 1960, and the Iranian hostage crisis in 1980 tested the ability of the incoming and outgoing teams to work together, but in all three cases partisanship was largely avoided. With rare exceptions, the President and President-elect have established a relationship of trust and mutual respect. In transitions where there has been a change of parties, this is not easy because of the inevitable tension between the incoming and outgoing transition teams, one puffed up by victory, the other downcast and resentful from the humiliation of defeat. This is particularly true when the election is very close. In most cases, however, patriotism and respect for the legitimacy of constitutional succession prevail over partisanship.

The Guru of Transition

Richard E. Neustadt, the foremost analyst and historian of the modern Presidency, captured the spirit of this unique period better than anyone. "Everywhere there is a sense of a page turning, a new chapter in the country's history, a new chance too. And with it, irresistibly, there comes the sense, 'they' couldn't, wouldn't, didn't, but 'we' will. . . . We won so we can."[2] Having endured the waterboarding of an endless modern campaign, the incoming President may think that governing will be easy by comparison. As Neustadt noted, the President-elect can be forgiven if he wakes up the day after the election with the thought "I did this impossible, terrible and awful thing—I got nominated and elected. So I can do anything."[3]

For every incoming President, the stakes in a successful transition—both the initial eleven weeks and the first year after—are very high. The new President's reputation, policy prospects, quality of appointments, and not least the integrity of the institutions he inherits can be enhanced or jeopardized by how he manages the transition from campaigning to governing. For all these reasons, Dick Neustadt believed that transition studies mattered. Recognizing that all new Presidents are vulnerable to "arrogance in ignorance, their own or that of their associates,"[4] he hoped that risks to the nation rooted in the inexperience and hubris of new Presidents might be mitigated or avoided with greater anticipation and knowledge gained from the analysis of what has gone right and wrong in transitions. Teaching the lessons of transitions became a major focus of his work as a scholar and presidential adviser.

For over forty years, from 1960, when (with Clark Clifford) he was the junior member of a two-man transition team for President-elect Kennedy, to 2003, when he worked with me on early transition planning for 2004, Dick Neustadt was the leading expert on presidential transitions in America. Since 1935, when the Twentieth Amendment to the Constitution shortened the period from election to Inauguration Day from four months to eleven weeks, there have been seven changes of President involving a change of party (1952, 1960, 1968, 1976, 1980, 1992, and 2000). Except for 1952, Dick advised the incoming transition teams of every one. In 1952, as a member of Truman's White House staff he was an eyewitness to the passage of power from Truman to Eisenhower. As he said with characteristic modesty, "Every four years prospective White House aides for an incoming administration consult me about the transition, and every four years my advice is not taken."[5] The truth is that as a trusted confidant to a generation of transition advisers since World War II, Dick Neustadt had more influence on the way Presidents thought about and executed their transitions than any other scholar or practitioner before or since.

Neustadt's career as a transition adviser started with President-elect Kennedy, who asked Neustadt, then a professor at Columbia University, and Clark Clifford, a Washington attorney and former special counsel to President Truman, to help him think about preparing to be President. JFK met with them separately, made clear what he wanted, instructed them not to consult with each other, and not to obtain advice from or share their conclusions with the members of the Kennedy campaign team. Both reports also went to Ted Sorensen,[6] the future special counsel. At the twenty-fifth anniversary of Harvard's Institute of Politics, in 1991, Dick described his first encounter with Sorensen, in 1960: "I was summoned down to Washington on the Tuesday after the election. I went into Senator Kennedy's office, and there I found a bright young man from Nebraska. What was he doing? Lolling about, enjoying the victory? . . . Sharpening up his spite against the Republicans? Not at all. He was sitting in a chair, seriously engrossed in an academic monograph on an aspect of the Presidency that would materially affect him as special counsel. He was literally reading his way into his new job. An enormously impressive thing to do, six days after the election. And may I tell you the way I knew it was impressive? It was my monograph!"[7]

Although Dick was a lifelong Democrat, he saw his role as transition adviser as serving the Presidency, not a particular President or party. Dick was always available to Republican and Democratic transition advisers alike. Although the Eisenhower-Kennedy transition was regarded at the time as one of the smoothest transfers of power between parties in history,[8] Democrats typically have not excelled at transitions, much to Neustadt's frustration and chagrin. The standard for transition success, as judged by historians, was set by Ronald Reagan; the standard for transition disappointment was set by Bill Clinton and Jimmy Carter. Of the six "turnover" transitions since 1960, in which a challenger defeated an incumbent President, only John Kennedy among Democrats gets passing marks from historians, and then only if the Bay of Pigs is not considered a transition event. The most frequent terms used to describe the Carter and Clinton efforts are "disorganized," "amateur hour," "staff infighting," "failure to prioritize," and "delay."[9] The terms used to describe the Nixon, Reagan, and George W. Bush transitions are "disciplined," "competent," "experienced" and "focused." Dick was unsparing in his critique of transition blunders by Democratic Presidents, noting that "too many transitions like Carter's, too often, might indeed make the Presidency impossible."[10]

The transition records of Democrats and Republicans may in fact reflect each party's political culture and expectations of government. In a nutshell, the record shows that in the early days of a party turnover, Democrats focus on policy, Republicans on management.[11] Republicans traditionally approach government as something that must be tamed, controlled, and managed. It may play a dominant role in national security, but more often must be reined in to get out of the way of the private sector. Democrats see government as an instrument of change, a constructive force to be unleashed to execute policies which enhance the common good. The expectations of Democrats' constituencies propel them to initiate many new policies, the sooner the better. David Gergen, a veteran of both the Reagan-Bush and Clinton administrations, once described the Republican White House as having the authoritative calm of a corporate boardroom with the emphasis on hierarchy, management, and execution; and the

Democratic White House as more like a grade school soccer game where all the players run to whichever ball of policy is in play at the moment. This scenario aptly describes the early days of the Clinton transition.

Even if one accepts these snapshots of Democrats' performance as generally true, Neustadt believed that political culture need not be destiny where transitions are concerned. Even Bill Clinton can point to transition successes (economic policy and budget preparation) and the calm surface of the Reagan transition masked failures (budget estimates and deficit predictions). The history of transitions clearly shows that success is more likely when transitions are built on a foundation of good planning, management skills, and a ruthless focus on the President-elect's preparation to govern. As of the first Wednesday in November the President-elect faces an onrushing freight train of decisions—making scores of key appointments, organizing the White House and the Executive Office of the President, preparing the budget and Presidential messages, setting international and domestic agendas, preparing for the Inaugural, and many more that are more executive than legislative in nature. They come at him with a pace and complexity never experienced in running a Senate staff, a governor's office, or a campaign. As Sorensen noted, they would "benumb" the brain of an ordinary man.[12] For the incoming chief executive and commander in chief, these early decisions have long-term consequences that, unlike campaign decisions, cannot be remedied by a shift in rhetoric or policy nuance in the next news cycle.

One of the reasons that Dick was sought out by transition advisers from both parties is that he never jockeyed for a position of influence but would always respond when asked for help.[13] He sought no credit or recognition and his discretion was as secure as a bank vault. When I was a young transition adviser to Jimmy Carter in 1976, I was terrified of leaks that might destroy the tentative trust invested in me by a skittish President-elect, but I also desperately needed advice. Neustadt became my life raft, the most valuable source imaginable and the one least likely to take advantage. His advice was deeply imbued with respect for the institution of the Presidency and with heartfelt empathy for the flawed individuals who occupied it. He was therefore easy to trust and a joy to learn from. Like an all-star point guard, he made all the players around him—his advisees—better at their jobs.

How to Make Presidents Listen

Anyone who has been asked to advise a presidential nominee before an election or a President-elect afterward harbors the fear that the distilled wisdom in his memos either will never reach its target or, worse, will be judged irrelevant, boring, or banal if it does. Neustadt was exquisitely sensitive to this dilemma and had succinct advice for the advisers: take into account the personal style, strengths, and weaknesses of the President-to-be, show sympathy for the crushing burden of his office, and maintain your adviser bona fides by putting a tight leash on your ego.[14] He made these points to me when I first sought his advice in August of 1976 when I was part of Jimmy Carter's experiment in preelection transition planning. He asked me what I knew about Carter's personality and style in making decisions and working with staff. I was embarrassed to answer "very little." He suggested that the best advice started with a deep knowledge of transition precedents and case studies, which would then be filtered through a lens of idiosyncratic detail to make it relevant to the personal preferences, style, and circumstances of a particular President and his times. Neustadt believed that personality, more often than not, trumps process and structure and therefore generic advice on the Presidency, as opposed to advice tailored to a particular President's needs and vulnerabilities, had little utility outside the academic realm.

In 1976, had we understood Carter's decisionmaking style better, we might have put greater emphasis on the need for a chief of staff in the White House, although in the post-Watergate era, we would probably have lost the argument. Reflecting on his predecessor, Ronald Reagan noted that "the problem with Carter is that he tries to do everything at once and he tries to do too much of it himself."[15] During Carter's first year, this was true. A prodigious reader, Carter tried to be his own chief of staff for most of the first half of his Presidency, but his style—lack of wide access to staff, reluctance to chair meetings, preference for communicating through memos where the volume of his marginalia sometimes exceeded the original text—often made him more remote than engaged. Neustadt believed that the President needed a chief of staff, not as an all-controlling chokepoint for decisions going to the President, but more as a Washington-savvy, politically astute, intensely loyal filter who acted more as an honest broker than a deputy President. President Carter, for the first half of his term, preferred the "spokes of the wheel" model with himself as the hub, a decision process that he came to realize was impractical, but only after much harm was done.

In 2004, I drew upon this experience with Carter in preparing the pre-election White House planning memo commissioned by John Kerry. I asked Tim Todreus, a former Kerry Senate staffer, to discreetly interview Kerry's closest associates and former Senate chiefs of staff and prepare a memo on his decisionmaking style to guide our recommendations, an analysis that led us to strongly recommend an "honest broker" chief of staff, which was well received by the candidate.

Respect for the "Sacred Institution"

Neustadt also believed that advisers, to be successful and relevant, must have a deep respect for what he called "the sacred institution of the Presidency" and sympathy for the individuals who take on its burdens. He was particularly scornful of White House staff who, out of hubris, showed a lack of respect for the office. When Hamilton Jordan wore blue jeans to work and was photographed with his cowboy boots on the desk said to have belonged to two former chiefs of staff, Dick Cheney and Donald Rumsfeld, Neustadt called his action "silly and juvenile." In a conversation with me in 1992 comparing the experience of the Carter White House staff to that of Kennedy, he noted that Carter in the early months of his Presidency risked letting "amateur hour" become "animal house."

This theme of respect for the awesome challenges of the Presidency radiates through all of Dick Neustadt's writings on presidential power. No incoming President has any idea what he has gotten himself into. From the outside, everything looks easier. The powers of the Presidency seem more imposing than they turn out to be. Inexperience makes so many of the choices facing the President-elect virtually incomprehensible. As Barack Obama, responding to questions about his inexperience, said, "I'm not sure anybody is ready to be President before they are President."[16]

Staffing the White House

For these reasons, Neustadt was very protective of the incoming President's time and prerogatives. The transition should have one mission: preparing the President-elect to govern. As Neustadt advised Kennedy in his second transition memo, "Staffing the President-Elect" (October 30, 1960), "You are the only person you can count on to be thinking about what helps you." To this end, nothing was more important than helping the President-elect select his top team as soon as possible. He strongly advised Carter and Clinton to appoint the senior White House staff quickly and insulate them afterward. In both cases, however, internecine warfare at the staff level delayed the selection of the White House staff, the most important step that the President-elect can take to give identity, discipline, and momentum to his fledgling administration. Carter delayed appointing his senior White House aides until late in January. He commissioned a bottom-up review of the organization and decision processes of the presidential offices and seemed content to rely on staff in temporary positions with often overlapping mandates until the study was finished.

Clinton was even slower in selecting his key transition and White House aides. Indecision about his choices for transition director, White House chief of staff, and director of presidential personnel disrupted the flow of transition decisions and created an early impression of poor planning and disarray, which the new President found hard to shake. As Neustadt noted, comparing Kennedy's decisive staff appointments, "Kennedy's people leaped into governance" while Carter's and Clinton's held back, waiting for the dust to settle on internal struggles for power.[17]

Reagan, who had studied the misadventures of the Carter transition, turned immediately to senior aides from his campaign to staff the White House. Many of these individuals had worked together in the Nixon and Ford administrations and were comfortable members of teams in which pecking orders had long been established. As a result, they conducted the transition with extraordinary discipline, making judicious use of the President-elect's time while ensuring that cabinet selection, budget review, policy agendas for the first hundred days, presidential messages, and relationships with Congress and key constituencies were handled with efficiency and dispatch.

Putting a Leash on Egos

Neustadt had little patience for transition advisers who went into business for themselves. Neustadt strongly advised that transition advisers who want to ensure a market for their advice should not go into competition with the gatekeepers to the would-be President. In 1976 when I was asked by President-elect Carter to make recommendations for the organization of the White House staff and the Executive Office of the President, Dick gave me a piece of advice that he said Clark Clifford had given him in 1960. "Remember," he said, "you can accomplish anything you want in this town if you don't care who gets the credit." Neustadt faced the competition dilemma in 1960 when the Kennedy campaign staff assumed that he had eyes on a West Wing office after the transition period. Neustadt recognized that such ambition would spoil his usefulness and decided to demur, unless he were offered a major job "astride some key action-channel flowing to the President," an unlikely event.[18] Having learned from Neustadt, I followed the same approach in 1992 and 2000, when I was asked to prepare the preelection White House planning memos for Clinton and Kerry, respectively. I made clear that I had no interest in a post-transition job. I did briefly consider Chief of Staff Thomas "Mack" McLarty's overture to become a joint deputy chief of staff with Harold Ickes, but that was after the inauguration, and in any case I concluded that this role would not work (Neustadt mildly disagreed with me).

Preelection Transition Planning: Two Train Wrecks

Unfortunately, I was eyewitness to two wrecks where, despite Neustadt's good counsel, hubris and ego made roadkill of transition advice. In one case I saw it coming; in the other I was blindsided by bad information. Both occurred because of conflicts between campaigners and planners in the preelection period. This is a relatively new problem, which first surfaced in the Carter transition. The sheer endurance required to win the race, the total self-absorption in the campaign, makes it almost impossible to focus on the challenges of governing after the election. Most candidates for the Presidency are reluctant to begin planning for a transition before the election for fear of negative consequences if this leaks to the press. One fear is that they will be viewed as presumptuous or arrogant. Another is that, if preelection planners start matching people with positions, speculation about who may be appointed to top jobs will create an unhealthy anxiety within the candidate's team about division of the spoils, fostering tension between the planners and the campaign. Both Clinton and Kerry were initially concerned about the presumption of victory that preelection planning might convey. Jimmy Carter, famously, was not, nor was Ronald Reagan or George W. Bush.

Jimmy Carter was the first presidential nominee to organize a formal preelection transition team and acknowledge it publicly. He asked Jack Watson to put together a transition planning team in July 1976, immediately after the convention. Neustadt generally welcomed the preelection planning but warned me that parallel staffs before the election could be disruptive unless carefully managed. Carter appeared unconcerned when reports of the TPG ("transition planning group") activities made news by late September. Watson even gave interviews to *Time* magazine before the election, much to the consternation of Carter's campaign manager, Ham Jordan, and the campaign staff. In September 1976, when as Jack Watson's deputy I relayed grumblings from Jordan about the high profile of Watson's transition work, his response was that he had a mandate from Jimmy Carter and not to worry. Unfortunately, the Watson-Jordan rivalry disrupted transition planning after the election and helped delay key appointments to the White House staff.

Bill Clinton, while initially wary, commissioned discreet planning efforts that remained confidential until the election. Mickey Kantor, the nominal campaign manager, asked Ira Magaziner and me to form a small team to do preelection planning on budget and economic policy. Although the working group included Bob Rubin, Bob Reich, Roger Altman, and others well known to the press, we produced a full-scale "shadow" budget for the President-elect in almost total secrecy until the election. Unfortunately, in a bizarre reprise of the Carter transition, Kantor's fall from grace after the election (like Watson, he was pushed aside by the campaign staff) kept Magaziner's work from being fully embraced by the transition team. Like Watson, who was handcuffed by Jordan in the first week after the election in 1976, Mickey was shoved aside by George Stephanopoulos and other campaign leaders in the Little Rock war room. Much of Magaziner's very good analysis was dead on arrival because the campaign staff feared that dignifying it with attention would give Mickey a bargaining chip in the power struggle.

John Kerry, although skittish at first, accepted the advice of his Senate chief of staff, David McKean, that the benefits of a discreet planning effort outweighed the risks. With the help of an excellent team I developed a comprehensive plan for the White House and the Executive Office of the President under the leadership of Jim Johnson and David McKean and presented it to Kerry two weeks before the election. The campaign staff was consulted early and often and no tension developed. Unfortunately, the smoothest preelection transition planning effort in history was for a candidate who did not get elected.

Seeds of Distraction: Bloated Post-Election Transition Teams

With so much to do in so little time, Neustadt preached that an incoming President must be ruthless in setting priorities because on a date certain in January, he will be expected to govern, "ready or not," while the whole country watches.[19] Neustadt strongly advised shielding the incoming President from unnecessary distractions. Predictably, he cast a wary eye on the growth of transition teams funded generously by the government since 1976.[20] His nostalgia for the Kennedy transition where a two-person transition team presented the President-elect with two brief memoranda shortly after the election now seems almost quaint. While he thought discreet preelection planning could be useful, he was scornful of bloated postelection transition teams, the early vanguard of which emerged in the Carter transition and then metastasized into Reagan's four-hundred-strong occupation force, which tried to strong-arm the bureaucracy into early surrender to the Reagan revolution. Neustadt found the armies of former campaign workers and congressional aides "washing around Washington, doing busy work and seeking jobs" and producing reports that were both unreadable and unread to be both aesthetically offensive and politically dangerous. Neustadt was amused when I reported that coming out of a meeting at the Reagan transition team offices in mid-January 1981, I saw Dempsy Dumpsters piled high with black spiral notebooks, the hastily discarded reports from some of these transition teams. Attributing the growth of transition teams in part to congressional funding of Presidential transitions, Neustadt advised Clinton to return federal transition funds to the Treasury.

Hazards of Transition: Newness, Haste, and Hubris

Neustadt boiled down the hazards of transition to three key factors: newness, haste, and hubris. For anyone who survives the ordeal of campaigning and wakes up the day after the election as President-elect, the euphoria of victory is almost impossible to avoid. Victory, Neustadt wrote, produces an overdose of adrenaline leading to "self-intoxication." Although it is most potent in the immediate aftermath of the election, its effects often last well into the new President's first year. This exuberant arrogance, while very human and therefore unavoidable, is a major hazard of transition. Neustadt warned that the combination of haste and hubris pushes the new President to rush into things before his team is ready to analyze risks or execute decisions.

He analyzed the hazards of "newness" in a series of case studies such as Kennedy's stumble in the Bay of Pigs invasion; Carter's scattershot legislative agenda, which squandered his short reserves of political capital; Reagan's "rosy scenario" on budget policy, which condemned him to a deficit explosion that only an FDR Democrat could love; and Clinton's "Don't ask, don't tell" policy on gays in the military. The hazards of newness reflect the fact that incoming occupants of the most important and challenging job in the world are condemned to on-the-job training. No President-elect with a change of party since Grover Cleveland has had any prior experience with the challenges of transition. Noting that the weeks between the inauguration and the President's first message to Congress are especially vulnerable to miscalculation, Neustadt advised caution. He recalled that Kennedy's new staff came to him on January 17, 1961, with an urgent question: "What will we do with him on January 21?" Neustadt advised them to give the President "reports to read and invent harmless choices for him to make."[21] This scenario is inconceivable today. Any new President in the twenty-first century will have his time and choices minutely programmed from Election Day to Inauguration Day and will find his first weeks scripted and rehearsed by zealous aides to ensure that the President will get a good report card at the hundred-day milestone.

It follows that Neustadt also strongly advised against making hasty commitments during the transition, which could limit the President's options after taking office. One hardy perennial in the field of transition missteps is the tendency of some incoming Presidents to promise to cut staff or agencies by some percentage often derived from campaign expediency, not organizational analysis. In the past, this has been mainly a problem for Democrats; Republicans have felt less need to prove themselves as managers, although the well-documented incompetence and corruption of

George W. Bush's second term may have changed this. I remember well the dismay of Dick's son, Rick Neustadt (a former Carter White House staffer who worked for me in the 1992 transition), when Warren Christopher relayed to us a request from Little Rock to cut the White House staff by 25 percent. Like his father, Rick was a staunch advocate of keeping options open for the incoming President and noted that it made no sense to promise to cut the staff of agencies before you have had the chance to study them and shape them to your priorities. President Carter had gone further in 1976 and pledged to cut the number of federal agencies by 30 percent as well. This sparked a doomed exercise to find obscure agencies such as the Battle Monuments Commission to add to the body count. These transition commitments, like Clinton's pledges on diversity, prompted a numbers game with the press, which was relentless in holding the new Presidents to their promises.

Greater Risks in International and National Security Arenas

The transition perils of newness, hubris, and haste are magnified in the international arena. The consequences of failure are both more severe and longer lasting. Neustadt believed that the mostly one-dimensional, "stovepipe" nature of government agencies exposed the President and the nation to high risks from the failure to integrate foreign and domestic policy and intelligence. For new Presidents, especially those without foreign policy experience, learning whom to trust and what questions to ask of the national security advising system is a perilous endeavor. Neustadt saw the Bay of Pigs fiasco as a classic illustration of the hazard of newness in national security. Inexperience with the processes, institutions, and personalities of his national security team set President Kennedy up to fail in his first crisis. Specifically he failed to understand the organization of the CIA, particularly the lack of communication between operations and analytical staff, and its relationship to the Joint Chiefs of Staff. Kennedy thought he was getting an independent second opinion from the Joint Chiefs on invasion strategy and tactics without understanding their reluctance to second-guess the quasi-military operations of another agency beyond their control. He also relied much too heavily on a small cadre of untested White House staff for changes in the location of the landing site, with disastrous results.

Kennedy learned from his mistakes and took full responsibility for them. For example, he used his brother, Robert, as a sounding board because he could stand in the President's shoes and filter advice without a specialist's agenda. Eighteen months later, Kennedy performed brilliantly in the much more challenging Cuban Missile Crisis. Neustadt passed these lessons on to the Carter transition team in 1976. He praised the recommendations for integrating foreign and domestic policy and politics in Carter's "Reorganization Plan No. 1," a reorganization plan for the White House and the Executive Office of the President submitted to Congress in the spring of 1977, which he believed would help the President avoid the risks of myopia in the national security agencies.[22]

Do Good Transitions Make Good Presidents?

For transition scholars, who like to think that transitions matter, it would be comforting if the record showed that good transitions make good Presidents. Neustadt was doubtful that it did. With respect to the Kennedy transition, he wrote that "doing well in the eleven weeks did not keep him from doing badly afterward. Indeed, the sense of having mastered those exacting weeks brought on euphoria, itself a source of trouble."[23] The Presidency of George W. Bush presents a greater challenge for transition scholars. No other President prepared so early for the transition from campaigning to governing. Karl Rove told the presidential scholar Martha Kumar that his staff had studied seven presidential transitions trying to draw lessons about what would make the first 180 days after the inauguration successful.[24] If one looked at the list of "best practices" recommended by transition scholars to guide incoming Presidents, George W. Bush's team checked all the right boxes. Preelection planning began more than six months before Bush was nominated, and Cheney was picked to lead transition planning immediately after the convention. Andrew Card was designated de facto chief of staff while the Florida results were still in flux, and the key White House staff, with pecking order clearly established, was in place by Christmas. Card struck the right notes of loyalty, discipline, and discretion when he called a meeting of 150 White House aides on January 8. He advised his team to tuck their White House security passes away when they left the grounds and "be among the most humble people in Washington."[25] To build a sense of team spirit among the cabinet designees and give them some distance from departmental transition teams, they were given offices on "Secretaries Row," where they could interact for the month before the inauguration. Like Reagan, President-elect Bush had his transition team prepare a policy agenda that emphasized doing a few things very well, supported by a well-prepared communication and political strategy. By contrast, Presidents Carter and Clinton laid out laundry-list agendas without clear priorities during the transition period. As a result, the early months of their Presidencies were beset by disorganization, lack of a coherent message, and even a degree of chaos.

How can it be that the man who ran one of the most successful transitions under the most challenging circumstances is now viewed by some as potentially one of our most failed Presidents? Does this mean that the qualities that enable a President-elect to run a good transition are in some ways different from those it takes to run the country? Were there clues in the way George W. Bush staffed and organized his team, set early priorities, and structured the flow of decisions to the Oval Office that might have been early predictors of difficulties ahead?

Neustadt believed that incoming Presidents could learn from transition successes and failures of their predecessors and he welcomed the earnest study of transition precedents by the Bush preelection transition team. But he never suggested that transition "best practices" could be reduced to a recipe that guaranteed success. Success is often hostage to how a new President's challenges match up with the skills and temperament he brings to the office. As Roger Porter, former White House aide under the first President Bush, has pointed out, Presidents come to office as mature individuals. "They are not in the formative stages of their life; they are not figuring out how they're going to do things. . . . Given [that and] and all the pressures . . . [of the] job, the notion that they are going to adapt is rarely the case."[26]

Few Presidents were less prepared by experience and temperament than George W. Bush to be a war President in an extremely complex international crisis. Dick Neustadt died before the full tragedy of the Iraq misadventure was revealed, but he had seen enough to be deeply skeptical about the whole affair. He was also concerned about Bush's lack of foreign policy and national security experience and his well-documented lack of curiosity about world affairs. He said to me in the run-up to the invasion

of Iraq that he feared Bush, unlike his father, might be one of those leaders "who did not know what he did not know" and therefore might be led
astray by experienced advisers with strong ideological agendas.

The transition period between Election Day and Inauguration Day provides few clues on how Bush would react to a foreign policy and national
security challenge. Although the key appointments of Colin Powell, Donald Rumsfeld, and Condoleezza Rice happened swiftly in December, the
Bush transition did not highlight foreign and national security policy in
the first-year agenda.[27] The only foreign policy announcement in the transition came on January 2, when the White House announced that Bush
viewed the global war crimes treaty signed by President Clinton three days
before as "flawed."[28] The first eight months of Bush's Presidency was
devoted almost entirely to tax cuts, faith-based initiatives, education
reform such as "No Child Left Behind," and other domestic issues. His
preferred disengagement from international affairs and the absence of any
international crisis during this period provided little opportunity for him
to learn on the job, to get a feel for his role of commander in chief as well
as chief executive from working with his team on real events, which might
have mitigated the newness and hubris which Bush brought to the international and national security arena.

Any assessment of the impact of the transition process on the Bush
Presidency must deal with the fact that George W. Bush experienced two
transitions in his first term. The first began on November 27, when the
Florida secretary of state "certified" the Bush victory, and the second began
nine months later, on September 11. The World Trade Center attack rad-
ically changed the course of the Bush Presidency and brutally pushed the
new President out of his comfort zone in domestic affairs. No President
has ever faced a more formidable challenge in the first year of his Presidency. The Bay of Pigs for Kennedy does not compare. The Cuban invasion was a long-planned affair against a known enemy. September 11 was
an earthquake, a profound shock. No President could have been prepared
for the fear and uncertainty this event instilled in the American people.
That this event would lead in less than a year to a buildup for invasion of
Iraq that would fatally define the Bush Presidency was also largely unpre-
dictable except perhaps to a small cadre of neoconservatives in the Pentagon and the vice president's office.

September 11 was an extraordinary opportunity for Bush to define himself as a national leader who could rise above partisan politics and call upon all citizens to unite in mutual sacrifice against a common enemy. Before September 11, his Presidency was already adrift, with flat polls and little policy momentum. After September 11, he had for the first time the public support to take bold bipartisan initiatives. For example, he might have proposed raising the gas tax to reduce the nation's dependence on foreign oil, a "sacrifice" leaders of both parties and the American people might have gladly endorsed. But after an excellent start in which the President reached out to all citizens, his rhetoric, by early 2002, began to take on shorter-term, politically opportunistic tones, which convinced many Democrats who had rallied to his leadership in the first months after September 11 that he was using the national security crisis as a foil for partisan advantage, especially in the run-up to the 2002 midterm election. With hindsight, the roots of this political shift are visible in the White House staffing structure that began to emerge during the first transition period.

In retrospect, Bush's efficient, disciplined team of advisers, which performed so well in the first transition after the election, was poorly organized and staffed to serve and protect an inexperienced President in a national security crisis when his natural instinct was to substitute bravado for understanding and to scorn the pragmatism, conciliation, and nuance of diplomacy and alliances. His chief of staff, Andrew Card, embraced enthusiastically the "honest broker" model of his job, acting as a facilitator, consensus builder, tiebreaker, and orchestrator for strong policy advocates at Defense, State, the FBI, the CIA, and other national security agencies. By most accounts, he played a minimalist role in shaping the content of decisions flowing to the President. In staffing the White House, he enforced a strong emphasis on loyalty and teamwork.[29]

Condoleezza Rice adopted much the same approach to her job as national security adviser. Particularly in the first half of Bush's first term, she lacked the stature and experience to stand up to strong advocates at the Pentagon and in the vice president's office. As Jim Hoagland has noted in his superb analysis of national security decisionmaking in the White House, Rice "stayed out of the State-Pentagon-CIA battles and never established bureaucratic control over policy issues at the White House.

That left Cheney as the President's primary reference point when hard decisions had to be made."[30] Neither Card nor Rice, as gatekeepers for policy advice to the President, was prepared by either management style or experience to stand up to the determined push from the vice president's office for an invasion of Iraq. Dick Cheney, the strongest and, in terms of national security, by far the most experienced vice president in American history, had far more influence than Rice and was closely allied with Donald Rumsfeld and Paul Wolfowitz at Defense. Karl Rove and Karen Hughes, the other key confidants and advisers to the President, were focused on domestic policy and politics. Rove, as head of the Office of Strategic Initiatives in the White House, lacked any international or national security experience and reinforced Bush's natural instincts to focus on domestic policy objectives. From the earliest days, he had an expansive portfolio, which ranged over all policy issues coming to the President. Although trained as a pollster and campaign strategist, he became the de facto coordinator of domestic, national security, economic, and homeland security policy, a position that was institutionalized when he was named deputy chief of staff for policy coordination.[31] Karen Hughes, like Rove, belonged to the so-called "Austin group," former staffers in the Texas governor's office who made up over half of the White House staff. Her communications team kept the administration's officials relentlessly on message to support Rove's domestic political agenda.

Transitions are about the shift from campaigning to governing. The argument can be made, however, that George W. Bush, who is credited with effecting a model transition, and Bill Clinton, who was saddled with one of the worst, come out in the same place in one key respect: at first, neither really embraced the shift. At least in their first year, they preferred the permanent campaign to the serious work of governing.[32] Charles Jones, in his study of the Clinton transition, suggests that it is time to consider whether "an altered type of transition is upon us. The standard shift is from campaigning to governing, whereas the emerging progression may be from campaigning for office to campaigning for policy and status."[33] The latter requires a White House staff with a higher priority on managing opinion and enforcing political discipline than on using executive power to deal with long-term domestic and international problems. It also requires a different type of senior White House staff, for example a Karl Rove rather than a James Baker. Other recent Presidents, such as Carter and Clinton, in the early months of their Presidency also surrounded themselves with political cronies from their home state. One measure of the maturation of a new President is how quickly he makes the transition to more seasoned and Washington-savvy staff. Carter and Clinton had begun to do so by the middle of their second year. On the other hand, Karl Rove and to a lesser extent Karen Hughes expanded their influence throughout Bush's first term, and the weakness in the offices of the chief of staff and the national security adviser was not corrected. By the end of 2002, John DiIulio, director of the White House Office of Faith-Based and Community Initiatives, had concluded that the White House had no serious apparatus for making policy, foreign or domestic. What Bush had instead, he said, is "everything—and I mean everything—being run by the political arm. It's the reign of the Mayberry Machiavellis."[34] In retrospect, George W. Bush appears conditioned by temperament, lack of international experience, and a White House staffing and decision process to take a short-term, politically opportunistic approach to foreign policy and national security crises. Had the attack on the Twin Towers never happened, these fault lines in the Bush White House may still have crippled his Presidency, but with far less consequence to the nation and the world.

Neustadt saw evidence of the seeds of this failure months before September 11 in the style and attitude of Bush's early approach to international issues. Generally he advised new Presidents to show humility in reviewing the foreign policy legacy of their predecessor and not rush to repudiate hard-fought and long-term agreements for short-term political advantage. Instead George W. Bush, in the first six months of his Presidency, initiated a hasty and highly politicized repudiation of international agreements associated with the Clinton administration. In a speech given to a European audience in May 2003, Neustadt noted that "not since 1933, when Franklin Roosevelt sabotaged the London Economic Conference . . . have there been such reversals of international obligations undertaken, or at least ostensibly backed, by Clinton but repudiated by Bush."[35] Bush rapidly disengaged from policies and agreements initiated by the Clinton administration on international issues such as the Kyoto Protocol and cooperation on global warming, the nuclear nonproliferation agreement with North Korea, the Israeli-Palestine conflict, and U.S. support for a world tribunal on war crimes. His early break with these policies reflected an indifference rising to contempt for the process of international cooperation that would haunt him later in Iraq. Neustadt condemned the "angry, scornful, almost paranoid" tone of these announcements, where President Bush appeared to deny the importance, let alone the substance, of these issues. Neustadt presciently predicted that such paranoid reactions against predecessors can have boomerang effects.[36]

Dick had a front row seat in watching foreign reaction to Bush's first missteps as an international leader. He spent much of his last years splitting his time between Wellfleet, Massachusetts, and England. His second wife, Shirley Williams, was a founder of the by now well-established third political party, the Liberal Democrats, in the United Kingdom, and during the course of their marriage became her party's leader in the House of Lords. Neustadt was well aware that the radical shift in power in a "change-in-party" transition in the United States can provoke both shock and awe among our closest allies. He told me that this perspective deepened his concerns about the hazards of transitions in the United States and the impact they can have on the first impressions a President makes abroad.

At the end of a President's term, there is only one legacy that counts: how the President himself—not his vice president, not his national security adviser, not his secretary of defense, nor any other member of his cabinet or White House staff—has responded to the challenges and opportunities of his times. Neustadt understood that the American President ultimately sits alone with history. Hence his empathy even for failed Presidents and his emphasis on helping Presidents protect themselves against advisers, however well intentioned, with agendas more narrow and time bound than his. It is impossible to know whether George W. Bush could have avoided the mistakes that have crippled his Presidency in his second term if he had had a more experienced and able personal staff, Washington savvy and loyal only to him, to advise on international and national security affairs. His father and his senior advisers such as Brent Scowcroft might have helped, but by most accounts, George W. Bush studiously ignored them. In his compelling survey of presidential blunders in the first-term transition period, Neustadt concluded that in all of these instances, "The Presidents did not think hard enough, carefully enough, beforehand, about foreseeable, even likely[,] consequences to their own effectiveness in office, looking down the line and around corners." If in the aftermath of September 11, a McGeorge Bundy, a Ted Sorensen, or a James Baker had been available on his personal staff to "look around corners" in debates with Scooter Libby, Douglas Feith, and Paul Wolfowitz about the long-term consequences of going into Iraq, would George W. Bush have had the confidence to press home any initial doubts he may have had about the enterprise? Neustadt would probably have said no. As he noted in *Presidential Power*, "The professional reputation of a President in Washington is made or altered by the man himself. No one can guard it for him, no one saves him from himself."[37] If, like Kennedy, a President has the ability to learn quickly from failure, take responsibility for his mistakes, and hold the architects of blunders accountable, he can save himself and his administration. Unfortunately, George W. Bush was no John Kennedy, and not even Neustadt could tell us how to divine these qualities in our candidates before they are elected.

A good transition, alas, does not make a good President, although it may extend his post-inaugural honeymoon with the electorate. Personality trumps structure and process. If a President comes out of the transition with a well-organized staff and decision process that fits his needs, this may mitigate, but not remove, inadequacies rooted in personality traits and inexperience. When a weak staff serves an insecure President forced outside the comfort zone of his experience, the probability of failure rises exponentially. In 2000, many voters took comfort in the fact that George W. Bush's inexperience and untested temperament might be offset by the experience and mature presence of Cheney, Rumsfeld, and Powell. This was a mistake. Bush cultivated the image as a big-picture "CEO" President who valued order, process, and heavy delegation to his aides, but this leadership style can lead to overdependence on key advisers, particularly if the President himself lacks intellectual curiosity and has advisers who are either weak or motivated by strong agendas of their own.

Looking ahead to 2008, the transition hazard of "newness" for the incoming President will be even greater than in 1992 or 2000, because for the first time since 1952, no incumbent President or vice president will be on either party's ticket. If the President-elect is Hillary Clinton, her service as First Lady and domestic policy adviser is without precedent but is likely to be a plus. But more important than any particular experience is the ability of a new President to adapt, to learn from his inevitable gaffes and blunders. Ideally the new President will have the confidence to surround himself with people who are not afraid to bring him bad news and to make the tough choices that show that he can learn from his mistakes. Such was the case with John Kennedy after the Bay of Pigs.

If the DNA of candidates for the Presidency could reveal their ability to grow in office, mandatory testing should be required. Absent this, Neustadt, if he were still with us, would have this advice for Americans in 2008: "Choose your President very carefully because at the end of the day, no one can save him from himself (or herself, as the case may be)."

President Harry S. Truman is surrounded by his White House Staff in Key West, Florida, November 26, 1951. From the left, standing are John R. Steelman, Richard E. Neustadt, Donald S. Dawson, Milton P. Kayle, and Russell P. Andrews. Seated from the left are Kenneth W. Hechler, Dallas E. Halverson, Gen. Harry H. Vaughn, Truman, and David Noyes. Truman frequently went to Key West with his staff for working vacations.

for Richard E. Neustadt — in appreciation and best wishes John Kennedy

President John F. Kennedy in the Oval Office. Neustadt turned down a staff role in Kennedy's White House for a sabbatical in England with his family, and the independence that came with remaining a private consultant to the President.

An artful display of President Kennedy's reading material from a magazine in the 1960s. Among the President's choices is the first edition of Neustadt's classic *Presidential Power*. It was a wire photo of President-elect Kennedy on an airport tarmac, carrying *Presidential Power* under his arm, that first gave the book a nationwide audience.

President Lyndon B. Johnson meets in the Oval Office on June 7, 1966, with members of his administration to discuss an air carrier labor dispute. Johnson had appointed Neustadt to an emergency board in April to make findings of fact and recommendations regarding the dispute. Neustadt sits facing the camera, the first from the left. Also seated here, to Neustadt's left, are David Ginsburg and Senator Wayne Morse, the other two members of the emergency board. Facing away from the camera, from left to right, are White House aide Joe Califano, Assistant Secretary of Labor James Reynolds and Secretary of Labor Willard Wirtz.

A working meal with Johnson in the Dining Room in the Mansion of the White House, April 21, 1966. Neustadt is helping draft a message to Congress regarding ways to improve the quality of the government. A smiling Neustadt sits immediately to the President's right. Also pictured are Joe Califano, seated to Neustadt's right, Willard Wirtz directly across from Neustadt, and White House aide Bill Moyers.

Participants at the oral history interview with former President Jimmy Carter, in Plains, Georgia, November 29, 1982. Neustadt stands immediately to Carter's right. Charles O. Jones, a contributor to this volume, stands directly behind the former President. Carter acknowledged that his Presidency might have experienced a less bumpy road had he heeded more of Neustadt's advice. (Photo courtesy of the Miller Center of Public Affairs, University of Virginia)

DEPARTMENT OF HEALTH, EDUCATION, AND WELFARE
OFFICE OF THE SECRETARY
WASHINGTON, D.C. 20201

July 6, 1977

MEMORANDUM FOR THOSE CONCERNED

SUBJECT: Study Assignment to Richard E. Neustadt

I have asked Professor Richard E. Neustadt of Harvard University to review the whole course of decision-making and implementation for the swine flu program from the time of the initial outbreak at Fort Dix through the first months of the new Administration.

The purpose of this study is to help us better understand the problems involved and to seek lessons for the future decisions which the Department will have to make on these complex issues in public health. Professor Neustadt has had invaluable experience in studies of this sort for comparable purposes in previous Administrations. Working with him will be his close colleague, Dr. Harvey Fineberg of the Harvard School of Public Health.

I commend them to you and ask your full cooperation.

Joseph A. Califano, Jr.

GERALD R. FORD

August 30, 1977

Dear Joe:

Your letter of August 18, 1977 made sense. Please let Professor Neustadt know that I would be happy to see him sometime in the future.

He is in good hands if he is talking with Jim Cavanaugh. After he's done there have him contact Bob Barrett of my staff to coordinate the event.

As always, the problems of your department abound--good luck in working for their solution.

With warm regards,

Sincerely,

Jerry Ford

Mr. Joseph A. Califano, Jr.
Secretary of H.E.W.
Washington, D.C. 20201

Neustadt greets Nancy Reagan at a reception. "Never let your Nancy be immobilized" was one lesson Neustadt extracted from President Reagan's Iran-contra affair.

At left: Correspondence between former President Gerald Ford and Carter's Secretary of Health, Education and Welfare, Joe Califano. Ford authorizes his aides to cooperate with Neustadt's and Harvey V. Fineberg's investigation into the swine flu affair. Whenever possible, Neustadt sought to use the lessons from these consulting roles in his research and teaching on the Presidency.

The "little yellow house" at 78 Mt. Auburn Street, on the Harvard University campus. The property housed the Institute of Politics (IOP) between 1966 and 1978. Neustadt described securing this property to hold IOP-related events "the best strategic decision I ever made." (Harvard University News Office)

Jacqueline Kennedy meeting in October 1966 with Neustadt and other members of the senior advisory committee to establish the Institute of Politics as a living memorial to JFK and to change the name of the Graduate School of Public Administration to the John F. Kennedy School of Government. Katherine Graham, then publisher of the *Washington Post,* sits to Neustadt's immediate left. Averell Harriman is to the left of Jacqueline Kennedy. (Harvard University News Office)

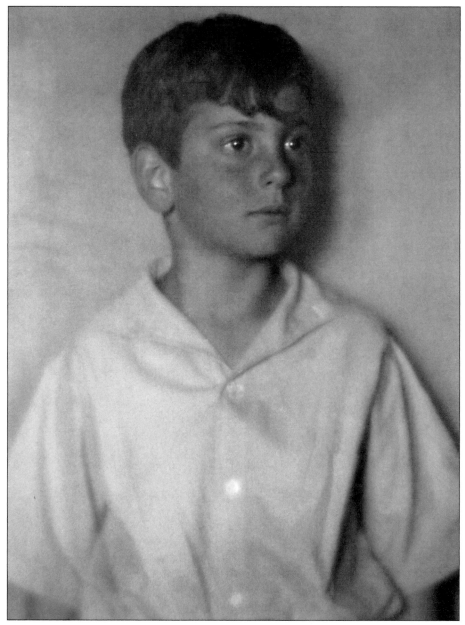
Little Richard, as the young Richard E. Neustadt was called by members of his family, in deference to his father, Richard M. Neustadt.

A self-described "political bureaucrat" turned professor, Neustadt taught several generations of students. A framed version of this photo, signed by many of his former students and presented to him in honor of his eighty-first birthday, is located in a classroom dedicated to him in the Rubenstein Building at Harvard's Kennedy School of Government. (Photo courtesy of Martha Stewart)

Neustadt was well known for his smoking, as well as the use of cigarettes as props during his lectures. Some listeners even kept track of how many were smoked during a fifty-minute talk. While at Harvard in his forties, having smoked since age sixteen, he gave up cigarettes because of a hacking cough and took up the pipe. In 1970 he gave up pipe smoking too, rather than risk being unable to lecture for a living.

Former President Truman at one of several breakfasts at the Neustadts' New York City apartment before giving the Radner lectures at Columbia University in 1959. Behind Truman are Bertha (Bert) Cummings Neustadt, married to Neustadt from 1945 until her death in 1984, and their son, Richard (Rick), then eleven years old. After one such gathering, the former President spontaneously seated himself at the Neustadts' old upright piano and launched into a Mozart sonata, sight reading the music open at the moment.

Probably in the mid-1960s, a smiling Dick listens to Bert make a point. Bert had always worn her hair short until she married Dick, who insisted she grow it. She wore it in a signature bun for many years.

When her multiple sclerosis began to affect her dexterity, Bert returned to a short hair cut. This photograph, taken by Rick probably in the late 1970s, is from the family's summer home on Gull Pond, Cape Cod.

Shirley Williams and Dick on the dance floor, celebrating the twentieth anniversary of the Institute of Politics in 1987. Francis Bator recalls that dancing, which Dick loved to do, epitomized Dick's "blending of fun and purpose." Invitations to IOP-sponsored dances (black tie, decorations allowed) kept alive a sense of "the nobility and fun of politics," Neustadt once noted. In all his roles, Dick remained light on his feet. (Photo courtesy of Martha Stewart)

Shirley Williams lecturing. After Shirley accepted both Neustadt's marriage proposal and a teaching position at the Kennedy School, Dean Graham Allison teased that by marrying her, Neustadt had done more to advance the hiring of women at the Kennedy School than the entire faculty had done in the prior decade.

CHAPTER FIVE

TWO OF JFK's AIDES REMEMBER KENNEDY's MACHIAVELLI

THEODORE C. SORENSEN AND ARTHUR SCHLESINGER JR., two of President John F. Kennedy's closest White House aides, provide intimate portraits of Richard E. Neustadt's role as Kennedy's Machiavelli, beginning with Neustadt's service as one of Kennedy's transition advisers in 1960 and 1961. But it would be a mistake to infer from the reference to Machiavelli that Neustadt's applied lessons were intended to show JFK—or any president—how to gain power for its own sake. The crowning lesson Neustadt taught generations of students and political practitioners is that Presidents work within a Constitution-based system of shared powers. It follows, as he reminded his readers in the preface to the 1990 edition of *Presidential Power*, that Presidents—and their aides—ought to think about power "in its symbolic and constitutional dimensions," and not just as an end in itself.

Neustadt's service to Kennedy, following so closely on the heels of the publication of *Presidential Power*, established his reputation as someone who moved seamlessly between the worlds of academia and presidential politics. In commenting on Neustadt's prominence as a "presidential expert" both Schlesinger and Sorensen also describe their own friendships with Dick.

RICHARD E. NEUSTADT, PRESIDENTIAL EXPERT
Theodore C. Sorensen

After receiving the Democratic nomination for President in 1960, John F. Kennedy—a prudent and curious man who was brainy enough to know that he did not possess all the brains he needed—planned well in advance of his election by asking two separate individuals to prepare for him reports and recommendations on how he should conduct the transition period between his November 1960 election and his January 20, 1961, inauguration: Clark Clifford, the skilled and renowned Washington lawyer who had served as special counsel to President Truman, and Richard E. Neustadt (everyone, without exception, called him Dick), a then little-known professor of political science at Columbia University who had also served in the Executive Office of the President under Truman—both in the Budget Bureau and on the White House Staff, if I'm not mistaken. JFK met with them separately, made clear what he wanted, and instructed them not to consult with or copy each other, and not to obtain advice from or share their conclusions with the members of the Kennedy campaign team.

Both reports were delivered to Kennedy, who distributed copies to me and others around Election Day. They took remarkably similar approaches and made remarkably similar recommendations. For example, both reports urged that the President-elect's immediate needs during the transition would include—in addition to a press secretary—a policy and program adviser, a position that could be combined with speechwriter and message draftsman. Neither report specified that this appointee be a lawyer, though Clifford—drawing upon his personal experience—suggested reviving the title "special counsel," last used during Truman's presidency, for this position. All indications were that both reports took into consideration the reality of the existing Kennedy team and had me in mind for the job. In any event, JFK, in our first postelection discussion, asked me to fill that post, and to initiate transition planning immediately. Soon thereafter I met with Dick Neustadt, and depended upon him for advice, counsel, and assistance throughout the transition and beyond. He suggested another Truman White House veteran, David Bell, as our director of the budget bureau, a superb recommendation of an invaluable appointee.

For many years, the presidential transition has been structured according to guidelines laid out in an Act of Congress, with a substantial appropriation to pay the expenses of those involved. The smooth and successful Eisenhower–Kennedy transition, to the best of my recollection, had no such Act of Congress as reference point, no appropriation, and no detailed guidance of any kind, except from Dick Neustadt and, in a broader sense, Clark Clifford.

Dick remained available for assorted Presidential assignments. When JFK wanted a special study on what went wrong in the U.S.-U.K. controversy over this government's failure to provide the British with Skybolt missiles, he appointed a task force noted for its members' professionalism, objectivity, integrity, and insights; it consisted of one man, Dick Neustadt. Dick played a key role throughout Kennedy's thousand days, and then played an indispensable part in guiding the Kennedy family and legatees in the establishment of the Kennedy Library, the Kennedy School of Government at Harvard, and the Kennedy Institute of Politics within that School. He also served as the IOP director. He was beloved as director by students and colleagues, but ran into some unfortunate misunderstandings—as would any new director—with those members of the Kennedy family who had their own firm ideas on what should be done.

Fortunately, our paths continued to cross. In addition to being my friend and colleague, Dick became the country's foremost presidential scholar, historian, analyst, and author. Inasmuch as I was occasionally called upon to speak and write on the subject of the Presidency, I drew heavily from his insightful books—extremely articulately, comprehensively, and authoritatively written, they reflected his academic studies, practical experience, organized mind, sense of history, and sense of humor.

Though he was not a lawyer, his writings on presidential power remain today more authoritative in their interpretation of both the U.S. Constitution and historical precedents than many books by renowned professors of constitutional law.

In the presidential campaign of 1976, the Democratic nominee, Jimmy Carter, also established a team to prepare in advance for the Ford–Carter transition, in the event that there would be one. That team was headed by Carter's aide Jack Watson, later Carter's chief of staff, and included two other members, Dick Neustadt and me. The three of us, working long and hard, produced a comprehensive report. Many of its recommendations and findings, sad to say, were ignored by those closest to Carter, people who had been with him on the campaign trail while we three were working on the transition report. (That is often the fate of transition reports. But I have reason to know that the report was read and appreciated by the President-elect.) In that context, Jack Watson asked Dick to write a separate memorandum for the report on the sensitive issue of the Central Intelligence Agency. In his otherwise excellent memorandum, Dick described the qualities he believed necessary for the position of director of Central Intelligence, concluding, unfortunately, that "the job should be filled by someone like Ted Sorensen." Watson passed that recommendation along to Carter, and Carter adopted it. The recommendation, in my opinion, was doomed for a variety of reasons. Flattered as I was by Dick's endorsement, the nomination caused substantial, maybe even predictable, controversy, and was ultimately withdrawn. Dick and I remained friends throughout the rest of his life, despite that little error on his part.

I have no doubt that in his heart, Dick identified with the Democratic Party. But he was such a meticulous scholar and so committed to the objectivity of the precepts about which he wrote and taught that there was no evidence of political bias—none that I could see—in any of his books or teachings. In that way, and so many others, Dick Neustadt was an extraordinary man who should, and will, be long remembered.

Dick Neustadt
Arthur Schlesinger Jr.

How did Richard E. Neustadt and John Fitzgerald Kennedy meet? Dick's *Presidential Power* came out in April of 1960, the year that JFK won the Presidency in November. Dick's book was shaking up the political science establishment much as JFK's victory was shaking up the political establishment. Neustadt was the first political scientist to describe the President as persuader and bargainer. Kennedy was the first President born in the twentieth century, the first Catholic to become President, the youngest man ever to be elected President.

Not long after Kennedy's victory, my wife and I were invited to Hyannis Port for luncheon. As we went in to lunch, the President-elect brandished a collection of memorandums on the issues of transition, prepared, he said, by Clark Clifford, a Washington attorney who had served as Truman's special counsel from 1946 to 1950, and a "Professor Neustadt of Columbia." Over luncheon we discussed assignments and appointments for the new administration. JFK had already raised such questions with

Clifford, his friend and sometime counsel: "If I am elected," he had told Clifford, "I don't want to wake up on the morning of November 9 and have to ask myself, 'What in the world do I do now?'" His own experience and that of his staff, he pointed out, had been on the legislative side. He needed to analyze the problems of taking over the executive branch, and he thought Clifford with his White House background in the Truman administration would be ideal. Clifford, impressed by Kennedy's foresight, had promptly accepted the assignment.

Clifford discussed the transition with Neustadt, an associate from their Truman days. After the Democratic defeat in 1952, Neustadt had ended up as a professor of political science at Columbia. By the time Clifford approached him, Neustadt had already been tapped by Senator Henry Jackson, chairman of the Democratic National Committee, to produce a memorandum, "Organizing the Transition," in anticipation of a Democratic win. On September 18, 1960, Jackson took Dick out to Georgetown to meet Kennedy and show him the transition document. JFK, sitting in his garden, flipped through the twenty pages of the memo in his usual manner. He liked it at once, and it is easy to see why. The presentation was crisp and methodical, and included a numbered list of specific actions. Dick began by questioning campaign talk about "another Hundred Days," a caution inspiring confidence in the sobriety of the memo's author. The memo constantly stressed the importance of flexibility.

JFK told Dick to elaborate his argument in further memos. "When you finish," JFK said, "I want you to send the material back directly to me. I don't want you to send it to anybody else." Dick asked, "How do you want me relate to Clark Clifford?" JFK replied quickly, "I don't want you to relate to Clark Clifford. I can't afford to confine myself to one set of advisers. If I did that, *I* would be on *their* leading strings." Once Kennedy said that, the author of *Presidential Power* was thereafter on *his* leading string.

Clifford and Neustadt, both equally hostile to the top-heavy bureaucracy that surrounded Eisenhower, ended up stressing the same points. After the election, Robert Kennedy tried to persuade Dick to serve as special assistant to the President, but in vain. Dick, having had practical experience in the Truman days, preferred the freedom to analyze and to speculate from not being tied formally to the administration, which may ultimately have increased his value to Kennedy. In 1962 the United States and Britain disagreed angrily over Skybolt, a two-stage ballistic missile launched from a bomber. JFK asked Neustadt in March 1963 to undertake a study designed to find out how two close allies could have miscalculated and fallen into a surely avoidable crisis. Neustadt spent the summer on the project and submitted the result to the President on November 15, 1963. JFK read it with care and on November 20 told his assistant, McGeorge Bundy, to tell Neustadt, "I want to see him after I get back from Texas."[1] He never got back from Texas.

Sometime later Jacqueline Kennedy gave me the Skybolt report to read, remarking how fond her husband had been of Dick Neustadt. I would judge that the bond between them was their sense of humor. They both were ironists—not passive, all-out ironists, but pragmatic ironists yielding to the need for action. That is why it was so much fun working with them.

CHAPTER SIX

AN AMERICAN IN ENGLAND

ANTHONY KING

DICK ARRIVED IN England along with Bert, Betsy—as Beth was then known—and Rick in the autumn of 1961. He was already a famous man, not famous in the movie-star sense but famous among his academic colleagues, among students, and, not least, among those policy-makers in Whitehall and Downing Street sensitive to developments in the outside world, especially in the world across the Atlantic. Not only was he famous: he was remarkable, and those of us who happened to be in Oxford at the time knew it.

It is now more than half a century since Harry Truman left the White House and since Dick, a staunch Democrat, had no option but to leave along with him. But at the time that Dick arrived in England in 1961, only eight years had elapsed. Truman was still alive, and we now had in our midst a man who had been with Truman during the years of the famous Republican "do-nothing" Congress, the first days of the anti-Communist witch hunts, North Korea's invasion of South Korea, China's crossing of the Yalu, and Truman's sacking of General MacArthur. The arrival in England for more than a fleeting visit of a man with comparable experience of American government would cause a bit of a stir even today, but in

81

that pre-jet-hopping age it was a major event. The Neustadt family had come all this way by sea, and the country to which they came was still called England. In those days, one did not have to call the country the United Kingdom or Britain—on grounds of either accuracy or political correctness.

Dick was not only an ex–White House staffer. He had written a book. It was called *Presidential Power,* and anyone who had not read it by the time Dick arrived on the scene certainly did read it soon afterward. How many of us not only read the book but understood it is another matter. Dick's prose style was deceptive: simple and straightforward on one level, subtle and complex—and based on a wealth of reflected-upon personal experience—on another. To this day, rereading *Presidential Power* invariably yields new insights. Trying to teach from it makes one realize just how subtle and, in the best sense of the word, how worldly it is.

There was the book, but there was also the world-famous man who had read it and who, remarkably, had allowed the world to know that he had read it. When Dick arrived in the autumn of 1961, John F. Kennedy had occupied the Oval Office only since the previous January. His formidable inaugural address was behind him. The Bay of Pigs—or Cuba I, as Dick later taught us to call it—was ahead of him. The sense of excitement of that time is still hard to recapture. If anything, the excitement was greater in England than it was in the United States. Kennedy was not the divisive figure in the United Kingdom that he was in the United States (what had *really* gone on in Cook County?), and Britons could not help contrasting the new President's youthful vigor with the physical and sometimes, it seemed, mental decrepitude of the aging British Prime Minister, Harold Macmillan. Kennedy *was* exciting, and some of the excitement inevitably rubbed off on Dick. Here was a man who knew Kennedy, who had worked with him and whose great book had even been read by him. In fact, Dick never traded on his acquaintance with Kennedy. On the contrary, he took care almost never to refer to it. Kennedy for Dick was never "Jack." He was always "Mr. Kennedy" or "the President." Dick's respect for the Presidency, for the heavy responsibilities that went with that office and therefore for whoever bore those responsibilities, was implicit in everything he said—and in the tone in which he said it. Dick always insisted that *Presidency* should be spelled with a capital *P.* If *Congress* merited an initial capital, the *Presidency* did, too.

Dick lectured on the Presidency at Oxford. His lectures were major events, remembered by all who attended them. He lectured from notes, and he spoke very . . . very . . . very slowly . . . with pauses between phrases and sentences that seemed insupportably long. Oxford students in those days prided themselves on thinking and speaking ridiculously fast. It was the local affectation. Dick's measured manner of speaking therefore came as a shock to the system. But no one ever made the mistake of supposing that, because Dick spoke slowly, he also thought slowly. It was obvious to the meanest intelligence that, precisely because he thought very quickly and also very subtly, he needed time to organize his thoughts and to decide how best to articulate them. Fortunately for him (though perhaps less fortunately in the long term), Dick always had a prop, or, rather, a whole chain of props. A cigarette—lit, unlit, about to be lit—was seldom far from his lips. The cigarettes, lighting them, pulling on them, holding them out at arm's length, validated his pauses and bought him time to think. Occasionally members of his audience tried to keep track of how many cigarettes Dick got through during his allotted fifty minutes, but they usually lost count. The content of what he was saying commanded—and soon secured—their undivided attention. Dick gave frequent lectures, but he also found time—he always gave the impression of having an infinite amount of time—to talk to students, mostly graduate students. He talked—and he listened—in common rooms, on college lawns, and on walks through Oxford's parks and lanes. In his own pensive way, he was the best of company.

But Dick had another life, one of which his Oxford contemporaries were only vaguely aware. Dick was a man of government, and he cleaved to other men of government. (They were almost all men in those far-off, unenlightened days.) He wanted to talk to them, and they certainly wanted to talk to him. The curiosity of each matched the curiosity of the other. Especially for British civil servants, it was fun to be able to talk, on a basis of equality, with someone from outside one's own system. Dick's being an outsider meant that people in Whitehall would talk to him more freely than they would talk to people in other government agencies—or possibly to the man in the next-door office. Some of them must sometimes have wished that Dick *was* the man in the next-door office.

The Oxford experience yielded personal results: friendships that, in many cases, lasted for the rest of his life. The Whitehall experience yielded personal results, and, in addition, it yielded results that were more professional. One such was a paper, frequently printed and reprinted in subsequent years, called "White House and Whitehall" (not, note, "White

House and Downing Street").[1] The paper bore witness to Dick's insistence, always one of the most important characteristics of his work, on thinking his way into other people's minds and professional situations: locating *them* in *their* working environment, identifying *their* stakes and *their* ambitions, working out what *they* could reasonably be expected to know and, not least, taking note of the expectations that they and those around them had of themselves and of each other. Men and women often assume that their own vantage point is also that of others. Dick never made that mistake. He had not only worked in government: he had drawn from his governmental experience a rare and precious set of analytic skills.

"White House and Whitehall" was a work of social science, but it was also a work of social anthropology: one old pro unobtrusively observing the tribal rites and customs of other old pros. He began by describing, on the basis of his own observations, the relationship that he recognized as being at the heart of the British system of government: that between government ministers and the permanent career civil servants who advised them. Senior civil servants, Dick observed, governed Britain in collaboration with their political superiors, the front-bench politicians who happened to command a parliamentary majority for the time being.

> Theirs [he wrote] is an intimate collaboration grounded in the interests and traditions of both sides. Indeed it binds them into a society for mutual benefit: what they succeed in sharing with each other they need share with almost no one else, and governing in England is a virtual duopoly.

This society for mutual benefit was, he believed, the product of a tacit treaty, an implicit bargain, expressed in self-restraint that was observed on either side:

> The senior civil servants neither stall nor buck decisions of the government once taken in due form by their political masters. "Due form" means consultation, among other things, but having been consulted these officials act without public complaint or private evasion, even though they may have fought what they are doing up to the last moment of decision.

For their part, Dick maintained, ministers of the Crown returned the favor in full measure, with only rare and transient exceptions:

The politicians rarely meddle with official recruitment and promotion; by and large, officialdom administers itself. They preserve the anonymity of civil servants both in parliament and in the press. Officials never testify on anything except "accounts," and nobody reveals their roles in shaping public policy. Ministers take kudos for themselves, likewise the heat. They also take upon themselves protection for the status of officialdom in society: honours fall like gentle rain at stated intervals. They even let careerists run their private offices, and treat their personal assistants of the moment (detailed from civil service ranks) as confidentially as our department heads treat trusted aides imported from outside. More importantly, politicians *lean* on their officials. They *expect* to be advised. More importantly, they very often do what they are told, and follow the advice that they receive.

But Dick's principal purpose in writing the paper was not to educate his American readership in the folkways of British government (even though those folkways were of far more interest to his fellow Americans then than they would be today). His principal purpose was to draw Americans' attention to features of their own system that, but for the Anglo-American comparison, they might overlook. "First," Dick said, "we have counterparts for their top civil servants—but not in our own civil service. Second, we have counterparts for their cabinet ministers—but not exclusively, or even mainly in our cabinet." To imagine that American civil servants and British civil servants performed the same political functions simply because they were both called civil servants, or to imagine that members of the American and British cabinets performed the same political functions merely because both countries boasted an institution that happened to be called "the cabinet," was to fall victim to semantics, to confuse function with form. The equivalents in Washington of top-level career civil servants in Britain were "*non*-careerists holding jobs infused with presidential interest or concern—'in-and-outers' from the law firms, banking, business, academia, foundations, or occasionally journalism, or the entourages of successful governors or senators—along with up-and-outers (sometimes up-and-downers) who relinquish, or at least risk, civil service status in the process."

Here [Dick wrote] is the elite-of-the-elite, the upper-crust of *our* "administrative class." These are the men who serve alongside our equivalents for ministers and share in governing. One finds them in

the White House and in the *appointive* jobs across the street at the
Executive Office Building. One finds them also on the seventh floor
of State, and on the third and fourth floors of the Pentagon: these
places among others. If they have not arrived as yet, they probably are
trying to get in (or up). If they have gone already, they are likely to
be back.

In the 1960s Dick cited Averell Harriman and Clark Clifford. Forty years on,
he probably would have cited (though not with approval) Paul Wolfowitz.

Similarly, the American equivalents of British cabinet ministers were
not mainly U.S.-style cabinet officers, though a very few of them might
attain that status, but those men, wherever they were located in Washington, whom the president had to square before he could achieve any of his
major objectives. A large proportion of those power holders—those who
must be squared—were to be found, needless to say, unlike their British
counterparts, not in executive-branch agencies and departments but on
Capitol Hill, in the House and the Senate. The pattern was long familiar
"of a President manoeuvring around or through the power men in his
administration *and* in Congress." Only occasionally did Britain's power
men include government backbenchers in the House of Commons, let
alone opposition MPs.

Dick, of course, could not resist entering the debate then raging in
Britain—it rages still—concerning whether the British system was, or was
not, becoming more "presidential," with the Prime Minister the man (or in
the 1980s the woman) in charge. Sure, Dick pointed out, British Prime
Ministers can often get their way, sometimes quite quickly, and he cited
examples from his own time in England. But hang on, British Prime Ministers often have no option but to square the people he called "influentials"
in their own political environment, and squaring them can be time consuming and political-capital consuming. Not infrequently they fail. More
to the point, American Presidents are not nearly as presidential as they
look. *They* have to square *their* influentials. Presidents as well as Prime
Ministers have to be artists in maneuver. He noted,

Underneath our images of Presidents-in-boots, astride decisions, are
the half-observed realities of Presidents-in-sneakers, stirrups in hand,
trying to induce particular department heads, or congressmen, or
senators to climb aboard.

The conclusion that needed to be drawn struck Dick as obvious: "The [British] PM is not yet a President. The President, however, is a sort of super Prime Minister. . . . This," he added triumphantly, "is what comes of comparative inquiry!" To this day, most British commentators on the alleged presidentialization of the British system are insensitive to the prime-ministerial features of the American system that Dick so long ago discerned.

By the time Dick wrote "White House and Whitehall" in 1965 he had become a regular, or at least a frequent, transoceanic traveler, renewing friendships, making new friends and acquaintances, and nosing and poking on both sides of the Atlantic. British politics, far more than American politics, has a village-like quality, and Dick had become a villager. The only thing he lacked was the vote, and that lack was actually an advantage because the Brits he encountered were not tempted to impute partisanship to him. An American Democrat like Dick could be, in Britain, a moderate Labourite, or a moderate Tory, or even a Liberal. No matter. Who cared? Dick was accepted for what he was—a quintessential man of government—and it did not greatly matter which of the two major British parties happened to be in power.

To begin with, he enjoyed (in his own words) "the vague status of sometime-Kennedy-consultant" ("It helps to be an object of curiosity"). Then, in 1963, President Kennedy asked him to provide him with a confidential report on how both he and Harold Macmillan had contrived to turn up at the Nassau conference of the previous year largely ignorant of each other's stakes and priorities ("Prime Minister Macmillan cooperated. I learned a lot"). In 1964 President Kennedy's successor, Lyndon Johnson, asked Dick to facilitate communications between the two governments in preparing for the first meeting between Johnson and the new British Prime Minister, Harold Wilson ("Again, I learned a lot"). Each flight across the Atlantic—alas, stately ocean-liner voyages were by this time a thing of the past—added to his store of knowledge. More than knowledge: understanding.

Dick's confidential report on the Nassau conference and the events leading up to it—submitted to President Kennedy in November 1963 but so sensitive that it was not declassified until April 1992—is a masterpiece of Neustadtian analysis, a set of elaborate variations on the single theme, a theme enunciated in one of his opening paragraphs:

"Skybolt" [a missile system the abrupt cancellation of which precipitated the awkward dealings between the President and the Prime
Minister at Nassau] as an issue between Washington and London
was caused . . . by successive failures on the part of busy persons to
perceive and make allowance for the needs and wants of others:
failures among "Chiefs" to share their reasoning with "Indians";
failure among Indians to sense—or heed—the reservations of their
Chiefs; failures among Americans to comprehend restraints upon
contingency-planning in London; failures among Englishmen to
comprehend imperatives of budgeting in Washington; failures on all
sides to consider how A's conduct might tie B's tongue.[2]

As always (well, almost always), Dick ascribed the specific pre-Nassau
Anglo-American misunderstandings not to the failures of individuals
(though individuals had failed) but to the characteristic failure of all decisionmakers everywhere to enter in imagination into the worlds of other
decisionmakers and to seek to view *their* worlds as *they* see them through
their eyes. Dick believed that his Skybolt report was one of the last state
papers—possibly *the* last state paper—that Kennedy read. He also believed
that it was one of the first state papers—possibly *the* first state paper—that
Kennedy ever gave his wife to read. Dick submitted his report on November 15, 1963. A week later the President was dead.

Years later, back in England, Dick could not resist trawling through the
now-open British archives to check his own interview-based account of
the events leading up to the Nassau conference against the contemporary
documentary record, at least the record on the British side. It says much
for Dick and President Kennedy, as well as for British ministers' desire to
remain on good terms with America, that Dick in 1963 was given permission to interview the Prime Minister's private secretaries and his minister
of defense as well as officials more distant from the center of power. Even
so, as Dick discovered to his amusement, Prime Minister Macmillan had
been extremely reluctant to grant him access:

Lord Home, the Foreign Secretary, and Peter Thorneycroft [the
defense minister], along with the Lord Privy Seal—Edward Heath,
who knew me—had to coax him into it. They decided, as the internal
record shows, that my interviewees "should not give Professor
Neustadt any paper. . . ." To make sure, the PM scribbled in the

margin of the Foreign Office memo before him, "I agree. But it is important not to have a document."

Otherwise, Macmillan feared, the whole transaction would soon find its way into the newspapers.

The upshot was that, while Dick could talk to people, and they could talk to him, he was not to be given sight of any of the communications that had passed between the British ministers.

Macmillan's instruction no doubt explains why the only papers I was shown in London during August 1963—as I pursued my inquiry for JFK—were transcripts of transatlantic or cross-channel meetings, and then only certain pages, one at a time, and literally shown—held out across the desk so I could read, by craning, while the owner kept a hand-hold (or kindly read to me).

Having thus craned, read, and listened at the time, Dick was relieved to discover three decades later that the passages relating to Britain in his report to President Kennedy, while they contained a few factual errors, contained none of great importance.

Dick's personal interest in things British, as well as the then importance of things British, led him in 1966 to give a series of lectures at Columbia—published four years later as *Alliance Politics*—in which he used two transatlantic crises, Suez and Skybolt, to explore "the task of maintaining friendly relations" between friendly allies such as Britain and the U.S.[3] The jacket of the book was adorned with a colored picture of the Stars and Stripes next to one of the Union Jack. Once again, Dick, ever the general-izer, disdained accounts of the two crises that attributed them simply to the vagaries of personality and differences of policy and priority. Such differences there were, of course, but to rest content with explanations along those lines would be to suggest that all crises in the relations between friendly nations are unique and that there are no future lessons to be learned from past mistakes.

Dick thought the core lesson to be learned from the fracas over Suez and Skybolt was, and is, that "foreign relations begin at home." The crises of 1956 and 1962 were brought on by each side's perceptions—that is, their misperceptions—of the other's concerns: "The villain of the piece is blurry vision by the light of hope, as each side looked abroad to gauge the other's bind and bite. These men made few mistakes when they took note of what the other side was *doing*. Perception of its actual behavior was not the problem. Comprehension of what lay behind the behavior was the problem." Each side projected onto the other an outcome that would suit its own convenience. Each side, in addition, imagined that the other side was subject to a set of political constraints that would conduce to its own, not the other side's, preferred outcome. Those in charge on both sides constantly judged each other's thought processes by analogy with their own. The fact of friendship itself induced misplaced confidence in each side's knowledge of the other.

Of course, Dick was able to write as he did because, if Britain's ministers and officials were invariably playing their own British game, and if America's "clever chaps" (as the British saw them) were invariably playing their own American game, and if each side was therefore invariably liable to misconstrue the other's game in terms of its own, Dick, having spent so much time in both Washington and London, was uniquely well placed to be able to identify the sources of these continuing misconstructions. "Uniquely" in the previous sentence means just that: uniquely. Even the two countries' most skillful ambassadors—and Dick in *Alliance Politics* graciously named several of them—lacked any full comprehension of the workings of the governmental machine in the friendly but yet foreign country to which they were accredited. Dick spent much of the rest of his working life helping to elaborate frames of reference in which the chances of such mutual misconstructions might be minimized—never eliminated, just, with luck, minimized. It takes little imagination to guess what Dick would have thought of Britain's and America's mutual relations in the run-up to the invasion of Iraq in 2003. It takes even less imagination to guess what he would have thought of the quality of the thinking at the top of both countries' governments about the situation in Iraq itself.

Dick spent less time in England during the 1970s and early 1980s than he had done during the previous decade. He visited often, but the visits tended to be short and more social than professional (insofar as Dick differentiated between the two). The Republicans were in power in the United States during much of this time; Dick's relations with the one Democratic President of that era, Jimmy Carter, were not close; and Dick was spending most of his time helping to establish the Kennedy School and developing its curriculum at Harvard. Latterly his wife, Bert, was increasingly ill and needing to be looked after. Dick's life for a number of years was largely Cambridge-centered (Cambridge, Massachusetts, not Cambridge, England).

But then, suddenly, he entered another English phase of his life. From now on he was to be at home, literally as well as figuratively, in both countries. After a prolonged and debilitating illness, Bert died of multiple sclerosis in May 1984. Dick's devotion to her, and his care of her, had bordered on the saintly. Friends had observed, marveled, and been moved. But Bert's death inevitably came as a release as well as a wrenching deprivation, and Dick soon had another woman in his life. She was Shirley Williams, a British politician and intellectual and a good friend of Bert's as well as of Dick's (before her death Bert actually recommended Shirley to Dick). The two married three years later, and from then on Dick lived—sometimes without Shirley (both of them traveled at lot), more often with her—in Cambridge, Massachusetts; on the Cape; in a London flat; and in Shirley's house in a Hertfordshire village. He became stepfather to her daughter, Rebecca, and step-uncle to her niece and nephew, Larissa and Alexander, all of which roles he played with sensitivity, skill, and devotion. Dick was never an Englishman—heaven forfend—but he certainly felt at home, because he was at home, both in political London and in the gentle English countryside.

To be married to a politician—and, moreover, a politician who was enormously popular and a former cabinet minister—was, for Dick, sheer bliss. Shirley, then still in the Labour Party, had lost her seat in the House of Commons as a result of the 1979 Conservative landslide but had then been reelected for another seat two years later, this time as a Social Democrat. She then lost that seat, as a result of another Conservative landslide in 1983, but a decade later found herself again a parliamentarian, this time as a member of the House of Lords. For three years she led her party, now rechristened the Liberal Democrats, in the Upper House. However, the important point is that, whatever the vicissitudes of politics and whatever her formal position, Shirley remained a public figure, in the midst of every political controversy, with a wide circle of political friends, pressed constantly to write newspaper articles and appear on radio and television. She was, in her own self-effacing way, a star.

Dick loved it. He was inevitably something of a consort figure, at least when he and Shirley were in England, but he did not mind one bit. He loved Shirley and was proud of her, he loved the company of her fellow politicians, and anyway he knew he was a star in his own right, with no need to concern himself with his star rating. In any case, he had never objected to just sitting and listening, unless someone asked him a direct question or was talking arrant nonsense. It gave both Dick and Shirley pleasure that some of the personal ill will generated at the time of the Social Democrat breakaway from Labour gradually dissipated and they were able to renew old friendships with people who had remained on the Labour side. As a retired man of government himself, Dick especially enjoyed the company of other retired men of government, such as Denis Healey, who had served successive Labour Prime Ministers as secretary of state for defense and chancellor of the exchequer. (Denis was credited with offering one of the best-ever pieces of political advice: "If you're in a hole, stop digging.")

But Dick by no means spent all of his time consorting. He traveled on his own, gave lectures, attended conferences, and saw friends in England as well as in the U.S. For several years he taught part-time at the University of Essex, and British students in the 1990s were just as thrilled to have Dick in their midst as they had been in the 1960s; he often found himself autographing copies of his own books that students had acquired for themselves. His occasional lectures—of which he gave many in London, Oxford, and elsewhere—were as well crafted and carefully prepared as any he had ever given, and his intellectual creativity and powers of observation never flagged. The only sign that he was getting on a bit was that, for the first time, he lectured from a written-out text instead of from notes. But of course, Dick being Dick, he continued to lecture standing up and the truth was that he digressed from his prepared text as often as he stuck to it. He continued to speak very slowly, but, if anything, he spoke just a trifle faster as time went on. The cigarettes had by now disappeared. So, therefore, had the long, cigarette-induced pauses. Thirty-five years after the first appearance of "White House and Whitehall," Dick published his "Later Reflections" on the same topic. He commented ruefully that in the mid-1960s he had had no idea that he was "capturing both systems at the tail end of a period of relative stability, about to be succeeded by continuing revolutions, still proceeding at the century's end."[4]

Dick died unexpectedly at his and Shirley's home in Hertfordshire at the end of October 2003, only a few days after both of them attended a memorial service in Cambridge in honor of Shirley's first husband, the philosopher Bernard Williams. Dick's funeral, attended only by family and close friends, was held in the crypt of Westminster Cathedral ten days later. A more public memorial service was held in the Royal Navy church of St. Martin in the Fields, on Trafalgar Square in London, at the end of January 2004. Dick would have loved the whole thing: the life of someone who had served briefly in the United States Navy being celebrated in the home church of the Royal Navy; the life of a nonobservant Jew being celebrated first in the crypt of a Roman Catholic cathedral and then in a parish church of the Church of England; the death of a quintessential American being marked so solemnly in the capital of another country. Dick would have rejoiced in the warmth of affection but also at the irony of it all. It is said that many Americans do not know what irony is. Dick did.

CHAPTER SEVEN

WAS NEUSTADT A JOURNALIST, TOO?

JONATHAN ALTER

AMONG HIS MANY talents, Dick Neustadt was an acute student of the news media, or "the press," as it was more often called in his era. This interest was initially peripheral to his understanding of the American Presidency, but it evolved and became more relevant with each updating of *Presidential Power,* especially the edition that followed the Reagan years.[1] Although Neustadt's insights into the impact of television on the White House were usually short asides en route to larger points, they illuminated his arguments and sometimes proved astonishingly prescient. And when he offered them directly to reporters and columnists in personal interactions, they carried great weight because many of those in the news business who knew him felt that in spirit he was one of us—his booming laugh, lively metaphors, and nontheoretical style felt familiar in the world of journalism.

In some cases, Neustadt served as a quasi-diplomat between the often-alien universes of academia and the media. He didn't shuttle back and forth—as between the academy and government—but he was fluent in our tongue, or at least the language spoken by the mandarins of the print press, which increasingly favors the historical analogies he helped introduce into public debate. He shared with the wider Washington press corps an abiding interest in the man at the top, though his was, of course, a more penetrating focus. But the lens he fashioned could work on many cameras. He strove simultaneously to make journalism more thoughtful and scholarship more accessible.

"He wrote with such clarity that even a journalist could understand it," says David Broder of the *Washington Post,* widely considered the dean of American political reporters. "And therefore his writing had more influence on me and our generation than [that of] anyone else in political science. It really influenced the way we look at the Presidency and the political process."

Any understanding of Dick's view of the press might fittingly begin with his view of Franklin D. Roosevelt. Not long before he died, Dick gave me a long interview for a book I was writing on FDR and his famous First Hundred Days. Dick had a passion for all things Roosevelt. Harry Truman was the President he worked for, but Roosevelt was the gold standard for him—the ideal of President as persuader in chief. FDR's famously "first-class temperament" was at the core of Neustadt's notion of effective leadership. "Experience will leave its mark on expertise; so will a man's ambitions for himself and his constituents. But something like that 'first-class' temperament is what turns know-how and desire into his personal account," he wrote in *Presidential Power.*[2]

Neustadt, whose temperament was also first-class, explained to me that he arrived in Washington in early 1933 as a teenager when his father took a middle-level job in the New Deal. Dick was full of heady tales about the most frightening and exciting presidential transition and debut in history. To convey the level of adulation for the new President, he told me the story of a woman named Ruth Sims. In Dick's uproarious version, Sims was so enamored of FDR that when she left home for a reception at the White House she brought along four handkerchiefs, so that after shaking hands with the great man she could wipe her hand on each hanky, preserving traces of her hero's sweat for each of her four children. Alas, the Secret Service made her check her handbag at the door.

Dick was no Ruth Sims; hero worship was never part of his makeup. But understanding the spirit of that time is important to understanding his reverence for public service. Neustadt described young New Dealers as so enthralled with their new jobs that they seemed to float several feet above Pennsylvania Avenue. He recalled a popular movie of the time, *Gabriel over the White House* (about a "good dictator" as President!), and how it truly felt as if an angel had descended to save the country.

Amid our conversation, Dick suddenly exclaimed, "Don't forget that first press conference!" On March 8, 1933, four days after taking the oath, FDR broke the tradition of having questions for the President submitted in writing. He announced to the assembled reporters that he would hold two press conferences a week, with his comments on background so he could speak more freely (most were quickly put on the record). Two a week! As Neustadt explained and other accounts confirmed, the grateful and excited reporters at this first press conference actually burst into applause for the new President. FDR kept his word, and from that day forward, even as Roosevelt's successors cut back on their interactions with the press, the balance of power shifted. Washington replaced New York as the principal source of news in the United States.

From FDR forward, Neustadt believed, the press became a critical player in the American system. In the very first paragraph of the landmark third chapter of *Presidential Power,* entitled "The Power to Persuade," he writes, "Many public purposes can only be achieved by voluntary acts of private institutions: the press, for one, in Douglass Cater's phrase, is a 'fourth branch of government.'"[3] And the only unregulated branch, as he liked to tell students.

In *Presidential Power* he writes about Presidents governing through a series of "choices," one of which is the choice of "whom he will tell and in what way and words." This role of the President as communicator is close to the core of Neustadt's notion of the true powers of the office. Communications choices, in his view, are the "only means in his own hands" to protect his powers. But although Neustadt believed that a President who failed to communicate would fail in the job, his definition of communications encompassed much more than just media relations. Particularly in the early editions of the book, he focuses on how a President communicates his vision and policy priorities to members of Congress and the executive branch in order to enhance his "professional reputation." Public communications, through speeches and the press, was part of this effort, but a subordinate part.

In fact, Neustadt wrote relatively little about the press as an institution in either his books or memos to Presidents. Because his focus was the Presidency, the press was mostly relevant to him as an instrument of, or check on, the executive. In his original conception, glowing press coverage and the high poll ratings that came from a strong television performance were more often manifestations of "Presidential prestige" than causes of it. The key factors were external events and the President's responses to them. "Events determine audience attention for a President," he wrote. "They also make his actions more important than his words."[4]

Often those events aren't the ones we might expect to generate huge public reactions. For instance, Harry Truman preempted regular radio and TV programming eight times during his Presidency to talk about policy. Dick cites the old Hooper ratings to show that his largest audience (besides his World War II broadcasts) came not when he spoke to the nation about Korea or the dangers of communism but when the subject was meat prices.[5]

The importance of the President as communicator, Dick argued, is often overemphasized. He points out that Truman, Dwight Eisenhower, Lyndon Johnson, Richard Nixon, and Gerald Ford were all "mediocre" if not boring speakers, but this did not directly affect the accomplishments of their Presidencies. Given that, it was no great surprise that Dick's famous transition memos to John F. Kennedy offered considerable advice, for instance, on the proper role of the President's science adviser, but nothing on the role of the press spokesman. As for the new institution of the televised press conference (dating only from Eisenhower), he concluded blandly in late 1960 that it "serves some purposes well, others badly" and that "whether any changes could or should be made is an open question." In an early indication of his admiration for journalistic mandarins, he suggested that such changes were "worth pursuing with responsible journalists."

In 2000, Neustadt wrote in *Preparing to Be President,* a collection of his transition memos to Presidents, that "it never occurred to me to write a memo on press relations to JFK. He and his campaign aides seemed to be doing fine in that regard. There seemed to be more genuine affection for him among members of the press I knew than ever since Franklin Roosevelt's time, and he, like FDR, seemed to regard himself as almost one of them."[6] (Ironically, Neustadt's affection for JFK came more slowly. He originally supported Hubert Humphrey for the 1960 Democratic nomination before switching to Lyndon Johnson. Although he didn't support Kennedy until after the convention, Kennedy quickly came to request his advice.)

Once in office, of course, Kennedy validated Neustadt's confidence in his press relations and communicated brilliantly, especially in the give-and-take of press conferences, which allowed him to show his sense of humor. Thus did Kennedy transform himself, Dick wrote, from "pushy," "young," and "Catholic" into President of all the people. Like FDR, JFK rightly feared overexposure, as well as the risk of saying something publicly that might complicate his private efforts. So, for instance, he limited his televised speech during the Cuban missile crisis to two minutes—"spare and dry." Neustadt's point was that Kennedy's talents on TV had nothing to do with his success in handling the missile crisis. And those skills did not convert to mastery over the complex political forces necessary for civil rights legislation. That required the very different political talents possessed by LBJ, who usually bombed on television.

Neustadt went so far as to speculate that TV skills and managerial skills are often mutually exclusive. "The intricacies of motivating bureaucrats in complex organizations are likelier than not to have escaped the President with a talent for TV," he wrote. At the same time, administrators "grow up tongue-tied." Indeed, great performers like Roosevelt, Kennedy, and Clinton were famously sloppy managers, whereas organization men such as Eisenhower and the first Bush looked gray and buttoned up on television.

In later editions of *Presidential Power* Neustadt amended his view of the centrality of the news media and adopted a McLuhanesque respect for the medium as the message: "Nowadays, the medium itself is at the podium, another party to the whole transaction, molding Presidential words and even the events to its dimensions as an entertainer and to ours as spectators."[7] Jimmy Carter, whose speeches on energy he considered "soporific," was proof that if a President could not make the public care about his priorities, he would have big trouble governing, though Carter's political woes, as Dick pointed out, were more tied to a series of decisions that destroyed his "professional reputation" with insiders than to his poor public performance.

As for Ronald Reagan, Neustadt was struck by how his aides set out literally to "'produce' the President with scripts and pictures all connected to the 'theme of the day.'" Every cabinet department conformed to the President's produced news. Reagan was the first President "who subordinated his own appointments schedule to media relations." He was "happy to have a script," and to use his professional training as an actor as the centerpiece of his approach. Here Dick makes a sublime point that hasn't, to my knowledge, occurred to most journalists and scholars who have wondered what accounted for Reagan's temperament in the White House: "That approach required a remarkable degree of passivity in what the President himself said and did."[8] The connection between being scripted and being passive sounds obvious, until you realize that, like many of Neustadt's insights, you hadn't considered it before.

Just because he understood how television was changing the Presidency didn't mean he had to like it. Dick never succumbed to old-fogeyism, but he rightly perceived that this new emphasis on television performance was not good for either the President or the country: "A President's capacity to draw and stir a television audience seems every bit as interesting to current Washingtonians as his ability to wield his formal powers."[9] He might have expanded "Washingtonians" to include the wider public. In the 1980s and 1990s, American media culture was more focused on how the President "played" on TV than on the consequences of what he was saying. And the heat generated by the partisan echo chamber changed the climate in which Presidents must operate. By the time of Bill Clinton's Presidency, Neustadt was struck by the vehemence of the media's dislike of Clinton and—after the failures of the early months of 1993—by how "unfamiliarity with press relations" was "dangerous for newly elected Presidents and their close aides."[10]

Recent events may be validating Dick's original view that media relations and public performance are secondary factors for Presidents. In formal settings such as State of the Union addresses, the current President Bush has occasionally proved himself a formidable speaker. Think back to his speech to Congress after the events of September 11, 2001. He was greeted with almost uniform acclaim. But later in his Presidency, Bush's skills in that setting brought him no lift in the polls at all. What changed was not his ability to communicate but the external events (the war in Iraq) and presidential actions (again, the war in Iraq) that Neustadt rightly placed at the center of "Presidential prestige." Even as Bush attempts to hold more news conferences to explain his war policy, the limitations of the President's role as teacher in chief and communicator in chief become more apparent. Franklin Roosevelt himself, with two press conferences a week and legendary fireside chats, could not have sold a war as misbegotten and mismanaged as Bush's.

In 1979, Dick made a point of almost eerily prescient relevance for our current predicament. Most issues, he wrote, are "divisive, not consensual." But at least three issues "might contain the seeds of an old-style consensus: sustained fuel shortages, environmental risks and terrorism." Besides showing how much the problems of the 1970s resemble our own, this insight offers something Dick believed in—hope. With the right leadership, consensus and progress are possible on the major problems of our time.

How to build such a consensus was the focus of much of Dick's work. Neustadt viewed the elite columnists (he mentions Arthur Krock, Walter Lippmann, James Reston, and Richard Rovere in *Presidential Power*) as among those political players whom mid-twentieth-century Presidents needed to "persuade" in order to govern effectively. If only this were still true of those of us in the columnist dodge! Some have argued that the rest of the news business was not central to Neustadt's interests. "Journalists, with few exceptions—Reston would come first—didn't particularly fit into Dick's universe, his line of vision," according to Michael Janeway, a former editor of the *Boston Globe* and dean of the Medill School of Journalism at Northwestern University. "His tendency toward the practical, and often the technocratic, together with his in-born sophistication, made him uniquely reliable and effective in his life-long 'of counsel' role to those who governed long after he moved back to academe. These distinguishing characteristics didn't have much to do with journalism."[11]

Or did they? Janeway is right that because Neustadt came of age when the American press was still trying to professionalize itself out of the sensationalist era of *The Front Page,* the journalism he knew was, in Janeway's words, "not noted for the depth, training, specialization or the kind of intellectual apparatus, including thesis, that is instrumental to distinctive research or carefully reasoned case studies." But Neustadt's gifts were so abundant that he became deeply relevant to the work of journalism anyway—an indirect, almost accidental, influence on a whole generation of political reporters and commentators.

David Broder recalls his own experience coming to Washington during the Eisenhower administration: "I didn't have any kind of framework for understanding what powers the President does have, and how he is using them." But with the publication of *Presidential Power,* "He made it so clear that this was a political office and the constitutional bounds were so narrow. You didn't have to rely on your own application but could rely on Neustadt's."[12]

Nearly a half century after its publication, *Presidential Power* remains essential reading not just for political scientists but for any reporter covering an American President. Richard J. Tofel, formerly of the *Wall Street Journal*, goes further: "The realism and appreciation for practical politics of *Presidential Power*—a book that described itself as being 'about the power problem of the man inside the White House'—also set the tone for the book that revolutionized journalistic coverage of politics, Theodore H. White's *The Making of the President*, the first of a long series of books about the 'power problems' of men *seeking* to be inside the White House."[13]

An equally influential book for journalists is *Thinking in Time*, which Neustadt coauthored with Professor Ernest May of Harvard in 1986.[14] The book grew out of a Kennedy School of Government course they taught together called The Uses of History, which I took as an undergraduate. This course, in which I was the youngest student (Neustadt, though he barely knew me, happily threw me into the pool with thirty-five-year-old midcareer fellows), changed my life. It brought together my two main interests, journalism and history, in ways I didn't completely understand until a few years later. From the time I began my career at the *Washington Monthly* through my more than two decades at *Newsweek*, I have found myself returning to the ideas of the class and the book again and again. I'd go so far as to argue that the angle of vision that I try to bring to my column is a direct outgrowth of *Thinking in Time* and the conversations I had with Neustadt on the subject.

To offer just one example: Within a month of the invasion of Iraq in 2003, I wrote a column about the validity of a comparison between Iraq and Vietnam.[15] Under the influence of Neustadt and May, I made it clear that there can be no perfect parallels, and that historical analogies are often misused to make political arguments. But I went on to suggest that Vietnam-era buzzwords such as "pacification" and "infiltration" were likely to reemerge in different form as part of the Bush administration's efforts to make its case, as indeed they have. Think of all the talk of "clear and hold" and the threat posed by Iranian infiltration.

Columns and news analyses with historical context and a feel for complex motivation aren't new, but they aren't common, either. Such articles are not exactly scholarly, but they move a fair distance beyond straight reporting and old-fashioned opinionizing. They attempt to bring a different level of insight to the workaday press—an analytical tone, illuminated by fresh reporting, that is essential if the old-fashioned mainstream media are to have any chance of providing added value for readers who suddenly have endless Web options. And by bringing a deeper and more intellectual flavor to our work, this journalism is more professionally fulfilling for those of us lucky enough to practice it.

I am hardly alone among journalists in crediting Dick with inspiring us to think more ambitiously about our craft. Phil Bennett, managing editor of the *Washington Post,* says flatly that the Kennedy School course on the uses of history and his relationship with Neustadt were what gave him his first interest in journalism. He recalls that Neustadt's "teaching style was anecdotal, probing and wonderfully unpretentious. He asked more questions than he answered."[16] The frame he put on his analysis was, perhaps unconsciously, journalistic. It offered a way of understanding history and politics that relied on detached observation and penetrating questions about character and worldview. "Dick was fascinated by how people in government were self-conscious actors in history with often unconscious historical narratives shaping their understanding of events," Bennett remembers. "What still seems so original was applying it to the study of, say, the decision to send U.S. troops to defend South Korea. Or, for that matter, the decision to invade Iraq." Bennett continues:

> One lesson from Dick's teaching that's been present for me nearly constantly at the *Post* since September 11, 2001, is this: It's what's in people's heads that matters. This is true of al Qaeda; bin Laden, Zawahiri, even the hijackers nurtured their strategy and tactics from a particular reading of history and their place in it. The West's failure to understand this allowed them to develop. A similar process unfolded before our eyes in Washington. The road into Iraq was paved with untested analogies, unexamined assumptions, and the misuses of history. How this happened has been the subject of some of our most important journalism. (Failing to appreciate it earlier probably also contributed to shortcomings in coverage of the prelude to the invasion.)[17]

This gift of Dick's to journalism was largely inadvertent. It wasn't as if he sat down and decided to help reinvent analytical reporting. And the other trends coursing through the news business did not seem to engage him directly. Over the years, Neustadt was not deeply involved in assessing the impact of changing technology on the media, though if his son, Rick, a veteran of the Carter administration and an expert on telecommunications, had lived, he might well have brought Dick with him to the cutting edge of the information revolution.

In one case, however, Dick's contribution to the press was explicit and enduring. Neustadt built media relations into his vision of the Institute of Politics, the "living memorial" to President Kennedy established by the late President's family as part of Harvard's John F. Kennedy School of Government. Broder was one of the first members of the press to become an IOP fellow. He, Robert Timberg of the *Baltimore Sun,* and dozens of others stayed in contact with the Neustadts over the years. "Dick and Bert were wonderfully hospitable to any journalist wandering through," Broder remembers. "Here he really was like a journalist. He just loved talking politics."

Michael Janeway recalls:

He was utterly free of hauteur or condescension and, with Bert playing Ginger to his Fred, had a sharp sense of humor in the bargain. But his attention and intimacy went to people who knew the score (or a score), not to those who, professionally, were on the outside, looking for "just the facts" on a daily basis. Dick was a natural raconteur. He told friends, colleagues, and students stories (not all of them fully discreet) about those he dealt with that were, in a way, first drafts of his case studies and revisions of his *Presidential Power.* He often spoke of how a powerful individual's "inner compass" worked. Dick's art and style in such narratives did indeed make him attractive to journalists as a source, usually off the record.

From the mid-1960s on, the press recognized Neustadt's importance. A *New York Times* profile from 1965 quoted Bert ribbing him for being unable to function in the morning. He brought a thermos of coffee to class that belonged to his children and "had a picture of Roy Rogers on it." Students adored him. In 1986, the *Wall Street Journal* wrote that his class The

American Presidency, which he taught on and off at Columbia and Harvard for more than twenty-five years, is "one of the country's great courses." Neustadt summarized his approach to teaching this way: "Everyone else looks at politics from far, far away. I want to snuggle up. There ought to be one course where students get to look at power up close, to see how it can be used, to understand the risks of failure."[18] Thousands of students over the years watched him "snuggle up" in the lecture hall, in walking conversations as he happily bounced down the path, or during friendly dinners at his home. They were privileged to experience not only a priceless view of how things really work in Washington but also the company of an exceptionally warm man who defied their stereotypes of pretentious professors.

Neustadt was constantly on the lookout for fresh ways to increase interactions between Harvard students and the real world. By the mid-1980s, this idea evolved into the Joan Shorenstein Center on Press, Politics, and Public Policy at the Kennedy School, which also bears Neustadt's imprint. Had he taken a less expansive view of the role of the press, it would have been easy for Harvard to downplay its importance.

On at least one occasion, Neustadt had arguably too much respect for the opinion of journalists. In 1987, as chairman of a subcommittee of the Commission on Presidential Debates, Dick formulated what he called a "realistic chance" standard for deciding which candidates should be allowed to participate in debates. This became an issue in October of 1992, when the independent candidate Ross Perot decided to reenter the campaign. One way Dick used to determine Perot's prospects was to ask several journalists, including me. (The consensus was that Perot should be included, and he was.) Although I was flattered, this was not the right way to make such an important decision. (Broder agrees: "I really had qualms about it.") In 1996, the standard caused controversy when Perot was excluded from the debates for supposedly not meeting it. An advisory report to the commission prepared by Newton Minow, a former chairman of the Federal Communications Commission, and Clifford Sloan found in 1999 that Neustadt's standard gave too much power to what Minow called "an aristocracy of unelected journalists, pundits and academics."[19] Since 2000, inclusion in debates has been determined by a quantitative standard—a mathematical chance of being elected and at least a 15 percent standing in national opinion polls. This is arguably more fair.

Even so, Neustadt's larger distrust of knee-jerk quantification was well placed. On the occasion of the fortieth anniversary of the publication of *Presidential Power,* he raised the question of why political science had not been more influential among political practitioners during the twentieth century. To him, the answer was obvious. Politicians didn't have much use for academics, he wrote, "because so many of us cease to discipline ourselves to write in accessible language—a harder task, to my mind, than writing in professional code, to say nothing of mathematics."

This was a simple but nonetheless critical insight. Although Dick was always open to different approaches in the field, he believed that true discipline lay in not using mathematical language any more than absolutely necessary. He knew that making an arcane point with a regression analysis is no substitute for offering an acute and lucid observation, and that jargon and math are often incomprehensible for the real-world policymakers whom Dick was always urging political scientists to reach.

In other words, Dick was trying to make his own profession more, well, journalistic. He had the standing to make this argument because his own writing was so clear. "His prose was light and spare, unburdened by cant or jargon of any kind," notes his friend Tofel. "He loved to tell stories and wasn't afraid to use exclamation points. And the stories always had two elements usually missing in political science: narrative drive and well-sketched characters. Only Neustadt, for instance, could have reduced the lessons of the Iran-*contra* fiasco to the memorable political injunction: 'Never let your Nancy be immobilized,'" a reference to how First Lady Nancy Reagan was briefly boxed out of decisionmaking by White House aides, with disastrous consequences.

For political scientists as well as journalists, the larger lesson is clear: the only way to have enduring influence is to develop an instinct for what might be called the anthropology of politics—the complex ways in which Presidents and other political players interact and manage their professional lives. Dick knew that graphs do not always bring insight, that accessible does not imply superficial, and that good questions are often more "rigorous" than easy answers. In that sense, he was more than a remarkable scholar, teacher, and adviser to Presidents. He was a first-class journalist, too, though I'm not sure he would have regarded that as a compliment.

CHAPTER EIGHT

TRIBUTE TO A TEACHER

AL GORE

I'M PAUSING BECAUSE . . . this is one of two occasions when the image of Dick Neustadt has surprised me. I don't normally get emotional at occasions like this—no matter the depth of respect I feel for the individual we are remembering or honoring—but I am emotional today, because . . . Dick played such an important role for me, personally.

The first time Dick's image surprised me was a few years ago, when I was in conversation with close friends on the subject of trust. And the question was posed: If you could close your eyes and imagine all the people you have encountered in your life—men, women, and children—and you could select one person as a trusted adviser to guide you, whom would you pick? Several people went through this exercise; I closed my eyes and thought—Dick Neustadt was that person for me.

He changed my life.

I encountered him, first, when I was an undergraduate. I was confused, not knowing what I wanted to do in life (not an unusual condition for

Remarks presented originally on April 15, 2004, at the Richard E. Neustadt Memorial Service, Memorial Church, Harvard University, and edited for publication.

undergraduates). I had a lot of complicated feelings about the "majesty" of American democracy, because of my experience, growing up, as the son of a senator. My father was a hero in my eyes; he'd shown wisdom and courage when he was in the midst of being rejected by his constituents because of a temporary triumph on the part of the politics of fear. Having seen that—the dark side of politics—as a young man had convinced me that I wanted nothing to do with it. Or so I thought. I was headed in the opposite direction. I was an English major at the time.

And then I took Dick's course on the Presidency, and it lit me up with enthusiasm for learning, and admiration for his ability to deliver penetrating insights in a humorous and homespun way. It seemed to me that, as an intellect, Dick had a certain "Goldilocks" quality: He was not too theoretical. He was not too mundane. He was just right. He could mix idealism and lofty theories with the most brutal practicality, and then embed gems of wisdom that resulted from this blend into a very engaging and humorous presentation. But as powerful as his teaching style was, what led him to play such a unique role for me personally had to do as much or more with his heart than with his head—with his character even more than with his intellectual stature.

I remember spending time at the Neustadt family's home on Traill Street in Cambridge; Dick and Bert (God bless her memory) drew students in, there, like members of their extended family. I remember spending time there with Beth and Rick (and God bless Rick's memory)—Rick was also an undergraduate at Harvard when I was there, and became a friend. I took Tipper, whom I was dating as an undergraduate, to dinner there, almost the way one brings one's girlfriend home to family. One year I brought her with me for Thanksgiving dinner, and the Neustadts' traditional, after-dinner game of charades. They had lots of the raw material one needed for a world-class game of charades. They were all very good at it. There was wit, and fun, and—sure—competition. But most of all, there was an underlying sense of real warmth.

The year after I took Dick Neustadt's Presidency course, because he had inspired me, and in doing so had reignited my attraction to my own father's field, I changed majors; I became a government major. But then I was very distressed to find that there was no other course taught by Dick Neustadt that I was qualified to take. In that case, I thought, what was the point of being a government major? So I went to see him. He was so understanding

and so solicitous; he devised a special course just for me. I had to understand that I would not get credit for this course—that it would never be a
part of my transcript and no record of it would ever appear anywhere—but
he would teach this course to me. And he did. And honest to goodness
every week he met with me and asked his young Ph.D.-candidate assistant, Graham Allison, to come and help him carry the burden of this one
persistent student. He would assign a reading list for the following week
that would choke a horse, and for this one course, that had no credit, I
promise you without any exaggeration I did far more work than I did for
all the rest of the courses I had, put together. And once a week I came to
the "little yellow house"—a great little place down near the Lampoon
building—and for three hours we would meet and discuss all this material
he'd had me read, and more. It was an amazing experience.

He then agreed to be my thesis adviser for my senior year, and that, too,
was an experience I shall never forget. Throughout those years, the Vietnam War, which had played a prominent role in my father's politics, and
ultimately caused his defeat for reelection, was playing a prominent role in
the lives of all the undergraduates here at Harvard (as it was on other university and college campuses). I'm sure my contemporaries will remember,
mass meetings in the football stadium, the incredible intensity of debate at
that time—it marked our generation.

I remember thinking, as a freshman, in 1965, "Thank goodness this war
is going to be over by the time I graduate." But graduation loomed ever
nearer, and the disappearance of my draft deferment confronted me with a
dilemma that is hard to convey, in this day and time, as the moral dilemma
that it genuinely was for me, then. And as I wrestled my way through to
my decision to volunteer for the Army and subsequently go to Vietnam,
notwithstanding the fact that I opposed the war, I went often to talk with
Dick Neustadt. He was always there for me. I remember one very long
walk in particular, one evening when he used his famous Socratic method
to enable me to sort out what were, for a young student, such very difficult
and complex issues. Not with any kind of directive—that was never his
style—but he helped me find my way to this decision, just as he'd helped
me find my way back into the field of politics.

I turned to him frequently in the years that followed, to get the same
kind of advice—when I went to Congress, when I went to the Senate, and
when I was in the White House as vice president, and in the presidential

campaign, and then again a little over a year ago, when I was wrestling with the decision of whether to run for President again or to become—as I am now—a recovering politician. And at every point, he was there for me; even now, he remains a light that will never go out of my life.

He had the power to persuade, and the dedication to teach us not just so we'd learn, but so we'd use what we learned. He advised presidents, and students, and lots of others, in between. And he listened to us all, and gave us all his undivided attention, and asked us the kinds of questions that made us feel understood, and that made us better understand ourselves and our circumstances. He made us all feel that we mattered. Every one of us. That is really something.

The poet Wallace Stevens wrote: "After the final no there comes a yes, and on that yes the future world depends." The power to persuade is the power to bring that yes after the last no. And I stand here as a representative of thousands of students who said yes to life in a way they would not otherwise have done, if not for Dick Neustadt.

CHAPTER NINE

MASTERFUL MENTOR

HARVEY V. FINEBERG

As A YOUNG man, Richard E. Neustadt embarked on a career in public service. He did not originally intend a life as an educator, much less as a scholar. Yet Neustadt transformed scholarly discourse on the Presidency, reshaped higher education for public service, influenced the thinking of thousands through his writing and lectures, and profoundly shaped the careers of hundreds of his students. All of his adult life, Neustadt advised Presidents, cabinet secretaries, and senior government officials. Over time, as a teacher and mentor, Neustadt also produced a new generation of leaders who served in public administration, electoral politics, academic institutions, nonprofit organizations, philanthropies, and civic life.

As one who feels a deep personal indebtedness and closeness to Dick Neustadt, I am frequently struck by how many feel similarly influenced by this man. One can describe a special relationship with Neustadt and be confident that the sentiment will resonate with hundreds of others he embraced as undergraduates, graduate students, course assistants, research collaborators, intellectual fellow travelers, and academic colleagues. Does not this kind of relationship require a degree of attention and intimacy that cannot be so generously distributed? I was advantaged by long years and many hours of association with Dick Neustadt. Yet, one tribute published after Neustadt's death in 2003 acknowledges that "I heard him lecture only once."[1] How did a little of Neustadt go such a long way?

This chapter is a reflection on this question: What made Richard E. Neustadt such an effective teacher and mentor to so many? I relate some of my own interactions with Dick Neustadt over thirty-eight years to give a flavor of the range and variety of his personal impact on others. I met Dick Neustadt when I was in college, and in time became his graduate student, course assistant, coauthor, colleague, and friend. I claim no privileged position in any of these roles, as so many students and associates of Neustadt have their own compelling experiences to relate. Indeed, it is in part his widespread and sustained impact on others that makes Neustadt such an intriguing subject.

Institute of Politics

My first meeting with Dick Neustadt was a chance encounter. He literally came knocking at the door. In the spring of 1965, Neustadt arrived at Harvard from Columbia to become the founding director of the Institute of Politics. One evening, unannounced, he stopped by my sophomore suite in Lowell House to say hello to a cousin of his who happened to be a roommate of mine. It was the first and only time any faculty member had visited our room, and I was intrigued by what the professor had to say about the new institute he was designing. The Institute of Politics was to be situated just around the corner, and I took advantage from time to time in the next couple of years to attend the informal, vigorous, and illuminating sessions that Neustadt hosted with visiting government leaders. I later learned that he had practiced this style of "education through conversation" at Columbia, and it was a welcome shift from the typical classroom lecture-and-listen instruction of the day.

The Institute of Politics and the newly named John F. Kennedy School of Government were a paired tribute to the late President and his example of public service. The institute introduced a host of us undergraduates to the human side of public affairs, rendering remote, government stick figures into flesh-and-blood personalities. In those days of military buildup in Vietnam, even the most air-headed undergraduate paid attention at some level to government. In Neustadt's hands, an evening with a cabinet secretary, a governor, a senator, a bureau chief, a journalist, or a future presidential candidate was stimulating, informative, entertaining, and often provocative. Whatever institutional development remained to be done within the university, from the vantage point of a student, the Institute of Politics was a hit from the start.

Public Policy Program

In the fall of 1967, I matriculated at Harvard Medical School, interested in the combination of social and medical dimensions of health that would come to characterize much of my work. In the winter of my second year, a notice appeared on our dormitory bulletin board inviting applications to a new master's degree program in public policy at the Kennedy School. A stellar cast of faculty had been assembled, headed by Neustadt, and the program seemed tailor-made for my interests. As instructed on the notice, I promptly made a date to talk with the dean of students. Although the dean of the faculty of medicine had endorsed the idea of a joint degree in public policy, word had apparently not reached the dean of students by the time I visited with him in his office a couple of days later.

When I sat opposite the dean at his large desk, he was flipping through a folder open in front of him. I realized it must be my student file. Most students who entered that office were in some kind of academic or personal difficulty, and he began by asking me what problem brought me in to see him. (It is a question doctors often use to open an interview!) I explained that I was interested in applying to the new public policy program at the Kennedy School and described what I had read about the program. He glanced up as he continued to leaf through the record in front of him.

"Let me get this straight," he said. "You want to take a year off from medical school."

"That's right," I replied.

"Fine," he allowed, "Every year, some students take a year off between their preclinical and clinical training, work in a laboratory, and learn a lot. It can be worthwhile, even if you are not going to pursue a career in bench research."

"I understand that," I persisted, "but I was thinking of applying to the new public policy program at the Kennedy School."

He stared at me for a few seconds, peered down at the folder, turned a page or two, and then looked again at me. "But," he said slowly, "your record here isn't all that *bad*."

This vignette illustrates the kind of skepticism that Neustadt and his fellow pioneers in the public policy program must have encountered in faculty across the university. At the time however, as a recent college graduate, I found the prospect of studying with Richard Neustadt, Thomas Schelling, Frederick Mosteller, and Howard Raiffa intellectually irresistible. After the year began, I also came to know and appreciate such remarkable individuals on the senior faculty as Francis Bator, Bill Capron, and Phil Heymann and on the junior faculty, Graham Allison, Henry (Jake) Jacoby, and Richard Zeckhauser. The adventure of a new program was an attraction to me, just as the prospect of a newly invigorated Kennedy School of Government and Institute of Politics had initially drawn Neustadt to Harvard.

Fewer than twenty of us enrolled in that first public policy class in the fall of 1969. Some entered directly from college, a few had been out and about in the world, and a handful were joint degree candidates in law, medicine, and business. Neustadt purposely sought this variety, for he and his colleagues intended to prepare individuals for public-policy work in any substantive area. Perhaps this reflected Neustadt's experience in the Bureau of the Budget and the White House, where he worked on a wide variety of topics. Neustadt later confided that he was especially glad to have some candidates from the several professional schools because they would have something to fall back on if the public-policy training experiment proved to be a flop. Neustadt consistently urged thinking about contingencies, whether in one's personal career or in public decisionmaking. And he lived by this advice: Neustadt completed his Ph.D. in the late 1940s at the urging of Roger Jones at the Bureau of the Budget, a step that opened the way for his later move to a faculty position.

The inaugural year of the public-policy program was intense and exhilarating. This was the first academic year after the student unrest, demonstrations, and strike at Harvard in April 1969. An increasingly unpopular war consumed the nation's attention, health costs were rapidly rising, and the environmental movement was gaining momentum (*plus ça change . . .*). Some members of the class were compelled by the urgency of these problems, and a couple dropped out the next spring to help organize the first

Earth Day celebration. Against this backdrop of social and institutional upheaval, the public-policy program offered a set of analytic tools, principles, and perspectives that were intended to be of enduring value. All of us were keenly aware of the experimental nature of the program, and the faculty, led by Neustadt, brought us into the process of our education as active contributors. What did we think, Neustadt constantly wanted to know. What was working? What not?

Exceptional though the classes were, the most memorable events of the year occurred in the homes of our faculty, where we students were frequently received and welcomed. Neustadt set the pace. At the Neustadt home on Traill Street in Cambridge, the events could be social and there could be serious group conversations as well, with us sprawled around the floor in a rough circle. Reflecting on those occasions at the twenty-fifth anniversary of the first graduating class from the public policy program, I remarked that all of us in that first-year class felt like we had three homes: one where we lived, one at Littauer in the room where we spent every weekday together, and one on Traill Street at the Neustadts'.

I vividly remember the initial gathering at the Neustadt house when I first set eyes on Dick's wife, Bert, and thought I had encountered Katherine Hepburn at Harvard. Bert was as gracious and accommodating to students as it was possible to be. Herself an accomplished teacher of English as a second language, Bert had a genuine and abiding interest in students' ideas and adventures. Some years after, when my fiancée and later wife, Mary Wilson, and I would visit the Neustadts at their home on Gull Pond in Wellfleet, Bert would warn us not to start any interesting conversation at the luncheon table until she had gotten all the food on the cart and sat down with us. And to Bert, practically every subject was interesting.

After the first year of the public-policy program, I remained in regular contact with Neustadt while I completed my M.D. and remaining parts of the master's of public policy requirements. As I was embarking on my own academic career, Dick invited me to become the junior instructor in his political analysis course in the public-policy program. I leapt at the chance and discovered that one does not truly understand material until one tries to teach it. I learned from Dick Neustadt about the detail of preparation and planning that goes into a successful class and a coherent course. Managing a case discussion requires a different set of skills from delivering a lecture, and Neustadt had mastered both art forms.

Dick regarded me, his student, as a colleague, seeking my opinions and taking them seriously. As a teaching colleague, Dick treated me as a partner with complementary skills and abilities. This was not quite true, of course, but it was how he treated me, thus simultaneously showing how to teach students and how to guide a junior colleague. In this period, spending more time together, our friendship grew, and my affection for him with it. In May of 1975, Dick and Bert stood as our witnesses when Mary and I exchanged marriage vows at Highland Light in Truro, on the Cape.

The Swine Flu Study

The swine flu immunization program was heralded in March of 1976 when President Gerald Ford announced a national campaign to immunize the American population against the threat of swine flu. The virus had been detected in soldiers who had fallen ill that winter in Fort Dix, New Jersey, and experts believed this was the type of virus responsible for the catastrophic pandemic of 1918–19. Between October and December 1976, 40 million Americans were immunized against influenza, more than in any previous flu vaccine effort. However, the program was marked by controversy, delay, administrative difficulties, legal complications, and a loss of public confidence in public health leadership. The epidemic never materialized, and the venture ended because of an unforeseen medical complication.

Soon after Joseph Califano took office as Jimmy Carter's secretary of health, education, and welfare in January 1977, he faced a vexing policy choice: whether, in response to a flu outbreak in a Miami nursing home, to release the influenza vaccine. The new outbreak was influenza type A/Victoria, and all available A/Victoria antigen had been formulated the previous year in a vaccine combining swine flu and A/Victoria antigens. So releasing vaccine against A/Victoria meant releasing the discredited swine flu vaccine. In the end, on the advice of experts, Califano released the vaccine. But he was keenly aware that the swine flu program of 1976 had been widely viewed as a fiasco, and he anticipated facing other difficult public health decisions that would require weighing scientific evidence, ethical considerations, and policy judgment.

When he joined Robert McNamara's Defense Department in the early 1960s, Joseph Califano read the classified report on the Skybolt missile

crisis that Dick Neustadt had prepared for President Kennedy. The Skybolt was to be an air-to-ground missile—a predecessor to today's cruise
missile—and Eisenhower had pledged to Prime Minister Macmillan that
the British would have full access to it. The system proved technically
unworkable and expensive, and the Americans scrapped the program. The
British were outraged, and when he entered office, Kennedy faced a diplo-
matic kerfuffle over the unexpected cancellation. The President asked
Neustadt, who happened to be in Oxford on sabbatical, to sort out what
happened, and he read Neustadt's report on the flight to Dallas that fate-
ful November of 1963. Portions of the Skybolt report were described in
Neustadt's *Alliance Politics* (1970) and more was published later, but Califano had access to the complete, original, classified version. When he
called Neustadt in 1977 and said, "I need a Skybolt report on swine flu,"
both men knew precisely what was sought and what was required.

Neustadt enlisted me to collaborate on the project, and it was an unsurpassed learning experience. Califano provided enough funding for a couple of research assistants, Thomas Kinsock and Michael Holt, and a
remarkably capable secretary, Sally Makacynas, who went on to work with
Neustadt for the rest of his years at the Kennedy School and continues
there today. As President Kennedy had done for Neustadt sixteen years
earlier, Secretary Califano provided a letter of introduction asking everyone to cooperate with us, and everyone we asked, did.

In the next six months, we interviewed scores of major and minor participants, observers, advisers, and decisionmakers; reviewed thousands of
pages of documents, legislation, scientific articles, and press coverage; and
watched every hour of pertinent news coverage from the three major net-
works. We visited together a number of the major players, including President Ford, Jonas Salk, and David Sencer, the director of the Center for
Disease Control, in Atlanta; others we met with separately. Neustadt was
a masterful interviewer. He prepared assiduously and knew precisely what
questions he wanted to have answered. At the same time, he always maintained an open mind and followed up the leads offered by the interviewee
without losing sight of our own objectives. He posed direct and inviting
questions to every person. For many of the officials involved, the program
had been a searing experience. Neustadt was a sympathetic listener, able to
retain with fidelity the words and sense of the speaker, yet without accepting the other's rationales and without betraying his ripening judgments. A

coauthor on a different project, Ernest May, once characterized Neustadt as "a very contemporary historian who got information from watching people and talking to people."[2] As a scientific observer of *Homo politicus,* Neustadt prodded his subjects and recorded faithfully, but neither provoked nor distorted the response.

Once at the end of a long day of joint interviews, we were seated on an airplane sharing our impressions of what we had heard. At one point, Neustadt stopped in midsentence and looked down the aisle of the plane. A flight attendant was assisting a passenger from a wheelchair to a seat. After watching carefully, Dick turned to me and said, "I have started to pay more attention to that sort of thing." He said this as a matter of fact, without a trace of emotion or hint of self-pity. Dick knew that I was well aware of Bert's diagnosis of multiple sclerosis and that her condition was deteriorating. Dick was not merely stoical; he was an immensely practical and perceptive observer who regarded his own condition with the same analytic eye he applied to the Presidency, the university, or political decisionmaking. One of the qualities I believe that Dick, as a lifelong Anglophile, most admired in the British is their culturally ingrained sense of duty. Whether caring for his ill wife, creating a new learning environment, or responding to the call of a President, Dick Neustadt exemplified the fulfillment of duty. I learned many things from Dick in the course of our swine flu project, not all of it about field research.

When it came time to craft the report, we developed the main features and lessons to be derived from the swine flu program. Dick was clear from the outset that the form of the report was to be a vivid narrative, one that would engage the intended reader, Califano, and convey the key messages in the course of telling the story. This was precisely the Skybolt model, with Califano now substituted for Kennedy. In fact, Califano was the only intended audience for our original report, though we expected eventually to produce derivative case material for teaching purposes. Once he read the document, Califano declared it should be published as is by the Government Printing Office. Since we originally told interviewees that their comments were exclusively for the secretary, we cleared every quotation prior to publication, and none required any alteration. To enliven the original text, we had occasionally inserted asides to Califano. For example, after a speaker mentions that Vice President Nelson Rockefeller's idea to consult with the military on implementation was not followed up, we wrote, "In

Ford's Administration, few of Rockefeller's were." Califano wanted not a word changed, and we published the report as submitted to him.[3]

In a later, commercially published, edition, we added an author's introduction, a foreword by David Hamburg, new case material, and teaching notes.[4] The original report is reproduced in its original form, enhanced, we felt, by the addenda in the book, but remaining intact. In the new introduction we wrote, "We think our report must remain what it was, infelicitous phrasing and all, a government document of given date, belonging to a certain time, open to criticism 'as was.' Anything else seems Orwellian" (p. xxii). Neustadt similarly enlarges upon an original publication without distorting the original in successive editions of *Presidential Power*, where he added chapters on later Presidents while retaining the original text.

Neustadt's direct style of writing was the antithesis of scholarly circumlocutions that spiral into a thicket of obscure subjunctive clauses. Although confounding in its simplicity to some academic readers, Neustadt's narrative style—concise phrases, declarative sentences, balanced cadence, pungent asides, abundant wit, and sublime choice of words—makes compelling reading. Neustadt as writer teaches the difference between serious writing and somber writing. He shows that one can be subtle and profound without being dense or convoluted. Dick was a disciplined writer. The Wellfleet routine, familiar to those lucky enough to be guests at the Neustadt cottage on Gull Pond, involved an uninterrupted morning of work, light lunch, afternoon swim or canoe ride, a nap, and animated conversation at every meal. Dick took pleasure in the craft of writing, always applying black ballpoint ink to a lined yellow pad. No other tools satisfied him. When page proofs arrived with an error or a phrase that begged to be replaced, Dick would countenance the change, but only if the number of letters and spaces matched nearly perfectly enough to limit reprinting to the single page. It was a game he relished, and it incidentally saved on printing costs.

Beyond form, there is a notable thread of consistency in Neustadt's work on the Presidency, presidential transitions, and government response to crises: he is constantly reminding decisionmakers to consider the effects of what they do today on their longer-term prospects to effect the changes they seek. Early impressions and actions count especially in preserving power over time. In the swine flu case, this guidance applies to department leaders and health officials who thought almost exclusively about the worst case and not enough about the most likely case. In presidential transitions, the advice applies to early, correct choices of people and priorities. In the swine flu affair, early impressions of the media about the impetus for the program were telling and lasting. One network pursued the initial story that universal immunization was being ordered through White House contacts, found none enthusiastic, and concluded that the politicians had been forced to do the doctors' bidding. Another pursued the story on background at the Center for Disease Control, found many skeptics, and assumed the decision was tainted by politics. Throughout the year that followed, the first network was sympathetic to a program it perceived to be based on scientific evidence and medical judgment; the second remained skeptical of a program it perceived to be driven in part by political calculations.

Lasting Impact

Neustadt's impact on students and colleagues went far beyond what he taught in the classroom and wrote in his books. The ideas Neustadt propounded about the Presidency and, more broadly, about the exercise of power, decisionmaking, and effectiveness in government were radical, insightful departures when he wrote *Presidential Power* in the late 1950s. Eventually, his ideas became mainstays of instruction about government and public service. However, to reduce Neustadt's influence as a teacher and mentor to his ideas would be as incomplete as ascribing the power of a President to Article II of the Constitution. Dick Neustadt had a lasting effect on so many he touched because of his temperament as much as his intellect, because of his abiding respect for the views of others regardless of their status or station, because of his striking ability to clarify and synthesize the essence of any situation, because of his personal integrity and forthright dealings with everyone, because of his empathy and patience with students, and because of a deep self-confidence that presented itself as humility.

Neustadt was pragmatic and accustomed to the rough and tumble of public life without ever growing cynical about it. He was guided throughout by a devotion to public service that pervades and motivates his many years as an academic. A lifelong Democrat, Dick advised leaders from both political parties. He believed most deeply about answering the call to public service. "When the President asks you to do something," he would say, "any President, you should do it if you possibly can."

For Dick Neustadt, the university was an instrument, not an end. He valued scholarship not for what it meant to the world of ideas, but for what it meant to the world of action. He sought to expose students to the joys and challenges of public service, and to make them more effective public servants. In April 1996, at the celebratory dinner for Dick Neustadt on the twenty-fifth anniversary of the first graduating class of the public policy program, Dick endured an evening of tributes to his leadership. Toward the end of the program, Nels Ackerson, on behalf of the alumni, announced a new student fellowship in honor of Richard E. Neustadt and invited Dick to the podium.

"Well," Dick began, "that makes it all right. I would rather, above all things, be honored with something that helps one real, honest-to-god student." Looking around the audience, Dick observed, "So many of your faces matter so much to me. No matter what you gained in dignity and years, you are identifiable. You are the bottom line. You're my bottom line."

Metaphorically speaking, I had observed earlier that evening, "filling out the line in just the right way" was what Dick Neustadt accomplished for his students as for his page proofs. More than anything, Richard E. Neustadt taught by who he was and the values by which he lived and worked.

CHAPTER TEN

INSTITUTION BUILDER

GRAHAM ALLISON

You HAVE "a tail, but you haven't got a dog."[1] So declared Kay Graham, publisher of the *Washington Post* and a member of the Institute of Politics' Senior Advisory Committee, about Richard E. Neustadt's newly named Institute of Politics. Formally, it was part of the newly named John F. Kennedy School of Government. But that body did not exist.

Neustadt agreed with Kay. Indeed, he liked her image so much that he made it his own, using it to describe his strategy in successive stages of institution building at Harvard.[2] A conventional strategy it certainly was not. As Neustadt stated in the last year of his life, had he to do it over, he might have just built the Institute of Politics as a memorial to President Kennedy, leaving the shell of a Graduate School of Public Administration to carry on as it had for a generation before he arrived.[3] In his entrepreneurial leadership, which led to the creation of both institutions, he was in fact a strategic adventurer, even gambler.

A colleague once quipped that Neustadt was an academic Christopher Columbus. Columbus set out for India without a map of how to get from here to there; arrived in the New World without knowing where he was; and did it all with someone else's money. Neustadt laughed deeply, as he often did, and acknowledged a certain similarity. But, he noted, Columbus did discover America.

Neustadt did establish something new under the sun in the world of great universities. Without Dick Neustadt, the Institute of Politics and the Kennedy School of Government we know today would not exist. Full stop.

The philosopher Alfred North Whitehead described Harvard University as "uniting the young and old in the imaginative pursuit of learning."[4] In that juncture between young and old, Neustadt created an institution committed to the imaginative pursuit of learning about electoral politics, governance, and public policy. As the cliché about Columbus says, the rest is history.

This chapter explores how Neustadt did it. This account is not a history of either the Institute of Politics or the Kennedy School. Those histories have been written by others.[5] Rather, it seeks to examine the role of an individual in those larger stories, to the extent possible, through his own eyes. It does so from the perspective of one who had the good fortune to know and work with him from the time he arrived at Harvard in 1965 until his death. I was a student in the first course Dick Neustadt taught at Harvard, his head course assistant, and later his Ph.D. thesis advisee. I was lectured to, examined, tutored, and mentored by a master. When, as director of the Institute of Politics, Neustadt decided to create the first Institute of Politics study group to examine how the plans of the "best and brightest" for Vietnam had so badly gone awry, I was selected to be "rapporteur" of the "May Group," as Neustadt named it, for its chair, Ernest May, a Harvard history professor. When, in 1968, Dean Don Price, and then Associate Dean Neustadt, decided to launch a Public Policy Program within the shell that had been named the John F. Kennedy School of Government, Neustadt recruited me to be a junior faculty member and his partner in creating the core course in political analysis. When I wrote my thesis, published as *Essence of Decision: Explaining the Cuban Missile Crisis*, which became a best seller in political science, I stood on Neustadt's shoulders, and the result reflects his insights and guidance throughout.[6] After Robert Kennedy was assassinated, Ethel Kennedy asked Neustadt to write an afterword to complete RFK's memoir of the missile crisis; Neustadt chose me as his coauthor. When the Kennedy School came to the point at which it had to swim, if it were to avoid sinking, Neustadt determined—over my strong objections—that I should become dean. And when, in 1977, I became the youngest dean in Harvard's history and set out on one of its most daunting undertakings—to reinvent a viable vision of a professional school of government and then build it—my greatest consolation was his counsel and support every step of the way. This chapter thus relies on a professional lifetime of experience and friendship with this extraordinary man, as well as the recollections of many of his other colleagues who worked with him and the historical record.

When he agreed to come to Harvard to try to create an unprecedented vital link between the academy and the world of government and politics, Neustadt sought to apply all he had learned and taught about the exercise of power to the achievement of his purpose. Thus in searching for clues to his operational code as entrepreneur and institution builder in the context of a great university, and assessing what was—and was not—accomplished—this chapter relies, wherever possible, on Neustadt's own writings and recorded interviews he did for the Institute of Politics' oral history project. I recount incidents and anecdotes to highlight bright threads from what was in his real life an infinitely more complex and subtle tapestry. The attempt to combine explicit insights and telling illustrations follows the principle Neustadt proposed in the preface to his classic study of the Presidency, where he illustrates "every major step in the analysis with cases from the record of recent Administrations."[7] The reader should be aware that Neustadt subscribed to his colleague John Kenneth Galbraith's view that no story worth telling was not worth improving in the retelling. Unlike Galbraith, however, Neustadt's retellings often erred in the direction of understating his own contributions.

Purpose and Ambition

What were his purposes and did these run with or against the grain of history; how relevant were they to what would happen in his time?

RICHARD E. NEUSTADT, *Presidential Power and the Modern Presidents*

In his afterword to the 1990 edition of *Presidential Power*, Neustadt explains how readers can use that book's frame of reference to appraise leaders. The first among four questions to be answered is, "What were his purposes and did these run with or against the grain of history?" (p. 167). In his own appraisals of Presidents, Neustadt clearly gave the highest marks to those who had faced great challenges and summoned great responses.

Having been persuaded by Robert Kennedy to become the founding director of the Institute of Politics at Harvard, he was frighteningly aware that he had accepted a challenge of the first order. His charge from the head of the family, Robert, and a group of former Kennedy colleagues who had agreed with Harvard's President Nathan Pusey to launch this undertaking, was to build a "living memorial" to the recently assassinated John F. Kennedy. But what did "living memorial" mean? Operationally, no one knew. Conceptually, what Robert Kennedy and his colleagues had in mind was the functional equivalent of a vigorous fifty-two-year-old former President who, after two successful terms, would, as JFK had put it, be "too old to begin a new career and too young to write my memoirs."[8] JFK had been planning to build his presidential library at Harvard. He would be there to enliven it himself, engaging students, writing, perhaps even teaching. Without John Kennedy at the center of this enterprise, how could a memorial come alive?

Certainly the authorities at Harvard did not know. The agreement to establish this institute at Harvard, to locate it within the floundering Graduate School of Public Administration, and to break with three hundred years of precedent by affixing a name other than Harvard to the lot reflected an awkward compromise. The January 1965 *Harvard* press release announcing Neustadt's appointment was a model of mission ambiguity.[9] It expressed President Pusey's hope that Neustadt would eventually become the director of "a new kind of institution in American life within a university setting, which will furnish a meeting place for scholars and for individuals pursuing careers in practical politics and public service."[10] But how to link the ivory tower of scholarship to the combative world of action? Beyond what had evolved over centuries, Harvard certainly did not know. So: Over to Neustadt.

Legend had it that during his undergraduate years at Harvard, the young John Kennedy had somehow been turned on to electoral politics. A living memorial should therefore inspire future generations to follow in his footsteps. Troubled by the trends in academic economics and political science that rewarded abstract theorizing and devalued clarification of real-world problems, Neustadt believed the academy, as well as the world, needed an institution that would combine academic rigor and practical relevance by linking scholars and practitioners. He was also fearful that in a sea of partisan Democrats, he (proudly a card-carrying Democrat) would become the madam of what he called a "Democratic brothel." At the "Kremlin on the Charles," in Massachusetts, with two sibling Democratic senators (and likely future presidential candidates), in a school named for a Democrat, such an outcome would be hard to avoid. But he believed that would be unworthy of a living memorial to JFK. He thus fought relentlessly, though often unsuccessfully, to keep his venture demonstrably bipartisan.

For the first phase of his entrepreneurship, Neustadt decided to build the Institute of Politics as a stool with three legs: IOP fellows would come from the real world of politics and government to campus for a semester and teach noncredit study groups for undergraduates; faculty "study groups" would engage senior faculty members from across the university who had a serious interest in government and policy; and high-profile, short-term honorary associates would come to campus for one- or two-day visits to talk to undergraduates and faculty at small off-the-record dinners and lunches.[11] Neustadt secured the "Little Yellow House" at 78 Mt. Auburn Street as a locus for this activity—smack in the flow of undergraduates as they made their way back and forth between the undergraduate houses in which they lived and dined and the Yard, where they took many of their classes. He later called this "the best strategic decision I ever made."[12] For his governing board, he recruited Robert Kennedy, Jackie Kennedy, Kay Graham, former Secretary of Defense Robert Lovett, former Secretary of the Treasury Douglas Dillon, former Senator John Sherman Cooper of Kentucky, and Senator Henry Jackson of Washington to form a Senior Advisory Committee. Averell Harriman was the chair. All shared great admiration for the former President; all had grand expectations for the venture that bore his name. Though this group supported Neustadt, they were suspicious of Harvard: fearful that its dominant culture would either reject their implant as a "foreign body" or, alternatively, devour its resources without a trace. Neustadt sought simultaneously to prevent them from interfering unduly with his plans, while using their weight to counter Harvard currents that posed even greater dangers for his mission.

Harvard's reservations about bringing the real world of politics into the hallowed halls of a great research university reflected a brute reality: politics and governance are inherently controversial. Public service is not simply a noble calling. It is a combat sport. People who compete to lead the nation in different directions disagree. Their disagreements are often about matters of life and death. Moreover, in American government, controversy is not accidental. It is built into the structure by design. "To what expedient," the *Federalist Papers* ask, "shall we resort, for maintaining in practice the necessary partition of power?" Madison answers: "[B]y so contriving the interior structure of the government that its several constituent parts may, by their mutual relations, be the means of keeping each other in their proper places. *Ambition must be made to counteract ambition.*"[13]

If anyone needed a reminder of this truth, the arrival of the first honorary associate three weeks after the inauguration of the Institute provided it in a flash. Secretary of Defense Robert McNamara symbolized Harvard's "best and brightest" struggling with the cardinal issue of the time: the war in Vietnam. A graduate of Harvard Business School who had risen to become CEO of Ford Motor Company (then one of America's leading and most admired companies), McNamara had been selected by JFK to be his secretary of defense. After the Cuban missile crisis of 1962, President Kennedy judged McNamara "the most valuable public servant in his administration and in the government."[14] Legendary for applying analytical intelligence to public-policy choices, McNamara introduced the Planning, Programming, and Budgeting System, "PPBS," to the Pentagon. President Lyndon Johnson later made McNamara's PPBS a requirement for the entire U.S. government.

This stellar secretary of defense landed on campus for a day-and-a-half visit at a time when the Vietnam War was as unpopular at universities as the U.S. war in Iraq became a generation later. Unlike Iraq, however, during the Vietnam conflict Harvard students were subject to a mandatory draft that could send them to fight, even to die. For students at that time, the war was not just a matter of principle. It was personal.

After having lunch with undergraduates in Quincy House, as McNamara walked to the chauffeured car that was to take him to his next event, at the Law School, he was surrounded by an angry mob of several hundred students organized by the leading radical group on campus, S.D.S. (Students for a Democratic Society). McNamara climbed on top of the car and sought to engage students in answering their questions. He was quickly drowned out by bullhorns and boos from the crowd shouting "murderer," "fascist," and worse. Concerned for his safety, Harvard's police rescued him, spiriting him and his graduate student escort Barney Frank through

Harvard's underground steam tunnels in an undignified escape. At dinner that evening at Neustadt's Traill Street home, one of the guests recalls, "I saw McNamara wipe tears away as Dick's guest undergraduates and graduates criticized his Vietnam policy, fierce and relentless, and Dick smoked and watched with that rare talent in realpolitik, to let a story run without interference."[15]

Like a flash of lightning that illuminates the landscape for an instant, the "McNamara affair," as Neustadt called it, awakened the Harvard community to the fact that his Institute of Politics had arrived. As the fortieth-anniversary *History of the Founding of the Institute of Politics* concludes, the IOP, "in its first public event, had made a formidable, but not altogether favorable, impression."[16]

This incident symbolized the extent to which Neustadt's venture flew in the face of the winds of his times. As he observed in an interview just three months before his death, "Politics is a noble calling. But that's never been a majority view in the United States. It was perhaps more widely held in 1964. But it went out of fashion very soon thereafter in the course of the Vietnam War." He concluded, "The Institute and the School have lived almost their entire lifetime in an unfavorable climate, a negative climate, a climate that thinks politics is a place for rascals."[17] After Vietnam came Watergate and the sharpest decline in respect for politicians and government ever seen in America. Nixon was followed by Jimmy Carter, and then Ronald Reagan, who expressed this zeitgeist best in his 1981 inaugural when he declared: "Government is not the solution to our problems. Government is the problem." So much for timing, Neustadt would say.

Strategic Adventurer

I think if I were doing it all over, I might have said, "This is too hard. Let's link the institute to Harvard: to the Faculty of Arts and Sciences or the President's Office. Let's not link it to this non-existent School."

I became an advocate of what got to be known as the "Big Plan" that would take over the [MBTA] car-barn site and put the library, the museum, the institute and the other Harvard facilities together. . . . But we could never get Harvard to find the money. . . . From my point of view, it was very sad, indeed.

RICHARD E. NEUSTADT, unpublished interview, August 2003[18]

The IOP's five-year financial commitment had elapsed, and by the mid 1970s the Kennedy School had severe financial problems running an annual deficit. . . . "The new [Master's in Public Policy degree program] would soon have to close down and the new faculty [would] have to be dismissed," says Neustadt. "The whole thing was going to collapse. All that would be left would be the Institute and the mid-career program."

CRAIG A. LAMBERT,
"The Origins of the John F. Kennedy School of Government"[19]

Remember: At Harvard, nothing ever fails.

OBSERVATION BY OSCAR HANDLIN,
recounted frequently by Neustadt

Return to the tail without a dog. Neustadt used this metaphor to explain his core strategy not just in building the Institute of Politics, but for creating the Public Policy Program, pursuing the Big Plan, and launching the Kennedy School itself.[20] In each case, he set out on a journey without a map that specified how one could get from here to there. He knew that the small ship on which he had ventured forth would face swells and storms he could not forecast, and that were in any case beyond his control. So he focused on doing what he could, leaving the next challenge for tomorrow. For someone who conceived of himself as a "political-level bureaucrat," as he often said, such adventurism felt foolhardy, even frightening. But when the goal is a destination to which no one has previously traveled, what is the alternative?

Ira Jackson served as the school's assistant dean for everything in the late 1970s and 1980s. He recalls that when others were tempted to despair, Dick "with his charming grin and avuncular reassurance . . . put his arm on my shoulder and said: 'At Harvard, nothing ever fails.'"[21] I must have heard Neustadt use that line a hundred times. He got it from an old Harvard lion, the history professor Oscar Handlin. For Neustadt, the observation was a double-edged sword. While reassuring others, Neustadt recognized for himself a deeper truth. Harvard included its share of walking wounded: individuals and institutes that had never come close to realizing their possibilities. Of course, as Neustadt once chuckled, rarely at Harvard did anyone ever own up to failure, especially in their own case. But he saw the world of Harvard without illusions and was brutally honest about what he had, and had not, done.

Having committed himself to an undertaking whose success he could not guarantee, he was counting on higher powers (at Harvard or beyond) to somehow see this through. In another of his oft-stated reassurances at junctures where others were tempted to despair, he would say, "We'll threaten to collapse, and Harvard will have to come to our rescue." When Neustadt handed me the baton at a point when the larger venture was in jeopardy, I inherited that angst. (At similar moments of uncertainty, I would remind colleagues that "God looks after drunks, little children, the U.S.A.—and Harvard.") "An agnostic on an optimistic day," as his daughter recalls, Neustadt nonetheless admired the framed Breton fisherman's prayer, presented to JFK by Vice Admiral Hyman Rickover, that always sat on the President's desk in the Oval Office: "O God, Thy sea is so great, and my boat is so small."[22]

For a tactical genius who counseled students and Presidents alike to analyze every dimension of significant choices, the need to rely so substantially on the necessity for strategic improvisation made him deeply uncomfortable. It was "unnatural," he once put it, for someone of his temperament. As he wrote, "Roosevelt's sense of fun combined with Roosevelt's sort of confidence remain for me . . . a target at which to aim."[23] Succeeding Hoover in 1933 at the depth of the Great Depression, FDR was, as Neustadt wrote, "ready to try anything, within limits, constitutional and capitalist; and he did."[24] Given the circumstances, he had no choice.

But as Neustadt enjoyed reminding students, FDR was, in the words of Supreme Court Justice Oliver Wendell Holmes Jr., "a second-class intellect but a first-class temperament." For great leaders, Neustadt adds, "perhaps this is a necessary combination."[25] For someone of FDR's temperament, leading into uncharted waters in the midst of a storm seemed "fitting." As Neustadt put it, the White House seemed "almost a family seat. Once he became President of the United States, that sense of fitness gave him an extraordinary confidence."[26]

Not so for Neustadt, who was unquestionably a first-class mind, and who never imagined himself a man on horseback. Like FDR, Neustadt was forced by necessity to lead by experimenting. As he noted at the conclusion of his rocky first year as director of the Institute of Politics, "So we begin, this year experimentally, and so we shall proceed."[27] But, Neustadt knew in his gut, without FDR's confidence.

Parameters of Power

The constitutional convention of 1787 is supposed to have created a government of "separated powers." It did nothing of the sort. Rather, it created a government of *separated institutions sharing power.* . . .

RICHARD E. NEUSTADT, *Presidential Power*

Each government is a more or less complex arena for internal bargaining among bureaucratic elements and political personalities who collectively comprise its working apparatus. Its action is the product of their interaction.

RICHARD E. NEUSTADT, *Alliance Politics*

Entering any environment, Neustadt began by mapping the parameters of power. As he put it, he would "case the joint." By that he meant that he would seek to identify not just the formal structures of power, but every lever, formal or informal, that influenced decisions and actions. He was insightful about the similarities among different environments of power. But he was fascinated by the nuanced differences, whether between the White House and Whitehall, or the Bureau of the Budget where he worked in the late 1940s and the Office of Management and Budget today.

Dick often said that the university is "something else." As a leading twentieth-century student of organizations, Jim March, proposed, the university is best understood as "organized anarchy."[28] On the spectrum from organization to anarchy, Harvard is the limiting case—of the latter. Operationally, Harvard hardly exists. The university is a confederation of semi-independent baronies, squire-archies, and small farms—united by a common name. The president of the university is its titular head. His or her major source of power comes from the power to select deans of the schools: the Medical School, Law School, Business School, and so forth. Once appointed, deans become largely independent barons (if they inherit a barony), squires (at the School of Education, the Divinity School, or the Design School), or, in the case of the Kennedy School of the time, titled gentry but without land. In principle, deans report to the president, who can fire them. But when a recent president, Lawrence Summers, attempted to exercise that power to replace the dean of the Faculty of Arts and Sciences, he found that he had accelerated a process that ended in his own departure. Ironically, at Harvard's memorial service for Neustadt in the spring of 2004, Summers, then president, recalled that when he sought counsel before assuming that role, Dick had replied, "Larry, you'll never make *small* mistakes."

The most fundamental financial principle at Harvard is ETOB: every tub on its own bottom.[29] According to this principle, each dean in the confederation is responsible for raising and spending his or her own money. While good news for the wealthy barons, this is bad news for a dean or director who inherits little endowment or is unsuccessful in raising funds. Thus the collapse of Neustadt's Big Plan. It envisaged construction of a complex of buildings that would house not just the JFK Library and Museum but also the Institute of Politics, the Department of Government and Economics (then located in the original Littauer Building), and Harvard's International Studies Programs, including the Center for International Affairs. On the principle that "nothing propinquits like propinquity," co-location would not only enliven the IOP and assure use of the Library, but also pull professors in these departments toward the real world of policy. Robert Kennedy argued, "This makes so much sense that I can't bear not to see it done."[30]

But as the official history of the Kennedy School notes, "Pusey was reluctant to commit Harvard . . . [since] the Big Plan would require fundraising that would distract from other projects high on the university's agenda."[31] In the final exchange of letters between RFK and Pusey in June 1966, RFK and Neustadt won a tentative commitment to the Big Plan. That "treaty" established the partnership between the JFK Library Foundation and Harvard; provided $10 million to create the IOP; renamed the Graduate School of Public Administration the John F. Kennedy School of Government; and pledged that Harvard would "make an effort" to realize the Big Plan. In the end, neither Pusey, nor the Kennedy family, nor Neustadt raised the money to make it happen, so it failed.

In time, the JFK Library and Museum left Cambridge for a site on Boston Harbor, in Dorchester. Harvard, however, managed to retain control of the twelve-acre car-barn site—since the decision to extend the MBTA's Red Line to Alewife had been made and construction on that project had begun. As Neustadt's chosen successor as associate dean, I worked with a new Harvard president, Derek Bok, and his vice president for finance, Hale Champion, to cut a suit to fit the cloth we could stitch together. We bought the land from the MBTA at book value, created a JFK Memorial Park along the river, and paid for that by selling a parcel of the twelve acres to a developer for what would become the Charles Hotel. An intra-Harvard "sale" of the original Littauer Building to the Faculty of Arts and Sciences, together with a loan from Harvard against funds to be raised in the future, allowed us to construct a building on the site to house the IOP, the Mid Career Program, the nascent Public Policy Program, and future activity to be imagined.

As that story progressed, Neustadt often remarked on the extraordinary unrecognized role money plays in shaping universities—even at Harvard. Why did the Big Plan not happen? For the absence of funds. Had it been implemented, the papers in the JFK Library would have been combed by countless undergraduates and graduate students writing theses; the school would have shaped—and been shaped by—its parent departments of economics, government, and international studies, who would have felt a stronger gravitational pull from the real world of global developments; and today's Institute of Politics and Kennedy School of Government would have been quite different.

The four most important decisions in the university are: What is studied? What is taught? By whom? And to whom? Each decision is made predominantly by the faculty. Senior faculty of each school and each department are tenured—appointed for life. Since full professors rarely leave, the most important players in departments and schools are, as Neustadt observed, "inmates for the duration." They know each other's strengths and weaknesses, bear scars from earlier battles, and find opportunities for getting even over years and even decades. Neustadt was fond of quoting "Sayre's law," named for his former colleague in Columbia's political science department, Wallace Sayre, who quipped, "Why is academic politics so vicious?" His answer: "Because the stakes are so low." Another academic who proved more successful in the politics of Washington and the world than on the Harvard campus was asked what he learned when serving as Richard Nixon's national security adviser. Henry Kissinger answered, "Even paranoids have enemies."

The most highly valued virtue at Harvard, as at other leading universities, is intellectual distinction. Academic efforts that produce great research advances in the sciences or other fields of study are most highly esteemed. A former dean of the Faculty of Arts and Sciences, Henry Rosovsky, notes in his *The University: An Owner's Manual,* "Our constituencies are inhabited by extremely talented scholars, including some who merit the label genius. A significant proportion own difficult and childish personalities (remember that temperament is ignored at time of appointment)."[32] After a stint as dean of Harvard College, Ernest May observed even more pointedly, "At Harvard, men of principle greatly outnumber men of honor." Protagonists in the university invariably stand on principle. The combination of ingenuity and flexibility in crafting principles that serve their interests can be as entertaining as it is dismaying.

Suffusing this structure of power, especially at Harvard, is an aura of arrogance. Not accidentally, a local T-shirt reads: "02138: The Most Arrogant Zip Code in the World." The prevailing presumption is that if it deserves to be at Harvard, it is. Even more important, if something is not here already, it must not belong.

Having analyzed these parameters of power, Neustadt was acutely aware that his mission required successfully implanting a foreign object in the heart of the university. He had to overcome antibodies that would naturally seek to reject it. Stealthily, he started by seeking out arenas where no permission was required. For example, having been licensed by President Pusey to head an "institute," he asked for no further approvals when creating a program for fellows. He could unilaterally identify, choose, and recruit individuals who fit his bill. And so he did, especially in the early years of the Institute, when he brought to campus a stellar group, including the voting rights activist Vernon Jordan, the *Washington Post* columnist David Broder, and the State Department official Jonathan Moore. Neustadt, Vernon Jordan recalls, opened his eyes to the wide world beyond America's borders. For a civil rights leader from Atlanta, Cambridge was terra incognita. But Neustadt arranged for Jordan to be the first black man ever to attend a meeting of the Bilderberg Group—a self-selected elite of European and American leaders from business and government—in 1969 in Elsinore, Denmark.[33]

Others suggested that Neustadt's fellows teach courses, but he rejected that idea, since it would require action by the faculty—authorization that would almost certainly be denied. Instead, he invented a functional equivalent, something he called noncredit study groups. If David Broder gave weekly classes on politics and the press, even if it were labeled a "noncredit study group," students would come. Who could stop them? Similarly, he

created Institute of Politics "faculty study groups" to engage specific scholars from across the university whom he suspected had an unscratched itch
to be more policy relevant. Senior faculty are free agents; he was the director of an institute; no further role permission was required in deciding
what would be studied or whom to include or exclude. So he built his tail
in cracks that were unoccupied or uncontested, assiduously avoiding gatekeepers or overt choices where others could say no.

Assessing the Opposition

Probably the price you have to pay for the assassination of a President, as
one faculty member said to me.

> RICHARD E. NEUSTADT, quoted in Craig Lambert, "Heart and Soul,"
> *Kennedy School Bulletin,* SPRING 2004

After the McNamara affair, the Institute became a source of trouble, and
a great number of conservative faculty members were increasingly outraged by the Institute's very existence.

> RICHARD E. NEUSTADT, unpublished interview, August 2003

In the core course on political analysis that Neustadt and I taught for the
Public Policy Program, one segment was called Assessing Foreign Governments. Later he developed this as a full semester course in itself.
Watching Neustadt apply this framework to his challenge at Harvard, four
points stand out.

First, Neustadt distinguished between a log floating downstream and a
salmon swimming upstream against a powerful current. He knew that he
was the salmon, and the dominant culture of Harvard, a river rushing in
the opposite direction. The fact that nothing like the Institute of Politics
or School of Government existed at any great university of the world was
no accident. At Harvard this concept had been explicitly considered more
than once—and explicitly rejected. At the beginning of the twentieth century, President Charles W. Eliot proposed a school of business and public
service. An influential Boston Brahmin, Lawrence Lowell, who was to be
Eliot's successor as president of the university, found Eliot's proposal unac-
ceptable, arguing, "We should not be holding ourselves out as training men
for a career that does not exist, and for which, if it did exist, I think our

training would very likely not be the best preparation."[34] The opposition triumphed, and instead, in 1908, Harvard created the Business School.

At Harvard's celebration of its three hundredth birthday, in 1936, the major gift announcement came from Lucius N. Littauer, a Harvard graduate, wealthy glove manufacturer, and former member of Congress. With Littauer's gift, Harvard announced the creation of a new Graduate School of Public Administration and construction of a building that would house Harvard's Departments of Economics and Government as well as the new graduate school. The speaker at the Tercentenary Commencement was Franklin Roosevelt, a graduate of Harvard College in the class of '04. Roosevelt linked Littauer's gift to Harvard's historic mission, calling on the University to "train men to be citizens in that high Athenian sense that compels a man to live his life unceasingly aware that its civic sense is its most abiding."[35]

However inspired the rhetoric, the reality of university politics proved otherwise. Predictably, these parent departments, of Economics and Government, moved swiftly to stifle the aspirations of those who would form an independent faculty in the school and even more decisively to capture its resources. Thus when Lowell's successor, James Bryant Conant, retired as president of Harvard in 1953, he identified the Graduate School of Public Administration as his "great disappointment."[36] There matters sat until Neustadt entered the picture—by which time the Departments of Economics and Government had grown accustomed to occupying 95 percent of the office space (and associated parking places) in the Littauer Building and using 90 percent of the income generated from Mr. Littauer's endowment as subsidies for their own faculties' activities.

During the 1950s and 1960s, Clark Kerr served as President of the University of California. Under his leadership, Berkeley, UCLA, and other campuses joined the major leagues, an achievement for which he was widely acclaimed. Reflecting on that experience, Kerr quipped, "The three major administrative challenges on a campus are sex for the students, athletics for the alumni, and offices and parking for the faculty."[37] Neustadt had no intention of disturbing the students or alumni. But he could not succeed in building a School of Government without dislodging some senior Economics and Government Department faculty members from offices and parking places at Littauer. On paper, this space belonged to the School of which he was Associate Dean. But especially in so decentralized an institution, possession is more than 90 percent of the operative law. I recall his glee on one occasion when he discovered an office of a professor who had died some years earlier. Full of unopened boxes of the deceased's papers, it was being used by a former student. When confronted, the student was eager to make his escape, since he knew he was in the wrong, and Neustadt chalked up one office.

Second, Harvard College and its Faculty of Arts and Sciences owned his key constituents: the undergraduates. That faculty was overwhelmingly opposed to what Neustadt had in mind. Hard as it may be to believe today, many shared the view that something bearing JFK's name was "the price you have to pay for the assassination of a President." He never doubted that if asked to vote on a proposal to establish a vibrant nexus between the academy and politics, the Faculty of Arts and Sciences would have decisively rejected it. Indeed, were a vote to be held today, the nays would likely greatly outnumber the ayes. Fortunately, the Faculty of Arts and Sciences was mostly an absentee owner of its undergraduates. Its neglect provided his opportunity to develop non-course courses that connected students to political animals in ways that often shaped their lives more than any class.

Third, the squires who chaired the key departments, particularly Economics and Government, and the senior faculty members of these departments, were naturally inclined to oppose bringing real-world politics and government inside Harvard's ivied walls. Some feared this would debase Harvard's currency, expanding the "trade school" mentality, as they referred to it, that they associated with the Harvard Business School (which, incidentally, they also opposed). Others suspected that such activity would compete for resources in ways that could threaten their interests. As a member of the Government Department and clearly the nation's leading political scientist who studied the Presidency, Neustadt could have been a heavyweight in the department. Instead, he attended meetings, but was mostly silent. His goal was to protect his undertaking, so he sought to avoid raising issues in ways that could give departments a veto. He limited fights over offices and parking places, mostly reclaiming territory only when someone left or died.

Fourth, countless numbers of assistant and associate deans and their minions stood as guardians of the status quo. Their operational catechism is decoded by the British scholar F. M. Cornford in his *Microcosmographia*

Academica: Being a Guide for the Young Academic Politician.[38] Cornford enumerates their arguments for doing nothing—nothing that is not already being done. These include the "principle of the wedge," according to which "you should not act justly now for fear of raising expectations that you may act still more justly in the future"; the "dangerous precedent," according to which "you should not now do an admittedly right action for fear that you, or your equally timid successors, should not have the courage to do the right thing in some future case"; and the "Principle of Unripe Time" that cautions against doing "at the present moment what they think right at that moment, because the moment at which they think it right has not yet arrived." Conscious of the faculty's catch-22s, Neustadt searched out cracks in the system, from "noncredit" courses to vacated offices. As a quintessential example of dealing with what he called the "guardians," Neustadt loved Heather Campion's story of the secretary to the corporation's outrage over the Kennedy School's logo for the celebration of Harvard's three hundred fiftieth birthday in 1986. Since the Graduate School of Public Administration had formally been established in 1936, even though it seemed a stretch, we chose to celebrate the School of Government's Fiftieth anniversary simultaneously. At the time, the chairman of the school's visiting committee was Frank Stanton, an acclaimed business statesman. Stanton had led CBS to its position as the dominant network, shaping a culture in which Edward R. Murrow and his colleagues defined the standards for highest-quality television journalism. Stanton also took a great interest in design, including CBS's headquarters in New York and the iconic logo, the CBS Eye. With Stanton's encouragement, Campion had added a flourish to Harvard's basic Kennedy School shield for this special occasion. When this came to the secretary's attention, he called Campion to his office to inquire on whose authority this had been done. When she explained that Dr. Stanton, a member of Harvard's Board of Overseers— formally the secretary's employer—had proposed the addition, the secretary responded, "But he was not even a Harvard graduate!"

Exercising Power to Make Things Happen: Bringing Camelot to Cambridge

Presidential power is the power to persuade.

RICHARD E. NEUSTADT, *Presidential Power*

Underneath our image of the President-in-boots, astride decisions, are the half-observed realities of the President-in-sneakers, stirrups in hand, trying to induce particular Department heads, or Congressmen, or Senators, to climb aboard.

RICHARD E. NEUSTADT, "White House and Whitehall"

The participants bargain not at random, but according to the processes, conforming to the prerequisites, responsive to the pressures of their own political system.

RICHARD E. NEUSTADT, *Alliance Politics*

As a scholar, Neustadt was the most penetrating analyst of power since Machiavelli. Few observers realized how skillfully he practiced what he preached. For Neustadt, power meant effective influence on decisions and actions. For him, the leader's "impact on the outcome" is the measure of the man.[39] In Neustadtian analysis, power is an elusive blend of three elements: bargaining advantages, skill and will in using these advantages, and other players' perception of the first two ingredients. Power is nothing to be sought, or held, or gloried in. Rather, it is a resource to be used to advance purpose. Wisely invested, exercises of power yield an enhanced reputation for effectiveness and thus added leverage for future use.

As the founding director of a newly created institute with no defined charter, Neustadt had formal authority enough, and sufficient funds ($400,000 annual income from the endowment of the Institute of Politics). With these, he could create a fellows program, select whom he wanted, bring them to campus, and have them teach noncredit study groups on topics that would attract students. He could invite honorary associates of his choice to campus, whether McNamara or, subsequently, Gerry Ford (at the time a Republican congressman from Michigan). He could hold lunches at the Little Yellow House, or stag dinners at his Traill Street home, as he did for RFK during the winter of 1968, when the senator from New York wrestled with his decision about running for President.

But if his fellows, such as Vernon Jordan, were to be allowed to live in one of the houses (the Harvard undergraduates' small residential colleges) like tutors, that required an invitation from the master of the house. If the senior faculty members across the university with the tightest links to policymakers in Washington were to come to view his Institute of Politics as a locus for their activities, he had to engage them in activities there that made this so. Later, when he decided to launch a new Public Policy Program that would grant Master's of Public Policy degrees and even Ph.D.s to students in the Kennedy School, that required a vote by the Faculty of Arts and Sciences. And when he concluded that a coup would be required to ensure that the Kennedy School could exercise independent authority to build its own faculty and appoint professors whose primary commitment would be to the school's mission, he engineered one to disenfranchise a majority of the Economics and Government departments' members of control.

The story of how he did this is mainly a history of tireless engagement of successive presidents of the university, deans of the various faculties, senior professors, assistant professors, and even occasionally graduate students in an endless series of breakfasts, coffees, lunches, drinks, dinners, and even Sunday brunches. Edith Stokey, secretary of the school through much of the Neustadt era, and herself no mean practitioner of quiet purposiveness at Harvard, cautions against revealing too many of Neustadt's secrets. But she notes that, while his classic, *Presidential Power*, is among the most-purchased, most-cited, and most-read books ever among students and practitioners alike, few will recall its subtitle: *The Politics of Leadership*. As a practitioner of his own prescriptions, he was relentlessly purposive, each engagement designed to advance his strategic ends. In instance after instance, he found ways to persuade those who were essential to his cause that what he wanted of them was what they wanted to do on the basis of their own appraisal of their own interests.

Neustadt would be the first to insist that many shared in the work from which these institutions emerged. He was fond of quoting JFK's observation that "success has a thousand fathers." In this case, mothers and fathers began with his first wife, Bert, who was his closest adviser and helpmate during these years. Colleagues-in-arms included the school's founding fathers, Derek Bok, president of Harvard University, and the dean of the Kennedy School, Don Price. While Neustadt was director of the Institute of Politics, he was the associate dean, not the dean, of the Kennedy School. Price, a gracious Tennessean, was a pioneer in the study of science, technology, and public policy. He was always a gentle gentleman. The relationship between Price and his associate dean, Neustadt, was symbiotic. As cautious as Neustadt was venturesome, Price built a reservoir of goodwill in relationships across the university on which Neustadt was able to draw. To what extent Price and President Derek Bok played "monarch" to Neustadt's "prime minister"—to use Fred Greenstein's metaphor in his revealing analysis of Eisenhower's hidden-hand presidency—will remain for others to explore.[40]

Of scores of examples that could be offered to illustrate the operational style of this entrepreneur in sneakers, six will have to suffice. From this distance, it is difficult to recall the magic of Camelot. But when Neustadt brought Jacqueline Kennedy to campus for Senior Advisory Committee meetings, the campus would light up. I can still recall taking the woman I was wooing (who subsequently succumbed to become my wife) to the October 1966 dinner at Holyoke Center that was the Institute of Politics' coming-out party. For a twenty-six-year-old graduate student, the thrill of attending a dinner with Jackie was greater than going backstage after a concert with the Supremes. No one who attended that dinner failed to say yes to Neustadt's next request.

Engaging the public policy influentials at Harvard was more complex. Some, like John Kenneth Galbraith, Pat Moynihan, Francis Bator, and Carl Kaysen, were veterans from the Kennedy administration. Each had views about what a "living memorial" should be and was eager to help. Other policy influentials and wannabes—for example, a professor in the Department of Government, Henry Kissinger—had to be courted.

As part of his relentless effort to scrape up bargaining advantages wherever he could find them, Neustadt hired an attractive English secretary with a very proper accent. Xandra Bingley was the wife of a graduate student, the Earl of Gowrie, who was studying with the Harvard poet Robert Lowell. She brought to the director and associate dean's office a combination of the exotic and the erotic. I can still recall her ordering pizza over the phone with the line "Lady Gowrie here." Have no doubt: the pizza was delivered much more expeditiously than when I called. She and the earl had a son during their stay in the United States and named him *Br'er*—a combination of Br'er Rabbit and the greeting "Brother," which was used by activists in the civil rights movement.

Xandra also had the longest and loveliest legs in Cambridge, portions of which were covered by her miniskirts—a rave in London that had not yet made its way to Boston. She would sit at her desk in Neustadt's front office on the first floor of the old Littauer Building typing or answering the phone. Occasionally, though, she had to roll her chair back from the

desk—a sight that could produce palpitations. Dick's office became a popular spot for graduate students and faculty members alike to drop by in
hopes of getting a glimpse of Gowrie. None was more frequent than
Henry Kissinger. At the time, he was secretly negotiating with the North
Vietnamese in Paris—a fact that emerged accidentally from the Parisian
baubles he occasionally brought back for Xandra.

For the purposeful director in sneakers, however, what seemed accidental to others was another thread in his plan. Kissinger became a key member of a faculty study group Neustadt created on Vietnam. This group
would spend Saturday mornings struggling with the consuming foreign-
policy issue of the day. Washington colleagues, including a former Harvard
Law School professor, John McNaughton, who as assistant secretary of
defense was McNamara's action officer on Vietnam policy, would often
return from Washington to Cambridge for those Saturday morning sessions. Participants, and even those who merely heard about the sessions,
discovered what Neustadt meant when he talked about linking the academy and practice.

A third of Neustadt's inventions was what engraved invitations called a
"small dance." The first was held at 17 Quincy Street, originally the home
of the president of the university, whose ballroom is the grandest at Harvard. The invitation said "black tie" and included the line "decorations may
be worn." For Harvard "decorations" was a first—at least, in modern times.
For Neustadt, it was, as he recalled in his final interview, part of "keeping
alive a sense of two things: the nobility of politics, and the fun of politics,
both of which were cardinal in Kennedy's belief and behavior."[41] Some
critics looked askance at such an extravaganza. But no one who received an
invitation declined, and the uninvited envied the invitees.

Francis Bator recalls that the "small dance" epitomized Dick's "blending
of fun and purpose. . . . I still recall Dick, resplendent in black tie, doing
the two-step with Bert—gorgeous. He loved to dance. And the dances
served a purpose."[42] Some of the older senior faculty at the university wore
distinguished decorations, among them a towering figure from the Government Department who had helped write Germany's postwar constitution. Neustadt wore a small blue ribbon he had won for finishing third in
a high school track meet.

For his larger purposes, Neustadt knew that he needed at least the
acquiescence, and in some case the active support, of barons and power

brokers. Chief among these was John Dunlop, a distinguished labor nego-
tiator and professor who had been chair of the Economics Department
during the first half of the 1960s, and subsequently became dean of the
Faculty of Arts and Sciences in the wake of the student disruptions in
1969. A project-oriented problem solver, Dunlop could rarely resist when
presented with a problem and asked for help, as long as it did not encroach
on his own interests or domain. The more intractable the problem, the
more irresistible he found it. He was perhaps Neustadt's most frequent
breakfast or lunch companion. When I became dean, Neustadt bequeathed
"Uncle John" to me. As Dunlop enjoyed reminding me, at his age "what I
enjoy most is getting recalcitrant bastards to do what I need them to do
without having the capacity to force them."

At the time, Dunlop was writing a book with the new dean of the Law
School, Derek Bok (fortuitously, the future president of Harvard). In the
wake of the Kennedy administration, numbers of law students imagined
they might also go to Washington for a portion of their careers. Bok was
thus a natural ally in helping Neustadt build a program that could help him
meet that demand at the Law School. Indeed, Bok had a deep personal
respect for public service, reflecting not only his career but also the values
of his wife, Sissela, and her parents, Alva and Gunnar Myrdal.[43] As dean
of Harvard's Medical School, Robert Ebert certainly understood the difference between a professional school and the Faculty of Arts and Sciences.
He also had a deep interest in the ways in which decisions in Washington—for example, about Medicare and Medicaid—would affect the
profession that was his constituency. He was thus enlistable as an ally
in support of instruction in public policy that could be helpful to a select
number of his medical students. Neustadt even targeted the dean of the
Business School, but eventually concluded that was for him a bridge
too far.

If there was to be life at the John F. Kennedy School of Government, it
would require students, a faculty, and a curriculum the faculty would teach
to the students. As he set about building a school to which the tail now
wagging as the Institute of Politics could be attached, Neustadt cherry-
picked and then courted superstars from across the university. From the
Department of Economics he chose Tom Schelling, a legendary scholar
and teacher; from the Department of Statistics, Fred Mosteller, to develop

statistics for public policy; from the Business School, Howard Raiffa, the leading decision theorist; from the Law School, Philip Heymann; and from the Kennedy School itself, the economist Francis Bator, whom he had recently recruited from the Johnson White House and who served as first chairman of the new Master's in Public Policy program. Other members of the initial crew included Joe Bower and Chuck Christensen, from the Business School, and three junior faculty members, Dick Zeckhauser, Jake Jacoby, and me.

The senior faculty was a group of "distinguished misfits," as Schelling called them. Each had sufficient standing in his core discipline that his choices were beyond being questioned by colleagues in the Faculty of Arts and Sciences. But each had an itch to do something more, to make a difference in the world of government and public policy.

How did each come to the view that he should devote the next several years of his life to building a pioneering curriculum to train extraordinary students in professional public policy? No doubt, many factors were important. But in every case, Neustadt invested countless hours of his own time in conversation that helped to connect the dots between where each thought he was and where Neustadt needed him to be. In Derek Bok's summary, Neustadt "had a real practical grasp of how the executive branch worked; his special strength was using those skills and combining them with an engaging and persuasive personality to inspire faculty members to believe they could pull it off."[44]

Ditto for the initial group of twenty-five students, many of whom were also personally recruited by Neustadt. This amazing group included Harvey Fineberg (a joint-degree student with the Medical School, who was subsequently dean of the School of Public Health and provost of Harvard University and is now president of the National Institute of Medicine); Robert Klitgaard (subsequently an associate professor at the Kennedy School and dean of the Rand Graduate School, and now president of the Claremont Colleges); and Mark Moore (subsequently a professor of public policy at the Kennedy School, who took the lead in building the public-management curriculum and the Executive Programs). This talent was important in sustaining the faculty's enthusiasm. Moreover, they would also establish the program's reputation in the eyes of their former professors and, in time, the world.

At each critical stage in advancing toward his goal, Neustadt waited until he had secured the support, or acquiescence, of the essential minimum coalition before raising an issue for decision—or allowing a choice to arise. When most effective, the director in sneakers maneuvered so masterfully that for most observers, things just happened. Another of Neustadt's oft-used lines—and his highest praise—was, "Look, Mom, no hands."

Beneath the two major formal choices that created the Public Policy Program and the independent faculty for the Kennedy School, one can unmistakably find Neustadt's invisible hand. The official history of the Kennedy School describes the process during the fall of 1968 leading up to the formal vote of the Faculty of Arts and Sciences on December 3 that approved the creation of a "Committee on Higher Degrees in Public Policy." That vote authorized the Public Policy Program. The school's forti-eth-anniversary history notes: "Neustadt managed eventually to allay most concerns among fellow members of the Government Department, and Dunlop saw to it that the economists did not interpose roadblocks. Thus at that faculty meeting, the new Committee on Higher Degrees in Public Policy was approved." The history concludes,

> For the Kennedy School, it was a stroke of luck that the necessary legislation reached the floor of the Faculty of Arts of Sciences when and as it did. . . . The issue might never have come to a vote if post-poned beyond December 3, for the next faculty meeting was, in fact, disrupted by demonstrations. And subsequent meetings were domi-nated by questions of whether and how the demonstrators were to be disciplined. Then came spring, the occupation of University Hall, and two years of seldom rational turbulence.[45]

What to the writer of that history appeared to be "luck" was to a con-siderable extent the result of Neustadt's calculation, cunning, and hundreds of hours of conversations.

Even more revealing was the coup Neustadt engineered that left the majority of faculty members in the parent Departments of Economics and Government without the power to make decisions about future develop-ments at the Kennedy School. Details quickly become too arcane for any but ardent students of academic politics. Suffice it to note that the faculty of what had been renamed the John F. Kennedy School of Government originally included all senior members of the two parent Departments of Economics and Government. As a result, the departments appointed faculty for their own purposes, some of whom had a secondary "joint appointment" with the Kennedy School. If the school was to appoint faculty members who were not primarily members of the parent departments, decisions about opportunities would have to be made by individuals committed to its mission. Neustadt thus designed what he billed as a "faculty reorganization." It distinguished between "full professors whose permanent tenure is wholly or partially the school's responsibility and who are willing to accept their full share of the school's academic and administrative responsibilities," on the one hand, and a number of other categories of faculty, including the majorities in the two departments, on the other. Price presented the proposal as an "administrative matter" on an agenda for a meeting held in December 1974. Few members of the official faculty actually showed up. The motion was passed unanimously. As a result, sixty full professors, formerly members of the Kennedy School faculty, no longer had a vote on appointments and other major developments in the Kennedy School.[46]

Finally, Al Carnesale recalls Neustadt's enjoyment when Al, then provost at Harvard, would explain how Shirley Williams, a star British politician who had joined Roy Jenkins in forming a new Social Democrat Party and who had a long association with the Kennedy School both as a teacher and as acting director of the Institute of Politics, became the first woman public service professor at the Kennedy School. The storyline came from Longfellow's "The Courtship of Miles Standish," in which the shy Standish enlisted his friend John Alden to propose to Priscilla Mullins in his stead. Alden duly made the offer, and Priscilla's response became famous: "Why don't you speak for yourself, John?" Alden came back, having married Priscilla himself. In Edith Stokey's version of that story, which Carnesale enjoyed retelling, Neustadt was heading off on sabbatical to England. Dean Allison, who had been trying to lure Shirley Williams back to the Kennedy School, urged Neustadt to seek her out and persuade her to accept a position as a professor at the school. But how to persuade her to leave England and move to Harvard? That was a problem Neustadt was happy to solve. Having lost his wife, Bert, after a long struggle with MS in which he became her constant caregiver, Neustadt had a void in his heart.

He offered Shirley not only the academic position but also his hand (the order in which these occurred is not clear); she accepted both offers and they came back together to Harvard.

It is true that I often teased Neustadt thereafter that he had done more in a single initiative to advance the Kennedy School's "affirmative action" recruitment of women professors than the entire faculty had done in the prior decade. Moreover, Edith Stokey recalls the heady days at KSG, when Dick and Shirley, now married, had to navigate through the impedimenta thrown in their path by the U.S. Immigration and Naturalization Service. As associate academic dean, Stokey was assigned by Carnesale to respond to periodic inquiries by the INS. She vouched for them personally and confirmed that their marriage was legitimate, not the sham the service must have suspected, set up for the purpose of permitting an alien—Shirley Williams—to enter and remain in the United States. No wonder Williams eschewed the "opportunity" to become a U.S. citizen! Stokey duly penned suitable letters, on Harvard University letterhead, once every two or three years, as required. "We were all delighted by their marriage and remain so," she wrote in one such letter. "I see them socially on a regular basis as well as professionally, and can testify that they are a happily married couple." It was, after all, part of Stokey's job at the Kennedy School to do whatever needed doing that no one else had volunteered to do.

As Neustadt watched the evolution of the Institute of Politics and the Kennedy School that he had invested so much of himself in inventing, he became decidedly uncomfortable. Since he bequeathed to me a school at risk of collapse and the challenge to reinvent a vision of the school that would prove viable, he was invariably generous about what he called "your baby." But as he stood further back from the school, especially after I stepped down as dean in 1989, he became increasingly vocal about his worries.

During the period in which he carried the baton, he had had not only goals but nightmares. His coordinates included not only objectives, but signposts about tempting directions that would lead the enterprise astray. At the top of this list were four, which in characteristic fashion he expressed epigrammatically. These were: first, that we not become the "third best economics department in Cambridge"; second, that we not settle for "applied social science"; third, that we not become "another

Woodrow Wilson School," by which he meant a captive of the Departments of Economics and Political Science; and fourth, that we not become a "Democratic brothel."

His worry grew that the enterprise was approaching, or had failed to avoid, one or more of these bogs. When he would return to Cambridge from England, where he had moved with Shirley when she was made Baroness of Crosby and joined the House of Lords, over lunch or drinks, he would voice these concerns. He knew the enterprise was now under new leadership, beyond his control. But that didn't mean he stopped caring about and worrying over "his baby." As Mark Moore, the Hauser Professor of Nonprofit Organizations at the Kennedy School, and a longtime and close colleague of Dick's, observed, Harvard's claim never to fail invites the risk of institutional complacency, and is antithetical to "Dick's uncompromising commitment to the goal of building an outstanding professional school of government. [Dick] refused to be satisfied with something that merely looks like the best that Harvard could do in advancing this goal. His was an entrepreneurial, exploratory spirit, animated by a vision of urgent public need that drove him forward."[47]

The school's continuing attempt to wrestle with these misdirections, as Neustadt saw them, is explored at greater length in the case on the Kennedy School that is now part of the Case Program—yet another facet of Neustadt's legacy.[48] These remain among the central challenges for the School's current dean, David Ellwood—and will for his successor. The dangers of which Neustadt warned arise from gravitational forces that are defining features of great research universities. Initiatives that require overcoming such forces demand sustained counterforce and perpetual vigilance. But the larger truth is that the Institute of Politics and Kennedy School of Government of which he was the entrepreneur-in-chief have become jewels in Harvard's crown. Graduates of the school are recognized contemporary world leaders, from the president of Mexico and prime minister of Singapore to the secretary general of the United Nations. Research at the school on topics from welfare reform and nuclear terrorism to climate disruption has informed and improved public choices. New methods for analyzing public policy issues advanced by KSG faculty were recognized in the award of the Nobel Prize in Economics to one of Neustadt's fellow "founding fathers," Thomas Schelling, in 2005. Other universities in the United States and around the globe seek to follow in the footsteps of

the Institute of Politics' and the Kennedy School's lead in building comparable institutions of their own.

This acknowledgment of Neustadt's disappointments, especially when
he was in his darker moods, should be understood in context. For the institute, the school, and most of all, himself, he held the highest aspirations.
As others applauded what had been accomplished, he focused on what
remained to be done. In that sense, he resembled the legendary twentieth-
century president of the University of Chicago, Robert Hutchins, who
when asked about the university answered, "It's not a very good university—it's only the best there is."[49]

His most important advice for all who would follow in his footsteps in
academic institution building came from the President he admired most,
Harry Truman. Of all those whose lessons he sought to apply, Truman
came first. Never has a university entrepreneur at Harvard better exemplified Truman's belief that "there is no limit to what an individual can
accomplish—if he is prepared to let others take the credit."[50]

CHAPTER ELEVEN

NEUSTADT IN BRAZIL

ERIC REDMAN

Good institutions for Poland can only be the work of the Poles, or of someone who has made a thorough first-hand study of the Polish nation and its neighbors. A foreigner can hardly do more than offer some general observations for the enlightenment, but not for the guidance, of the law-reformer.

JEAN-JACQUES ROUSSEAU,
Considerations on the Government of Poland, 1772

LIFE NEEDN'T IMITATE art, but may, on a whim, take a cue from it. Richard E. Neustadt's art—his academic writing and advice to Presidents—teems with life. For a biographer, however, Neustadt's life also teems with art, and no chapter more than the final one—which also imitates it.

In 2003, Neustadt was invited to journey from England to Brazil to advise on an unusual case: the transition to power of an improbable new President, the Workers' Party candidate known simply as Lula. Neustadt's real-life adventure mirrored one in art: In 1886, Sherlock Holmes traveled to Brazil to advise on another intriguing case, the theft of a Stradivarius the emperor of Brazil had given his mistress. The comparison shouldn't be stretched. Yet on both trips, famed observers applied their famous methods and left durable records of their work that repay examination. Both visits proved notable, too, for Brazil's invigorating impact on the visitors—and theirs on Brazil. Holmes's tale is told in *A Samba for Sherlock,* a best-selling 1995 novel.[1] Neustadt's is told here.

The 2002 Presidential Election in Brazil

To many foreigners, including international financial institutions, the election of the leftist President Luiz Inácio Lula da Silva—Lula, for short—in October 2002 came as a shock but no surprise. Lula never trailed in the polls. Indeed, his lead grew with every alarmist prediction (well publicized in Brazil) from the Northern Hemisphere. "When a giant falls, the noise is loud and the collateral damage wide," wrote Tony Smith in the *New York Times* before the election. "Fear of such a prospect is gripping Latin America."[2]

Latin America? Smith's article brimmed with Wall Street sources, references to bond prices, and fears for North American companies heavily invested in Brazil, such as General Motors and WorldCom. In retrospect, the fears seem like leachate, the product of Northern nightmares filtered through the contaminated gravel of Latin American financial history and political context. In the North, Enron had recently collapsed, WorldCom had gone bankrupt, the West Coast had suffered an economy-crushing run-up in electric power and natural gas prices—and the attacks of 9/11, with their economic impacts, remained fresh. Economic growth, reliable in the 1990s, had reversed. War simmered in Afghanistan and loomed in Iraq.

In Latin America, Argentina defaulted on $141 billion of debt. Uruguay briefly closed its banks, and in Montevideo riot police confronted looters. Hugo Chávez, a new demon for North America to conjure with, grew belligerent in Venezuela. Brazil's currency plummeted, interest rates soared, and Brazil sought emergency aid from the International Monetary Fund. The great concern was that after the election, Brazil would "renegotiate" its quarter-trillion dollars of public debt—in other words, walk right up to the precipice of default, forcing creditors to blink. Internationally, this might be cataclysmic. With 175 million people, Brazil was the world's fifth-largest country.

Brazil's financial problems weren't entirely self-inflicted. They also reflected a vicious circle of perception: international fears of Lula's election, when expressed, propelled Lula more surely to office, thus heightening international fears. Lula's opponent, Jose Serra, of the centrist Social Democracy Party—the party long in power—made the situation worse. As the *New York Times* article put it, "Mr. Serra may have also made a tactical mistake by warning voters that a failure to elect him would court an economic collapse like Argentina's. Instead of turning voters away from his rivals, the comment only further roiled Brazil's markets."

And what of Lula himself? If the North heard "Castro" or "Chávez" when crowds shouted "Lula," the error wasn't entirely inexplicable. Lula had risen from real poverty (although not the worst Brazil can offer). He'd known hunger. He'd received little education, worked at a lathe, and for two decades led the rough-hewn, red-flag-waving Workers' Party—the Partido dos Trabalhadores, or PT, which he'd help found in 1980. (Workers' Party members are known as *petistas;* the party has many factions, of which Lula's is considered center-left.) At one stage, Lula even declared support for renegotiating the debt.

As Lula's election became increasingly inevitable, however, foreign observers noted a few encouraging signs. Lula began wearing a coat and tie. (Yet hadn't Juan and Eva Peron dressed well amid throngs of *descamisados?*) He stopped talking about renegotiating the debt. (But was this a ploy?) He bowed to pressure from the incumbent president, Fernando Henrique Cardoso—the patron of his rival Mr. Serra—and announced he'd support the stabilization measures Cardoso had negotiated with international lenders. It began to be pointed out that Lula had run for President three times before, yet he kept leading his followers back to the ballot box, not the streets.

In the campaign's final weeks, the world took a somewhat different measure of Lula. He didn't seem such a hothead, a Castro, a Chávez. He began to seem like what he called himself: a democrat, a realist, someone willing to accept international and financial strictures, someone who just wanted to tackle what no one had yet tackled successfully—Brazil's poverty, its hunger, its disparities of income and shocking inequality. He won in a landslide, and took office in January 2003.

This was the man Neustadt—at eighty-four, living in England, hearing aids in both ears—five months later flew across the Atlantic to help. By then, Lula had been in office long enough for his advisers to agree: Things were not going entirely well.

Invitation and Acceptance

Invitations to experts often issue on the recommendation of a trusted source. So it was here. Sherlock Holmes's invitation came from Emperor

Don Pedro II himself, after he received a dressing-room tip from the vis-iting stage star Sarah Bernhardt. Neustadt's came from a Lula adviser, Helena Kerr do Amaral, the new president of Brazil's National School of Public Administration (Escola Nacional de Administrão Public, or ENAP), on the advice of Professor Michael Barzelay. Barzelay, an author-ity on Brazil, had met Neustadt at the Kennedy School and gotten to know him better after taking a post at the London School of Economics.

During a meeting in Brazil, members of Lula's inner circle confided to Barzelay their concern that the young administration was struggling a bit. Barzelay immediately thought of Neustadt. "Barzelay said that the most important person he knew that could be invited to talk about the role of early decisions on agenda, process, and structure [as these affect] Presi-dential success would be Professor Neustadt," Kerr later wrote of that meeting. "In June, he was here."[3]

Actually, it wasn't quite that simple. Kerr naturally wanted Neustadt's specific advice on how the new President and his team could do better— quickly. The Workers' Party had no experience with national administra-tion: *petistas* had held governorships and municipal posts, but never the Presidency. Nothing had prepared Lula or his party for this transition. In fact, Lula's inauguration marked the first time in eighty years that an elected Brazilian leader had succeeded an elected leader of a different party. (Previously, the dominant center-right Social Democracy Party had engaged in presidential transitions mainly with the military.) Neustadt cer-tainly would know more than the *petistas* about presidential transitions, Kerr felt. In fact, she believed, "He knew much more than anyone in Brazil about democratic government" in every respect.[4] Kerr could easily imagine how Neustadt might help.

Kerr and Barzelay failed to anticipate Neustadt's modesty. When, over lunch in London, Barzelay conveyed Kerr's offer—a paid consultancy to advise Lula and his aides on the Brazilian presidential transition— Neustadt was flattered but somewhat aghast. As he told his daughter, Beth, he knew something of the U.S. Presidency but nothing of Brazil's, and relatively little about Brazil itself, having visited the country only once, four years earlier, with his wife, the British political leader Shirley Williams. Firmly, Neustadt refused to become a Lula consultant.[5]

Barzelay must have sensed Neustadt's temptation, however. So he devised an alternative. The Brazilians, he suggested, should invite Neustadt to give a lecture. The topic should be U.S. presidential transitions, not the Brazilian one. Notionally, Neustadt would neither consult nor give advice to Lula's inner circle; rather, they could draw lessons from Neustadt's accounts of U.S. experience if they deemed the lessons relevant. Barzelay had the measure of his man. Then, as Kerr wrote, "In June he was here."

Neustadt's Lecture and Private Meetings in Brasilia

Neustadt arrived in Brazil on June 4, 2003. "He didn't look tired from the plane trip," Kerr reports: "My husband [a prominent *petista*] and I took him to dinner at an Italian restaurant in Brasilia. At eleven thirty p.m., he was still asking us marvelous and intriguing questions. The professor was gently teaching us already. We were deeply impressed by his curiosity. What a young 84 years old professor!"[6]

On June 6, Neustadt delivered a lecture at ENAP to an audience of high-ranking members of the Lula government. (Unlike schools of public administration in the United States, which are part of academia, ENAP is a government institute that exists specifically to train civil servants and government appointees.) The Brazilians received a simultaneous translation from a tag-team of interpreters. Intended for Lula's inner circle, the lecture falls into the class of works Neustadt prepared as advice for Presidents and their aides, rather than for publication. It is not among Neustadt's yet-published works, but ENAP recorded it and Neustadt gave Kerr the text from which he read.[7]

Neustadt's address is called "The Long Shadow of Presidential Transitions." Kerr says, "It took us a long time to find [an] adequate translation for this inspiring title of his lecture."[8] Those familiar with Neustadt's work can smile in recognition; it might take awhile to find an adequate English translation for this title. Neustadt used words with such precision that often the words of others cannot quite capture his meaning. But in this case, he didn't pick the title himself. As Professor Barzelay wrote later to Beth Neustadt:

I said [in an e-mail to the Brazilians] that basically they should just hear what your father had been saying over lunch [with Barzelay in London]. I then came up with the long shadow idea as a synthesis of [the] basic thesis of his luncheon musings—and I argued that idea should intrigue people to enter into his thinking because they were obviously trying to contemplate the longer term effects of decisions they were making at the time. The Brazilians accepted this advice— and your father was delighted with the invitation which asked him to give a lecture on that topic. I think the request endeared them to him. He did suspect I was behind the title and I did own up to it at one point.[9]

Neustadt's lecture is about how the first months in office, the management and mismanagement of those early days, can shape—and perhaps haunt—a President's entire term. The phrase "the long shadow" captures Neustadt's meaning exactly:

Tonight I wish to speak to you about a North American phenomenon, an aspect of politics in my country, the United States, which has important side effects on policy as well as public administration, namely the long learning time of new Administrations when new Presidents take office, especially if from a different party than their predecessor. We call this time the "presidential transition," encompassing not only the eleven weeks between election and inaugural, but also, after that, the next twenty-one months—almost two years—of governing.[10]

Neustadt limited the scope of his remarks as he'd promised: the entire presentation is devoted to experiences of U.S. Presidents, not to Brazil— at least on the surface. The lecture is less a new work than a distillation of familiar Neustadtian themes, a stitching together of illustration and observation on transition hazards Neustadt had offered privately to U.S. Presidents from Kennedy to Clinton (as we now know from the release and publication of Neustadt's memos of advice on transitions).[11] The Brazil lecture deals with Neustadt's lifelong concerns: the President's ability to get his way, to keep control, to have things turn out as he wants—and the ways the President's own actions determine his future power.

What makes the stitching together deft is that despite Neustadt's disclaimers, the lecture was tailored, if subtly so, specifically for Lula's team. It would have been unlike Neustadt simply to drop in on the Brazilians and lecture them on U.S. Presidents. The thought he devoted in advance to their situation and needs, as he understood them before his arrival—an important qualification—shows in the text, from small matters of English usage to the selection of particular "take-away points" (a term Neustadt would have hated, but understood).

For example, Neustadt nowhere refers to the "American President" or the "American Presidency," the conjunction of words with which he is most famously associated. Neustadt "was very polite and would always prefer to say US presidents instead of American presidents," Kerr noted. "He would argue that we were all Americans from the Americas."[12] Similarly, in choosing President Kennedy's debacle at the Bay of Pigs as the lecture's first illustration of a transition-period hazard, Neustadt mentions, seemingly offhandedly, "the Castro government's efficiency" in thwarting the U.S.-sponsored military invasion. Nothing in a Neustadt lecture is offhanded, of course. Here, at a stroke, and without pandering, Neustadt presumably established his objectivity (and neutralized any whiff of his U.S. government ties) before a powerful group of Latin American "leftists."[13]

Neustadt's historical illustrations of power-sapping mistakes by neophyte U.S. Presidents were carefully chosen—a point he wished the Brazilians to understand.[14] The particular illustrations offer an insight into what Neustadt, before his arrival, seems to have considered three major risks facing Lula:

—Simply continuing the policies of his predecessor, through lack of self-confidence or an excess of caution or failing to ask the right questions (as with Kennedy and the Bay of Pigs).

—Conversely, breaking too precipitously and contemptuously with those policies, as if they represented booby-traps left by a retreating enemy (a mistake Neustadt ascribed to George W. Bush on Kyoto and other international matters), or otherwise acting too adventurously too soon.

—Failing to seize the unique opportunity of the "honeymoon period" to advance, by legislation, the President's own domestic policy agenda (here Neustadt contrasted Carter's belated push for an energy bill with Clinton's timely 1993 tax proposal, although Neustadt said Clinton damaged his power by letting himself be "rolled" on another early legislative proposal).

All these mistakes, Neustadt argued, arise from failing to grasp the Presidency's nuances and subtleties, as newcomers are apt to do. All reduce the President's personal power. All are difficult to overcome later.

Neustadt may have considered these to be major risks facing any new President, but in Lula's case they seemed heightened. The outgoing administration had imposed fiscal and monetary measures that constrained, arguably severely, Lula's ability to undertake new domestic policies, and further tied Lula's hands by obligating Brazil to honor strict covenants with international lenders. Yet Lula had been elected overwhelmingly, with 62 percent of the vote, on the promise of sweeping progressive change: to reduce hunger, poverty, and economic inequality. Lula had won a mandate, but a mandate for changes that might, after the inauguration, seem impossible to achieve. Faced with this, Lula might give up too easily, failing to push with sufficient determination against the constraints he'd inherited—or, if frustrated, he might impulsively smash those constraints, plunging the country into who knew what. Neustadt's lecture implicitly warned against both extremes, and against the *petistas'* losing legislative focus on Lula's own policy objectives.

In keeping with his own constraints and objectives, Neustadt, after the lecture's first lines, never mentioned Brazil until his final paragraph:

> How, if at all, do these observations drawn from the United States translate into Brazilian terms? What likenesses and differences are relevant between Washington and Brasilia? Most importantly, does North American experience offer anything worth learning for your purposes? Those are not questions for me to address. Necessarily, they become questions for you. With keen interest, I await your answers.[15]

The answers, in effect, were as Neustadt must have hoped: *We're impressed; you seem insightful and worthy of trust; but we have not yet told you of our most worrisome problems.* For it turned out that the hazards Neustadt foresaw for Lula and discussed in his lecture were not those that privately concerned Lula's inner circle. This became clear once Neustadt stepped away from the lectern and plunged into a swirl of private meetings Kerr arranged with five of Lula's ministers and ten vice ministers and special presidential assistants. Notes of these meetings may exist (Kerr reports that an outline was prepared and provided to Lula personally), but they have not been compiled.[16] Nor do they seem particularly important here, for two reasons.

First, Neustadt listened in these meetings, rather than continuing to lecture. Then he thought about what Lula's team had told him. After his departure he distilled what they'd said and his own advice into a single major document (discussed later). Second, what's notable today is the very fact that his advice was sought, that Lula's inner circle immediately took Neustadt into their confidence, sharing their greatest worries and seeking help from this aged North American, a celebrated authority in his own land but nonetheless a stranger to them.

History abounds with foreign observers and commentators, such as de Tocqueville, and foreign volunteers in a national cause, such as Lafayette. The political thought of foreign philosophers and theorists, enshrined in the canon (as with Montesquieu and Locke) or augmented through correspondence (as with Jeremy Bentham's letters to the French revolutionaries), has repeatedly inspired domestic leaders from Jefferson to Gandhi. Rarely, however, have eminent living political thinkers been invited and trusted to provide actual advice to a foreign government on matters relating to its very formation. Imagine a first-term George W. Bush and his inner circle asking a European scholar to huddle with them at Camp David, hear their deepest concerns, and advise them on their agenda, staffing, and appointments. Jean-Jacques Rousseau, whose advice was sought for anticipated new eighteenth-century governments in Poland and Corsica, seems the closest historical counterpart to Neustadt in Brazil. Neustadt does not suffer by the comparison.

The Interviews

Back in England, Professor Barzelay learned from Kerr of the hectic schedule she'd arranged for Neustadt and became "somewhat alarmed," Kerr laughingly recalls. Barzelay sent messages urging that Neustadt's pace be slowed, that he be allowed to rest.[17] But Neustadt was filled with zest. In fact, in addition to meetings with Lula's inner circle, Neustadt met several times with the news media. This included two television interviews, one on his arrival and one following his lecture, and an interview with *Carta Capital* magazine.

The first television interview, which aired as a brief segment, forced Neustadt to confront unrealistic early expectations—and disappointment—about Lula's initial performance in office. Lula hasn't accomplished anything, the interviewer said; he's not doing what he promised and may fail. "But if you are able to explain to your people," Neustadt responded, "that this isn't the way you plan to do it forever, but this is what you have to do for now . . . [then] what more can they ask? . . . You meant to do what you promised *insofar as you could,* and in a time frame that was four years long. So you have to hope that they won't judge you until the next election."

Then you suggest the government engage in propaganda? the interviewer asked.

"Educating the public is not the same as fooling them," Neustadt replied.[18]

In the second television interview, conducted after Neustadt had spent several days in Brasilia, the host, Luiz Fara Monteiro, also asked Neustadt about criticism of Lula "for not doing much." Neustadt replied forcefully: "My opinion is that, as compared with North American Presidents, he's done a great deal in five months."

Asked about Lula's fight against hunger, which his host considered daunting (if not quixotic), Neustadt responded in Neustadtian terms: "I think it is, in Brazil's interest, the right fight. In his own interest, it is a fight he has to make." Other questions led Neustadt to predict that Bush and Lula might get along well ("They are both prone to candor"), that Hillary Clinton would not run for President yet, and that Bush would be reelected. Neustadt's most arresting observation, delivered with characteristic succinctness, came in reply to a question asked not about Brazil but about Bush in Iraq: "My views are that the Iraq war was a misfortune. Now that it has occurred, my personal view is that the only way President Bush can make a long-run success of it is to intervene seriously and persistently in the Israeli-Palestinian issue. And that one is almost as hard to get right as hunger in Brazil."

Of a factory worker becoming President of Brazil, however, Neustadt sounded an upbeat note, which became his refrain: "I think it's a marvelous situation. It's the most exciting democratic experiment to be found right now on the globe."[19]

Neustadt's interviewer at *Carta Capital* magazine, Luiz Alberto Weber, had the advantages of working in print and receiving a preparatory briefing from Kerr on Neustadt's work and thought. Perhaps as a result, Weber elicited from Neustadt a comprehensive assessment of Lula and his power in traditional Neustadtian terms—and one that reflected what Neustadt had learned in Brazil. The published interview could usefully be added to the reading list of any course that features Neustadt's work (although no English transcript was published, so we must retranslate Neustadt from the Portuguese). Yet what Anthony King wrote of *Presidential Power* applies here: "It deploys arguments that are subtle and intertwined and impossible to summarize."[20]

The headline writer does manage to summarize Neustadt's bottom line: "Bet on Lula and on Brazil."[21] And Weber gets Neustadt to explain that surprising conclusion. First, Neustadt lists Lula's advantages and sources of power that new U.S. Presidents "customarily do not have":

> He is surrounded by many sophisticated people, long-time companions, who have important administrative and political experience gained in the opposition and in several parts of the country. Lula's ministers and advisors appear as though they have been in power for more than a year, not just months. . . . Then, when you combine the qualities of the man, his personal prestige and powers of persuasion, with that team of the PT [Workers' Party], you have something formidable.

Even so, Weber counters, some say this isn't enough power to change Brazil. Neustadt says he heard that complaint from Lula's ministers, and considers it a good sign: it means the government still intends to pursue its ambitious campaign agenda, one that requires more power than Lula inherited from his predecessor. A skeptical Weber and patient Neustadt then explore the art of the possible for Lula and the *petista* government. Weber sees Lula's power diminishing as campaign promises remain unfulfilled; Neustadt considers Lula well equipped to achieve some of his agenda while explaining limitations and realities to his supporters. "The people may accept explanations," Weber concedes, "but they also want results." That's why a prompt resumption of economic growth is vital, Neustadt replies: it's important that Lula voters be persuaded conditions in Brazil are improving.

And what of distasteful alliances with other parties that Lula has forged in Congress, Weber asks? Don't deals and unsavory allies reduce presidential power? Do the ends really justify the means? "In a large and diverse country such as Brazil, you will never have a government consisting only of people with identical values," Neustadt responds. "Maybe that's not possible even in Norway. It's not Machiavellian when a leader holds his nose, creates a coalition, and carries out eighty percent of what he originally proposed. That is what I call good government."

"So Brazil still has a chance?" Weber asks, sounding unpersuaded.

"I believe that with a bit of luck, Lula's government will be very successful," Neustadt replies. "Lula combines the elements needed for success. . . . If Lula fails, my theories will be profoundly shaken [*profundamente abaladas*]. But I am an optimist, and especially about Brazil."

With that, Neustadt boarded a plane and flew home. He had spent less than ninety-six hours in Brazil. Yet he'd applied his methods, won the affection and admiration of his hosts, and—as time would tell—he also got things right. His best work on Brazil was yet to come. Sherlock Holmes, by contrast, had the benefit of several months in Brazil. He, too, applied his methods and won the affection and admiration of his hosts. But Holmes got things wrong, having failed—as Neustadt did not—to comprehend what he'd observed. And unlike Neustadt, once Holmes sailed home, there's no indication he gave Brazil another thought.

Neustadt's June 15 Letter and the "Three Discomforts"

Anthony King wrote that "Neustadt had a lightning-quick mind but, precisely for that reason, spoke very, very, very slowly. He weighed and ordered every sentence in his mind before uttering it."[22] This might have been apparent to those (including in Brazil) who heard him lecture or saw him interviewed. Neustadt found writing even more agonizing—slow and difficult.[23] Prose so precise—a writing style so "forthright, certain, and clear," as Professor Charles O. Jones put it—suggests a natural facility.[24] In fact, it reflected careful thought, and extensive polishing. Few who read Neustadt's prose watched him write it. Those who did witnessed real struggles.

Yet within a week of his trip, Neustadt composed and sent to Helena Kerr a 2,500-word letter of carefully organized thoughts for Lula and his inner circle (printed in the appendix to this book). That he could produce such a work so quickly may seem remarkable. He was, after all, not young. He'd flown far, worked hard in Brazil, slept little. (Indeed, in photos taken near the end of his trip, Neustadt looks exhausted.) Writing, for Neustadt, required painstaking effort, as we know. And what he wrote in his June 15 letter related not at all to his June 6 lecture. It was all new. The pretense of recounting U.S. presidential mishaps to enlighten the Brazilians, having served its purpose, now vanished. Neustadt's June 15 letter consisted entirely of original thought: his considered response to Lula's ministers having unburdened themselves to him in private. Now Neustadt offered pure advice, concrete and practical, the product of an unusual mind inspired to work overtime.

From the letter, we can surmise what happened when Neustadt and Lula's ministers met. The letter summarizes the opening advice Neustadt had offered: focus on "getting priority objectives straight, along with the mix of people to implement them." As Kerr do Amaral wrote, "In Brazil, he said that the main issue was the agenda."[25] This was consistent with his lecture, which effectively urged the *petistas* to seize their opportunity and push the President's policy agenda.

But, Kerr wrote, "Most of the senior executives and Ministers that met with him asked about the difficulties in governmental coordination."[26] When the ministers stressed the need for "coordination," Neustadt initially demurred: "He told them the problem was not management, but agenda."[27] Perhaps he took the word "coordination" to signify smoothing out and improving the efficiency of government *processes*—and process, isolated from its impacts on policy, rarely struck Neustadt as particularly important.[28]

There may have been a difficulty in translation. One minister made the point—"in what amounted to polite rebuttal," Neustadt wrote—that to Lula's inner circle the term "coordination" actually stood for "three different discomforts, each as important as, because impeding, effective choices of programs and people." The first of these, the ministers admitted, was their personal discomfort and that of Lula's closest aides with "the President's own activism, ebullience, honesty, and fresh ideas in the face of their need to get him focused." The tactfulness of this summary is suggested by Neustadt's dry remark, "Let me label the resulting problem, 'harnessing the boss.'"

Clearly, the *petistas* had revealed their concerns to Neustadt with disarming candor. Only the Brazilians know what advice Neustadt mustered on the spot. But in his letter Neustadt briefly restates the three "discomforts"—the others deal with distance and distrust between Lula's inner circle, on the one hand, and ministers from other coalition parties, as well as civil servants, on the other—then breaks them down into five separate problems. For each problem, Neustadt offers specific suggestions. These take up the bulk of the letter, representing a lot of hard thought—and hardheaded advice. At the same time, Neustadt does not lose sight of his original message. He emphasizes that the five problems "do not weaken the case for prioritizing the agenda or for reshuffling people. Quite the contrary. Tackling the discomforts help[s] with both."

The letter's final paragraphs concern the agenda itself, "the content of priority program(s) for the poor." In the meetings, Neustadt had expressed enthusiasm "for a simple assurance of one full meal a day for every child under 18, administered through the schools as far as possible." Neustadt now reported that his wife, Shirley Williams, had advised him of just such a program in India, "the chief source of [protein] for the children affected." Further, she told him that in wartime Britain, "Essential vitamins were distributed in school meals . . . by 'dinner-ladies' employed for the purpose," a concept Neustadt favored for full employment as well as nutritional reasons. Through Neustadt, Williams also recommended that Brazil consider South Africa's reportedly successful new health program for mothers and children. This litany of programs says much about the couple's shared interests and post-Brazil conversations. It also shows Neustadt working hard to help not just children or the poor but also Lula and the *petistas*.

Neustadt and Brazil in Context

If the complete Brazil-related work product that Neustadt produced and prompted is ever assembled and published, it will be found to represent not a departure from, but rather the seamless final extension of, his entire professional output and thought. What it means, and represents intellectually, in most respects hardly seems specific to Brazil, and can best be understood in other accounts of Neustadt, such as explanations of his work provided by Charles O. Jones and Anthony King, among others.[29] Yet in at least two respects, there's something special about Neustadt and Brazil.

The first is suggested by the comparison with Rousseau, which illustrates the singularity of Neustadt's Brazilian experience and achievement. Rousseau, world-famous at age fifty for the moral and political philosophy of *The Social Contract* (1762), was twice asked to apply his theories in real-world contexts and provide practical advice to prospective new governments. He took these requests seriously, producing *The Constitutional Project for Corsica* in 1765 and *Considerations on the Government of Poland* in 1772. Events frustrated both efforts: France occupied Corsica, and Poland was partitioned, so *Corsica* remained a fragment and *Poland* remained unpublished. Rousseau had intended neither for publication, however. He prepared both as private advice to individual political leaders.

If both works strike us as odd—and they do—it is not because of stilted prose (Rousseau wrote beautifully), mere passage of time (the Declaration of Independence and *Federalist Papers*, contemporaries to *Corsica* and *Poland*, have stood up well), any lack of intriguing insights ("Poverty did not make itself felt in Switzerland until money began to circulate there"), or dearth of fascinating details (such as the Corsicans making do, during a blockade, with "the pith of certain reeds" in place of cotton for candle wicks). Rather, the oddness of these works is that the advice Rousseau provides simply isn't practical—abolishing currency in favor of barter, for example, or restricting marriage and parenthood to those who till the soil. No one could have implemented Rousseau's suggestions. Even when "he could not resist the appeal of a people [the Poles] engaged in a life and death struggle against despotism," the great man proved unable to manage the shift from theorist to adviser.[30]

Neustadt showed greater agility than Rousseau, and always considered himself more adviser than theorist. More important, Neustadt believed better outcomes would be achieved by more enlightened leaders; he accepted as immutable, in the short run, both human nature and the political institutions a society happens to possess. Rousseau believed better outcomes could be achieved through more enlightened institutions; he considered immutable both human nature and the behavior it tends to yield. Neustadt's theories, focused on the effects of a leader's actions, allowed him to give concrete advice to political actors. Rousseau's theories did not. In this light, Neustadt huddling with Lula's advisers, then advising them himself, seems historically noteworthy, and perhaps unique.

Brazil as a Homecoming

When Sherlock Holmes visited Brazil, his amanuensis, Dr. John Watson, accompanied him, but Watson had not yet begun to chronicle the detective's exploits, as he later did in *The Adventures of Sherlock Holmes*. So we have only a novel to assure us that Holmes found his visit invigorating, that he fell in love with (and in) Brazil, and that, to Watson's relief—Holmes had been in a funk—he returned to England refreshed and rejuvenated. In Neustadt's case, we have the man's own words, and they almost sing.

This is the second respect in which Neustadt in Brazil seems special. The experience energized Neustadt completely. It did so by bringing him full circle, transporting him at eighty-four from semiretirement back to a bustling capital, back to a President's inner circle, back to a nation on the march, back to being *useful*. This was a great gift the Brazilians gave him, as valuable in its way as any he could possibly have given them. "He said it was difficult for him to work in Washington with Republicans in power, so he was delighted he could work with us in Brazil," Kerr recalls. "He intended to keep right on doing so."[31] Of course, at his age it would have been difficult for Neustadt, semiretired in England, to work in Washington even without Republicans in power. Brazil was a godsend.

Long before Neustadt's trip, Charles O. Jones interviewed him for a paper published in the *Annual Review of Political Science*. Neustadt's father had been a civil servant who "dived back into public service with enthusiasm" during the Depression.

> This meant [Neustadt told Jones], among other things, that I was in Washington all through high school from '33 to '36. And that in a way is the first part of my public service. People do not believe me when I say that no one walked on the sidewalk in Washington in 1934; they floated six inches above it. At night you could stand in Lafayette Park and look over at the White House and see that halo. So having a father with Teddy Roosevelt's ideas about public service and then being there during this glorious period: That did it.[32]

Consider, in this light, the first lines of Neustadt's June 15 letter to Helena Kerr: "What a set of interesting, well-motivated people! What a set of challenges! What a good time I had! Since I reached Massachusetts [where Neustadt had a summer home], I have told everyone in sight that touring Brasilia in these circumstances was like touring Washington DC in 1933 or '34—as invigorating as it was inspiring."

Neustadt's daughter, Beth, confirms this. On his return, Neustadt telephoned, ebullient, and told her it felt "just like the FDR era all over again. . . . These people are great," he continued. "They really want to eradicate poverty! Whether they can do it . . . well, what matters is, they're really going to try." His voice, Beth remembers, had a quality of "unadulterated happiness," something Shirley Williams remarked upon as well.[33]

None of this zest is apparent in the lecture Neustadt prepared before his trip, or in the television interview upon his arrival. His experiences in Brasilia had a rapid impact, however. By the time of his June 6 interview, Neustadt could say, "I think it's a marvelous situation. It's the most exciting democratic experiment to be found right now on the globe. . . . Certainly it is a great time to be here." And as he told *Carta Capital*, "The President and the PT know the social commitments they've made, and at the same time they know the practical restrictions imposed by the outside world. The solution to that problem is the most interesting experiment now in progress in the modern world."

Neustadt planned to remain in the thick of it. His June 15 letter brims with plans to return to Brasilia and meet with Lula, promises of research in London and information from Washington, travel arrangements for his wife as well as himself. "His enthusiasm was contagious," Kerr wrote. "He said he would like to be younger to be able to live what we were living. So did we."[34]

He wasn't younger. No one could change that. He died in October, before he could return to Brazil. Yet he had completed a circle, and experienced again, in his final months, the sensation of feeling fully alive. That is no small thing.

Aftermath

Lula and his government stuck to their agenda—insofar as they could. Neustadt would have approved. Constraints on the government's ability to bring rapid social change produced disappointment, and grumbling that Lula had abandoned the left.[35] Yet economic growth did slowly resume. Without breaching any covenants or renouncing any debt—the International Monetary Fund was repaid on time, if a bit disdainfully—the Lula government began delivering on its most important social promises.

To deal with hunger and poverty, the government adopted a Family Grant Program for the 11 million poorest Brazilian families, those with monthly incomes below $38.57 (U.S.). To receive benefits, families must enroll their children in school and take advantage of prenatal and pediatric health care at public hospitals.[36] Studies indicate a decline in inequality in Brazil, some of it from the government's income transfers.[37] Of course, there is a long way to go. If inequality continues to decline at the current rate, "it will nonetheless take more than two decades for Brazil to achieve the levels reported in other countries."[38]

"Harnessing the boss," as Neustadt called it in his letter, also proved difficult. Most famously, Lula expelled a *New York Times* reporter who wrote that Lula's drinking had become a national worry—then Lula reversed himself, regretting his momentary pique. According to Kerr, Neustadt had warned Lula's team in private, "The president is who he is; you can't change him. You must adapt yourselves to his style." This, says Kerr, was advice the inner circle took.

The greatest threat to Lula's Presidency turned out to be unpredicted: corruption. By the time Lula sought reelection, his party was mired in it.[39] Yet the word "corruption" nowhere appears in the record of Neustadt in Brazil. This seems, in retrospect, a curious omission. Among the hazards of transition Neustadt often stressed is the tendency of newcomers to imagine they are better than their predecessors—smarter, more capable, more in tune with the electorate, more honest. Corruption was a known pitfall for the politicians Lula succeeded. In his campaign, Lula had "boldly pledged to clean up the sordid politics of Brazil."[40] Yet some *petistas*—if not the President personally—having gained power, then succumbed.

Did Neustadt not foresee this danger? "No one asked Neustadt about corruption during his visit because no one in the PT imagined it could happen to them," Kerr says on reflection. "When it did happen, we were astonished and ashamed. 'Shame' is the word. But after that, we saw that the government was doing well otherwise, and the President personally was not involved."[41] One suspects Neustadt did foresee the risk. Yet he was in Brazil briefly, with much to do, a newcomer to Lula's team constrained to be polite—and caught up in the same enthusiasms as the *petistas* themselves. It would have been difficult to mention corruption on that first trip, and easy to wish it away.

Sherlock Holmes, the guest of an emperor surrounded by slaves, failed to foresee the Brazilian monarchy's imminent demise. Neustadt, the guest of the *petistas*, foresaw that Lula had presidential power within his reach, and could succeed. On October 29, 2006, after a difficult campaign, Luiz Inácio Lula da Silva was reelected President of Brazil with 62 percent of the vote: another landslide.

AFTERWORD:
A PERSONAL REMINISCENCE

ELIZABETH A. NEUSTADT

WHEN I WAS about three years old, Mom took both of us kids to the train station to meet Dad. He was returning from a whistle-stop campaign tour during which he'd been crafting the speeches. Apparently I spotted Dad descending from the train, broke free of Mom's grip, and went hurtling down the platform to greet him—only to be intercepted by some other man, who swept me off my feet and high into the air, saying, "That's my girl!" Unfazed by being airborne, I glared at this fellow and indignantly replied, "I'm not your girl; I'm my Daddy's girl!" The man was Harry S. Truman.

My older brother, always more inclined than I to toe the line, had internalized key Neustadtian principles by the age of four. On the morning following the 1952 presidential election, when he learned that Eisenhower had won, Ricky declared, "I do not like him but he is our President so I respeck him." Some years later, when our father's commutes back to D.C. from New York City took up half of each week, Dad took Rick along on one occasion, and they bonded during a tour of the Capitol as only Dick Neustadt could give it. It was surely no coincidence that Rick joined

Carter's White House staff at the same age—thirty-one—that Dad was when he joined Truman's.

For both Rick and me, although our responses differed, Dad's evolving career inevitably had a significant impact on our formative years, bringing mixed blessings that are the norm for children growing up in a high-powered family. On the one hand, he was away from home a lot, and when at home, was often preoccupied with work. On the other hand, we were privileged to make the acquaintance of, and in many instances establish friendships with, a great many quite extraordinary people as a result of Dad's work (including contributors to this volume). Of course, our childhood experience was also very much colored by the more consistently present parent, our mother. Readers of this volume have had only a few fleeting glimpses of her within its pages; although she probably wouldn't approve, I think it appropriate to offer something more about her here.

Bert Cummings was the only child of Jewish immigrants from Eastern Europe, and was the first in her family to attend college, graduating from Vassar. She never used her given name, Bertha, and as a teen made no protest when her father changed her surname from Kaminsky to Cummings—his effort to arm her for further education away from home. She subsequently obtained a master's degree at the University of California, Berkeley. Bert's father, Ben Kaminsky, who had traveled to the United States from Poland at the age of six, filled with the stuff of nightmares from early-childhood experiences and with dreams of a better future, had had to leave school at thirteen in order to help his parents make enough of a living to survive. Later, he felt that his dreams had been attained after all, when his son-in-law became a professor. The Neustadts, by contrast, hailed from Prague, and had arrived in the United States generations earlier; Dad's family was assimilated and well established. Mom used to say, with a twinkle in her eye, that she'd "married up."

As a young woman, Bert was quite overweight, but—unusually—she lost twenty-five pounds after the birth of each of her two children. From then on, she remained the slightly less-chiseled Katherine Hepburn lookalike that most of us who are still around remember. Her self-image never quite caught up with her new appearance, and her lack of self-assurance about her beauty simply enhanced her charm.

Bert was inventive and self-invented, with a romantic streak and a dramatic flair. In 1945, she and my father had something of a whirlwind courtship, although they'd actually first been introduced four years earlier, when she arrived at Berkeley just as he was departing. Later, she used to recount that when she encountered him again he had no idea who she was, and she vowed to fix it so that he would never forget her again. Over dinner on their third date, in D.C. (where she was visiting friends), he explained that he couldn't possibly make a marriage commitment until he'd established himself professionally. She countered that any woman "worth her salt" would of course want to be right by his side, providing emotional support during that period. She proceeded to describe the sort of woman she imagined would be right for him, who just happened to sound remarkably much like her.

He departed by train from D.C. for a business trip to New York. He must have thought long and hard during that train journey; upon his arrival, he sent her a message asking her not to leave, as he was coming back. When he returned, he proffered a bouquet of roses, got down on one knee, and proposed to her. In response, striking a dramatic pose, she gasped, "Why, Richard, this is so sudden!" which of course she intended as a joke. For him a commitment for life was no laughing matter; he threw down the flowers and stormed out, leaving her in a panic, fearing she'd blown everything. He came back after what must have been, for her, a very long hour and a half, and they got engaged. They were married on December 21, 1945.

Bert had made the case to Dick that, as his mother had died when he was just four years old, he'd missed out on being loved at a critical juncture, whereas she had grown up in a happy family, and knew all about how to be the sort of loving, supportive wife he needed and deserved. In fact, her parents' marriage had not been a particularly happy one; she'd left home at seventeen eager to escape the tensions there. Nevertheless, she now reinvented herself as the quintessential supportive wife, a role that she performed to near perfection for the whole of their marriage. In this role she was intimately involved as my father's confidante in his work and his evolving career. As Dad acknowledged in the 1990 edition of his first book, *Presidential Power*, "My late wife Bert . . . helped this book (and me) along at every stage" (p. xxvi).

Mom always downplayed her own career, but while Rick and I were still little, she enrolled at Columbia Teachers College and became certified to teach English as a second language, work she continued to do for the rest of her life. Although first and foremost Dick Neustadt's wife, behind the scenes she was, like my father, a devoted teacher; her students knew it, and loved her right back. Recognizing that adults were more self-conscious than children about making mistakes, she taught her international classes by raising topics for discussion (legalized abortion; the death penalty) that got these students so exercised they simply had to speak up. Of course, the only language in which they could all converse was English; as they argued with one another, she coached.

The longer she taught, the more indignant she became with textbooks that, in her view, treated intelligent adults as if they were morons or infants simply because they didn't have a thorough grasp of the English language. Perhaps being the daughter of immigrants fueled her passion. Her textbook, *Speaking of the U.S.A.: A Reader for Discussion* (1975), which broke new ground in the field when it was first published and went into a fourth edition, was designed to teach foreign students about contemporary aspects of society in the United States, while developing their English language skills and vocabulary. Sets of chapters treated topics as varied as U.S. libraries; the news media; the arts and architecture; education; the family; and, from the second edition on, the work force, work, and labor unions. Broad though Bert's coverage was, the influence of her husband's career remained clearly evident; fully one third of this textbook's chapters focused on U.S. government, U.S. politics, and the U.S. electoral process.

My father's students, too, benefited from my mother's love of students; she saw it as part of her supportive-wife role to make his students feel welcome in their home. Although thoroughly uninterested in cooking, she was determined to excel as a hostess, and was highly resourceful in finding others to provide the cuisine. In a later era, and with a less limited budget than she had to work with—particularly during the early years at Columbia—she'd have been a caterer's dream client. She regularly hosted meals in the spacious living room of our New York City apartment. Groups of Dad's students would come for seminars, and twos or threes would come simply to round out our dinner table. These mostly male undergraduate students were always happy to consume anything that might pass for a home-cooked meal, and initially she struggled with the problem that no matter how much food was prepared, there never seemed sufficient for everyone to have seconds. In due course she obtained, on the advice of an architect, the perfect solution: smaller plates.

As Dad's career took off, the guest list expanded to include increasingly well-known company, and Mom rose to each occasion with ingenuity and wit. In the spring of 1959, former President Truman arrived at our apartment for breakfast on three mornings running, prior to giving the first series of Radner lectures at Columbia University. Dad invited a substantial batch of students to each of these breakfasts, and Mom drafted Ted, the son of our downstairs neighbors David B. and Elinor Truman, to provide butler service.[1] Some years later, at 10 Traill Street, in Cambridge, Massachusetts, I recall one occasion on which Senator Ted Kennedy was a dinner guest, and graciously complimented my mother on the stuffed cabbage she served. When he gallantly inquired about the recipe, without missing a beat she replied, with equal panache, that it was a family secret.

As Chuck Jones recounts in this volume, Eisenhower's move to the White House precipitated ours away from Washington, D.C. We first went to Ithaca, where my father had obtained his sole job offer, a one-year lectureship at Cornell's business school. Having thus rather inadvertently launched his academic career, and under considerable pressure to make a go of it in order to support his young family, he turned his attention to the craft of scholarly writing. Mom, in her primary role, devoted herself to protecting his time for this work. Such writing did not come easily to him; he was excruciatingly slow at it. After his recruitment, one year later, to a tenure track position at Columbia University, an increasing array of academic demands competed for his time and focus. He worked on his first book every summer for seven years. We usually returned to Ithaca, where Rick and I were dispatched to day camps and he could write with minimal distraction. The book that resulted, *Presidential Power*, was, in its original edition, less than two hundred pages long. Dad developed and refined an approach to writing that was influenced by his early experience of speechwriting—he sought a particular rhythm for each sentence. He was equally relentless in searching for just the right phrase, or *mot juste*. Writing in this way was a craft that he honed, but it always remained a slow, deliberate process, page after page written by hand on yellow legal pads in an almost illegible scrawl. Many years later, long after he'd made a name for himself, I recall a moment, at the summer home my parents had by then acquired in Wellfleet, on Cape Cod, when he read a favorable review of a new book by his friend Arthur Schlesinger Jr., and let slip, sotto voce, "Damn! He's so prolific!"

My mother's support for my father's scholarship extended beyond protecting his time for writing. In Ithaca, my parents had become friends with

Clinton and Mary Ellen Rossiter. Clinton Rossiter, the author of *The American Presidency* (1956), was at that time regarded as the preeminent scholar in this field. In the index to his book there is an entry for Bertha Neustadt, which, it turned out, is for the blank page that falls between the end of the main text and the beginning of the index. Rossiter knew that my mother always went straight to the index of any book that might reference my father, so he knew that she would find this; it was a brilliant "gotcha," which, to Mom's credit, she subsequently delighted in relating.

The manuscript for *Presidential Power* was turned down by four publishers before David B. Truman persuaded Wiley & Sons to take it. In one instance, the rejected manuscript was returned with review comments enclosed, which stated that, as if it weren't enough that this book said nothing new, the author (Neustadt) made every point three times. When *Presidential Power*, finally published, found its way to JFK, who was photographed with it under his arm, and it suddenly rose to the *New York Times* best-seller list for two weeks, Dad could not but be aware of the serendipity. He never lost sight of this; perhaps it helps to account for his enduring humility—born not only, as Harvey Fineberg has intimated, of the self-confidence that comes from success in love and work, but also from a deeply ingrained sense of historical perspective.

My mother also saw it as part of her primary task, as the supportive wife, to preserve Dad's image at home, in his absence. She did so by idealizing him. She explained that he loved us kids very much and was absent only because he was off saving the world for us. During my adolescence, I took to quoting that back to him, and adding that I assumed this was why the world was so much better now. My father was very nearly always thoughtful and measured in his responses. I am pretty sure there were occasions, at least with me, when his long pauses were the outward appearance of an inner effort to contain himself while he regained his composure.

My mother was the first member of our family to take a stance against the war in Vietnam. In 1964, I recall a private family dinner during which, uncharacteristically, she was the one who raised the temperature with Dad. In due course, Rick joined that campaign in his usual measured, understated way. Having enrolled at Harvard as an undergraduate just before Dad was recruited there (we used to joke about how my brother got my father into Harvard), Rick often came to Traill Street for family dinners. On one occasion, in the mid-sixties, he discovered after arriving that

Henry Kissinger was also due to be a dinner guest that evening. When Kissinger appeared, Rick quietly walked out of the house and headed back to his dorm; as he saw it, it was not his place to challenge his parents about whom they chose to entertain, but he was not prepared to remain under the same roof with this guest.

During this politically fraught period, such dynamics also touched some who had become members of the vast "extended family" of Dad's students whom Harvey Fineberg once aptly described to me as my spiritual siblings. One of these, Dan Davidson, had been an undergraduate student of my father's at Columbia; he and his wife, Susan, established a lifelong friendship with our family. In 1965, as special assistant to William Bundy, who was then assistant secretary of state for the Far East, Dan's first meeting with the top men in the State Department involved a presidential decision on whether or not to stay in Vietnam. The meeting was at the State Department, presided over by George Ball, its number two man at the time. Dan had not expected Ball to know anything about him, and so was doubly surprised that, upon their introduction, Ball exploded with, "You are Dick Neustadt's protégé! He's the man who ruined the process! We used to tell the President what should be done. Now we have to give him *options!*"[2]

During his senior year at Harvard College, Rick and several of his college friends drafted a simple petition, deliberately low-key in order to generate widespread agreement, which called for no further escalation in Vietnam. They managed to obtain signatures of support from 70 percent of the Harvard-Radcliffe student body, and from a substantial number of the faculty. They sent this document to the White House late that spring. When our family arrived home from the Harvard Commencement, Rick's 1A reclassification letter was waiting on the doorstep.[3]

Dad was still working in an advisory capacity to President Johnson at this time. I have only a fleeting recollection of a conversation between my parents, in which he was evidently reflecting deeply on issues of ethics as well as protocol. Normally remarkably wise in such matters, in this instance my father found the conflicting pulls between his virtually instinctive allegiance to the President and his likewise natural loyalty to the members of his own family particularly difficult to reconcile. When his associate, Arthur Schlesinger Jr., came out publicly against the war, my father reacted with uncharacteristic irritability. Ultimately, Dad decided not to sign Rick's petition, and instead to write a confidential note to

President Johnson in which, in carefully crafted Neustadtian fashion, he privately offered his current views on the war. He never again heard from this President. (This tale is illuminated by the documents associated with it; see page 187 in the appendix to this book.)

Although a profoundly self-disciplined man, my father was not without ego. (Privately, he and my mother concurred that he was an inch taller than she, but while she knew full well that she was five feet, five inches, he was always adamant that he stood five feet, seven inches.) However, Dad was diligent about keeping his ego in check, lest it get in the way of things that mattered more, as Graham Allison describes in this volume. Dad was, likewise, remarkably strong willed (not to be confused with willful). He had taken up cigarette smoking at the age of sixteen, at a time, of course, before the dangers were widely known. In his forties, now at Harvard and chain-smoking up to four packs a day, he developed a hacking cough, which interfered with the flow of his lectures. He now determined that he had better cut down on cigarettes, and he succeeded, taking up the pipe as a substitute. This became a project; tamping down the tobacco was readily incorporated as a ritual that served him well in his professorial role. As some of his students who'd become friends of mine reported, they now had something to watch during his trademark long midsentence pauses. He even compelled the Kennedy School's glamorous, aristocratic English secretary, Xandra Bingley (then Lady Gowrie), to comply with his campaign, bringing in a second pipe for her, and informing her that *they* were quitting cigarettes. In due course, however, his dentist informed him that his gums had started to recede. "So what?" my father told us he said, undaunted by the prospect of eventually losing his teeth, which were anyway crooked and, well, not his best feature. "You lecture for a living, is that right?" the dentist replied. This gave Dad pause. But then the dentist suggested a solution: in order to protect the gums and teeth, why not try cigarettes? As it happened, having taken a leave of absence from college, I was staying at the family home on Traill Street at this time, on my way to California "to find myself," so I heard about this exchange at first hand. Dad left the dentist's office and arrived home, furious. Here was a perfect example of specialization gone mad. He was too intellectually honest not to recognize what he must do. He quit all forms of smoking that very day (though he was on Valium for a year, to cope). Later, he told me he'd quit smoking to set an example for me.

When an uncharacteristically late onset of multiple sclerosis disabled my mother, she had to lean on Dad in more ways than one. I was privileged to witness the silver lining of her illness—that their relationship became all the richer over those last years. Until then, he'd seen her as what he called a "love machine," while his primary role was that of breadwinner—a classic division of labor. It was only after she became ill that he began to discover how much *he* could give. Walter Sondheim had married my father's older stepsister, Janet, and so had known my Dad from his youth. A year or so after my father's death, Uncle Walter confided to me that Dad had been "a real itch" as a youngster. Juliet Brudney, a close friend of Bert's from Vassar, had used more colorful, less printable language to describe to me what my father had been like when she was first acquainted with him, in the early years of his marriage to her friend. Both Walter and Juliet independently observed that they'd never seen anyone change as much as my father did during the twelve years of my mother's illness. My father always had an enormous appetite for learning, and once he turned his focus to the art of loving, he became the most tender and devoted man imaginable.

Mom died in 1984. Letting go of her was a profoundly difficult, deeply private task for him. He retreated to their cottage on Cape Cod whenever possible. His loss was compounded by a freak car accident, just six months later, in which his younger stepsister, Minna, was killed in an instant. But even as he mourned, those wheels still turned. In 1986, I relocated to England for work. Dad phoned me there, and likewise phoned Rick, then based in New York City, to tell us that he had decided to go on living. In other words, he was taking Mom's advice, proffered shortly before she died, to marry again. Specifically, during one of their last conversations, as she lay incontinent and nearly completely immobilized, she asked him whether, had he known how it would go, he still would have asked her to marry him. His response was an unequivocal yes. Bert, physically disabled but intellectually as sharp as ever, and having had a great deal of time to do little but reflect, then gently observed that, if this was so, she wanted him to marry again, once she was gone. But, she advised, he mustn't try to replicate their marriage; rather, he should marry someone very different than her—someone, she suggested, like their longtime family friend, the British politician Shirley Williams. And it was to Shirley that he now proposed.

Shirley, of course, had a very full life of her own. But my father had given considerable attention to the study of persuasion and, it seems, had developed a modicum of skill in it. Shirley knew well my mother's compulsively immaculate style of housekeeping. Aware of her own tendency to overextend and, sans wife, to live in what she herself characterized as a messy environment, Shirley thought that my father would expect her to change her habits; she knew herself better than to think she would, and was too honest not to tell him. So she turned him down. As longtime friends, however, they were able to discuss this, and he persisted with his case, assuring her that he wanted to marry her for who she was, not in order to change her; he asked her to reconsider. Then her brother died, leaving two teenage children whose mother had predeceased him. Shirley felt that of course she must take them in, but she could not expect Dick, who was not far off seventy, with children long grown, to resume parenting all over again. He, however, held firm in his stance that when he proposed marriage he meant taking on whatever might come. And so, in the end, he persuaded her to marry him. This was a stroke of luck for me, since in this second marriage, by their mutual agreement, *her* career took precedence and in due course that brought him to England.

Some years later, I told Shirley that, if not for her, I suspected we'd have lost him much earlier; she conceded that perhaps I was right, but in characteristic self-deprecatory style then observed that she suspected the life he led with her was rather like being revived with a cold shower. Not so! Being married to a high-powered, indefatigable career politician was quite a switch for him, but that was the point: here was an entirely new role for him to learn about and master—that of Supportive Husband. He devoted himself to being her best staffer, ever. And his love and commitment transformed him into a family man, and fell like a mantle across all of our reconstituted tribe.

My parents had acquired what they always referred to simply as "the Cape house" a couple of years after they relocated from the Riverside Drive apartment in New York City, which Columbia University had provided, to the carriage house on Traill Street, in Cambridge, Massachusetts, which my father negotiated with Harvard University to obtain for the same rent as he had paid for the New York City apartment (little realizing at the time what a remarkable deal that was). With both children by this time at college, the Cape house had become my parents' regular weekend retreat and summer refuge. After my mother's death, my father continued to spend increasingly long summers there, reading, thinking, writing, canoeing to recharge his batteries, and trying, somewhat ambivalently, to curtail an endless stream of visiting colleagues, students, friends, and family. Overnight accommodation for these visitors was a privilege that remained limited because, unlike his Gull Pond neighbors, Dad never expanded the footprint of the little cottage. Indeed, after my parents' first summer there, which had proved far too social, my mother, always the protector, had hung a homemade black and white painted sign at the end of the drive which read "Man at Work: No Visitors Before 5 P.M."

Between the time of my mother's death and his own, nearly twenty years later, my father made few obvious changes to this cottage. Indeed, Shirley observed that Bert remained preserved in amber there. There was truth to that, and Shirley's willingness to embrace Dad's love of his first wife is both evidence of her own generosity of spirit and undoubtedly a factor in why this second marriage also proved successful. Nonetheless, close inspection of the cottage would have revealed that, in fact, some changes had been made. That sign had come down . . . the telephone number was now listed . . . Shirley, after all, was a British politician of very considerable stature; my father understood that, even when she joined him at his retreat on the outer Cape, she had to remain connected with the world. New sound speakers were installed, and the tape and CD collection expanded to include operas, side by side with older recordings such as *Ella Sings Cole*. New, longer windows in the master bedroom let in more light. The larger study, with both office telephone and fax lines, became Shirley's; Dad relocated into the smaller study, which had been Bert's. Shirley's study doubled as a second guest room, enabling sequential visits from her daughter, niece, nephew, and, over time, their spouses and children, all of whom Dad welcomed as family. In keeping with the role that, in this second marriage, he'd deliberately assumed—that of supportive spouse—he cheerfully made the necessary adjustments.

In 1995, we lost my brother, Rick, in a white-water rafting accident. Thereafter, my relationship with my father deepened into true friendship. This reflected a change in me as well as in him; after all, the role of younger sibling is very different than that of eldest child. The shift was not instantaneous. Dad's first reaction was to protect me; for twenty-four hours he held on to the information that Rick was missing, hoping against hope that he would not have to place the call that, when it came, changed forever the meaning of July Fourth for me. Dad insisted on making the trip, by himself, from the U.K. to Northern California to identify Rick's body. Later, even though, in accordance with Rick's will, I shouldered the role of executrix of his estate, it did not cross Dad's mind that I might wish to speak at my brother's memorial service. When I broached the subject, after a characteristic long pause he conceded that I could do so, as long as I made my tribute funny. This was a tall order, but was clearly all that he could bear. Thereafter, aside from sharing that event, and discussing various aspects of settling the estate, as required, we spoke only occasionally about Rick. Shirley, although of course worried about the impact on Dick of this sudden loss of his son, took a very English, stiff-upper-lip stance, actively encouraging Dad to soldier on. As Dad was naturally a stiff-upper-lip character himself, this seemed to suit him. Slowly, and as privately as ever, he came to terms with this latest loss. Just once, he told me he was glad that Mom hadn't lived to endure this. Thereafter, we always managed to meet or at least speak by phone, each February 4, without ever mentioning what we both knew—that we were acknowledging Rick's birthday. My father died on October 31, 2003. Still reeling from that, I was hit particularly hard by his absence on February 4, 2004.

As I look back on the times during the summer and autumn of 2003 when I saw my father, he was full of life. True, by then we'd had passing discussions about his estate, but in our wide-ranging conversations, numerous other topics invariably seemed more pressing. These included the state of the world; our reconstituted family; my interminable doctorate; and, especially, my daughter, Rachel, in whom this recovering-workaholic-turned-family-man took enormous interest, and with whom he played an active parenting role. That summer, for example, he collected his twelve-year-old granddaughter from camp and was in sole charge while I made a quick trip back to London for work. On such occasions, when she was littler, he would make up stories to entertain her—how Coca-Cola got its name, for example. As she grew older, he regaled her with anecdotes about his own youth. One of these, she recently reminded me, was that as a youngster he had trained himself to keep his upper lip curled in, because he thought it made him look more manly; he'd literally taught himself to have a stiff upper lip.

Two weeks later, Rachel and I waved him off from Boston to London, where he met Shirley and accompanied her on to Moscow to attend a seminar. He then returned to Wellfleet, where in early October he spent time with Matt Dickinson, as described in the preface to this volume. Dad then closed up the Cape house for the season and, first stopping off at the Kennedy School, headed back to the U.K. Upon his arrival in London, he had dinner with Rachel and me before traveling to Hertfordshire and returning to London with Shirley. Then, representing the family, he took a train up to Northumberland to greet my English cousin Larissa as she came out of hospital with her newest baby, John. In a subsequent phone conversation with me, I remember well how Dad marveled at Larissa's ability to arrive home after giving birth, and immediately prepare and serve a delicious dinner for the family; she was, he thought, "quite a girl." Dad then traveled back to Hertfordshire, to accompany Shirley and her daughter, my stepsister Rebecca, to the memorial service held on October 25 at Cambridge University's King's College, for Bec's father, who'd succumbed the previous summer after valiantly fighting a protracted case of bone cancer.

I had been lulled—perhaps my father had, too—by his continuing energy and good health into thinking that we still had plenty of time in which to deal with the fine points of his estate. That said, his natural humility seems likely, under any circumstances, to have precluded focusing on his legacy. One of his legion of former students who'd transitioned into family friend, Ric Redman, had campaigned particularly persistently and wittily to convince my father to write his memoirs, to no avail. On the one occasion when I directly asked Dad to appraise his overall professional contribution, after a characteristic pursed-lipped pause, he replied, "I suppose I might be a footnote in history."

I recall my father, now, as unpretentious, restrained, and remarkably down to earth for someone so cerebral, with a deep reflective capacity and a comparably great capacity to enjoy life in all its irony. Highly skilled though he was in the fine art of unobtrusive observation, his personal presence was such that he nonetheless gave the impression of being a larger man than his physical stature might suggest. And, indeed, his spirit was enormous. Summer neighbors on the Cape still speak of how they miss hearing his wholehearted laugh ring out across Gull Pond.

APPENDIX

June 15, 2003

Ms. Helena Kerr
ENAP, Brasilia

Dear Helena,

To begin with, let me say thanks once again, in the strongest terms, for your hospitality, your friendliness, and the extraordinary pains you took to make sure I was properly introduced to your marvelous circle in the PT around President Lula da Silva.

What a set of interesting, well-motivated people! What a set of challenges! What a good time I had! Since I reached Massachusetts, I have told

Editors' note: Since Neustadt did not intend this letter for publication, we have not identified "X," who was one of Lula's ministers at the time. In addition, the last section of the letter, where the writer cited several public welfare programs, has not been reprinted. Here he described a program in India where children were assured a substantial daily meal; the public provision to children, in Britain, of free vitamins and milk; the Works Progress Administration program, part of Franklin D. Roosevelt's New Deal; and a preventive health program for mothers and children established under Nelson Mandela's government in South Africa. Some of these were programs he had heard about from his wife, Shirley Williams.

everyone in sight that touring Brasilia in these circumstances was like tour-ing Washington DC in 1933 or '34—as invigorating as it was inspiring. Your troubles, of course, are mostly ahead of you; I understand that very well. Yet circles such as yours do not form often in this world, and only around extraordinary people, of which your President must be one. Next time I really must meet him. But it is well that I didn't meet him this time. I certainly needed to meet the others first, and then to learn more of the history and prospects, which I shall try to do in London this fall.

You will recall that early on I made a comment to the effect that I thought "coordination" as a general proposition less important than getting priority objectives straight, along with the mix of people to implement them. But one of your ministers made the point to me, in what amounted to polite rebuttal, that the term coordination as used currently in the circle, actually was a metaphor for three different discomforts, each as important as, because impeding, effective choices of programs and people. These three discomforts he identified—you will remember, you were there—as follows:

—1. The discomfort of presidential personal aides with the President's own activism, ebullience, honesty, and fresh ideas in the face of their need to get him focussed on decisions flowing in and up to him from others. We heard about this also in another session. Let me label the resulting prob-lem "harnessing the boss." (Although my thought of cloning him would actually serve better.)

—2. The discomforts of those well inside the PT inner circle with two separate (but sometimes related) groups, a) Ministers from other parties in the present coalition, and b) Federal civil servants in the permanent min-istries with their own established "culture," sense of mission, timing, and rou-tines, which turn out to be different from those long encountered by the PT even in Sao Paulo. Different and perhaps unfathomable. Let me label these two problems as "broadening one's reach," and "deepening one's empathy."

—3. The reverse discomforts of Ministers from other parties and of senior civil servants who may perceive the PT circle as exclusive, indiffer-ent (to them), unfriendly, even hostile, and may see the President himself so, since he is unlike his predecessor in so many respects. Let me label the twin problems that result as "widening the sense of circle" and "strength-ening civil service sympathy."

The five problems, stemming from those discomforts, do not weaken the case for prioritizing the agenda or for reshuffling people. Quite the contrary. Tackling the discomforts help[s] with both. So I have tried to think of United States experience in new Administrations which might be helpful to you, specifically in one or another of those five respects. The results are not world-shaking. Such as they are, I offer them to you under the headings indicated above.

Harnessing the boss

It can only be done as he allows and understands, and more, commits himself. It took Bill Clinton's staff the better part of two years to persuade him to stop wrecking his schedule. He tended to talk too long and he frequently invited people in on his own. Only when he was convinced that the results were hurting *him*, eliminating choices he might wish to have made, or damaging his reputation where it mattered, did he grudgingly accept the need to have a daily schedule and stick, more or less, to it.

President Lula evidently drives his close aides wild by refusing to address their agendas of decisions brought to him to make, and instead unleashing fresh ideas for them to comment on and follow up. Perhaps he does this to avoid decisions, either out of boredom or in order to buy time. If so there's no stopping him, unless his aides can make him sympathetic with their problem. But perhaps he does it out of genuine desire to articulate an idea and hear challenges to it, as a stage in firming up his own views. Lots of able people think that way, stating and testing on others. If so, perhaps he can be persuaded that the best way to get an intellectual test is to try his ideas out on people whose minds are not filled to the brim by what they are trying to get him to do. Better to separate, somewhat, his sessions for decision-making and those for hammering out new thoughts. Better for him because his interactive audience for new ideas is thus enabled to be livelier and more attentive.

Might that give him an incentive (more powerful than sympathy) for arranging such separations and for sticking to them?

Broadening one's reach

After six months, the time has certainly arrived for key members of the circle to extend a welcoming hand to coalition ministers with the potential to be friends (and perhaps also to any with potential to be serious enemies).

How to do that? In the United States, one way is family socializing. Another way is the informal working lunch. A third way is informal consultation. In North America, at least, most people love to be consulted. From the standpoint of Brasilia, the President's residence affords other opportunities: invitations to informal soccer? To join a weekend trip? To tea (or whatever spouses like)? I recognize the limits. President Kennedy could not make full use of such social means because, for one thing, his wife was a very private person, and for another, he himself preferred to socialize with old, personal friends.

Within whatever limits, these things should not be altogether random but ideally should be planned comprehensively, in a wholly private, unpublicized way. If the President takes the lead, others of you will no doubt follow, and the accidents of human friendship then take over. But it ought to be quietly audited so no coalition partner is ignored by inadvertence.

Deepening one's empathy

[X's] deputy is a civil servant, I was told, which seems entirely reasonable. Less reasonable is that I was also told he was the only one in the three Secretariats. He was said to be somewhat beleaguered, mistrusted by both sides. If he really is alone, that's no wonder. And to give your circle some feel for the world in which the civil servants work, their "culture," their procedures, their ambitions, their constraints, you need far more than one right on the cusp of your immediate circle. That sort of understanding is important whether you wish to use the civil service or go around it in particular cases. Either way your people should not have to act in ignorance. But to act knowledgeably you'll need more deputies than one. Five, six, seven, at a minimum, to interact informally and informatively with their seniors in the circle. Without such an outer circle in the immediate neighborhood of your inner one, I don't see how most of its members will ever get to be as knowledgeable about the civil service as they'll need to be for full effectiveness.

In Washington, whenever we have big changes of party at the White House, it turns out that a great part of the Federal civil servants voted with the majority and look with keen anticipation to the coming of the new regime. Then they are disappointed by the newcomers' suspicions of them. Only gradually do some of the permanent people prove themselves not only competent enough but sympathetic enough to be taken into the new-comers' camp. No doubt that will occur with you in time, for I gather that in your case also, many of the civil servants voted for you, or at least were excited by the prospect of your take-over. So you have only to watch, test, and select those who are best suited by temperament and sympathies to join you.

The trouble is that you have less time than would we in North America. Your impending choices are so crucial and fundamental that your need for knowledge about all your assets, civil servants included, is higher than at any time I can recall in Washington. Even in 1933, at the worst of the depression and the banking crisis, the new President himself had been in virtual charge of a great ministry of government as recently as twelve years before, and knew more about civil service folkways than almost anyone around him. That's a luxury you lack.

Widening the sense of "circle"

You people are so used to working with each other, and so unused to working equally intimately with anyone else, that it will be hard to summon up the grace—amidst all your other worries—to treat those "other" ministers, and civil servants "on the cusp," in such a way that they no longer feel you view them as "outsiders." Of course you do and will. None of the foregoing suggestions stops that. The only thing that stops it will be shared experience as your regime runs its course.

But maybe ENAP is an organization that could heighten experience, perhaps quicken it, not by formal courses for the many but by informal interchange among the few, mingling members of the inner circle with their civil service deputies, for off the record dialogue on subjects of high mutual interest. Is that worth pursuing?

Strengthening civil service sympathy

"They" ought to remember, but won't, that it is you who are the newcomers, deserving of their sympathy and tolerance as you find your feet in the strange new Federal world. They should be helping you on their own initiative. Mostly they will be holding off, while waiting for you to help, or at least instruct, them. Curious, perhaps, but that's a professional deformation, so to speak, of civil servants everywhere. So your inner circle has to try to make them think about your problems from your perspective. Judging from Washington, that can only be done by giving them real-life glimpses of what you do and why.

From my own Washington experience, I judge that nothing thrills a civil servant more than watching one of his political masters wrestle seriously with a real dilemma, whether or not the result is what the servant himself may have sought. Does this have an echo in Brasilia? If so, can ENAP help in any way to spread that opportunity?

Now for a wholly new subject, namely the content of priority program(s) for the poor. You'll recall my enthusiasm for a simple assurance of one full meal a day for every child under 18, administered through the schools as far as possible. . . .

Once again thanks. Regards to all. Not least to Professor Arbix!

Warmly,

Richard E. Neustadt
Douglas Dillon Professor of Government, Emeritus
Harvard University, Cambridge, Massachusetts, USA

HARVARD UNIVERSITY
JOHN FITZGERALD KENNEDY SCHOOL OF GOVERNMENT

Institute of Politics   Littauer Center
                                                                          Cambridge 02138

January 13, 1968

Dear Mr. President:

My son Dick (Richard M.) has been the sparkplug of a student-faculty Ad Hoc Committee on Vietnam for Harvard and Radcliffe Colleges. He and his associates have solicited signatures for a letter to you expressing moderate dissent from current policy in political, not moral, terms. Their aim has been to hold the "middle" hereabouts, against extreme forms of dissent. They have sought signatures from faculty and student ranks alike. I gather they have gained a substantial response from both.

Naturally my signature has been solicited in my capacity as faculty member. I have declined to sign. But I foresee that once the letter is delivered to the White House and subsequently released to the press, my son's connection with the venture will prompt local press inquiries about my own non-signature and hence my attitude toward his activity.

Accordingly, I have prepared the enclosed form of response which I shall use if that contingency arises. Hopefully it will not, but one must be prepared. I have wanted you to see the formulation in advance of possible use. As I imagine you are aware, if I am "called" in this fashion, I cannot conscientiously pretend all-out support for current policy. But neither do I wish to violate what I regard as proper reliance [hand corrected to "reticence"] in a sometime-consultant. Hopefully this formulation walks the line.

Forgive me for bothering you with so personal a matter. Let me add the warmest of regards for the new year.

Respectfully,

Richard E. Neustadt

The President
The White House
Washington, D. C.

Enclosure

[handwritten note]
Forgive the typing also! My secretary did this while I was out of town, & left it for me. Now she's out of town!

Attachment to Letter

For response to questions on Richard E. Neustadt's non-signature in light of Richard M. Neustadt's Chairmanship:

"I am very much in sympathy with the objectives my son and his associates pursued in seeking wide support for a thoughtful letter to the President. And although I might question some of its assumptions, I applaud the letter's emphasis on redefined war aims. However, having served from 1961 until last year as a Consultant to the President under both Messrs. Kennedy and Johnson, and having still the privilege of communicating privately, I think it inappropriate for me to start communicating publicly."

THE WHITE HOUSE
WASHINGTON

January 18, 1968

Memorandum for
The President

This confirms what I have suggested for almost 20 years:
That Dick has an I.Q. problem.

To mix metaphors, it is a silly effort to have an ear to the ground on each side of the fence.

The newspapers—to his probable dismay—did not note the absence of his signature or its significance.

I would file it away—and convert him from a "sometimes consultant" to a "onetime consultant."

John P. Roche

Editors' note: John P. Roche, a former Brandeis University professor, was sometimes described as Lyndon Johnson's "in-house intellectual." He had been chairman of the liberal Americans for Democratic Action and identified himself as a Social Democrat. He was also a fervent anticommunist and staunch defender of LBJ's Vietnam policy—as illustrated here in his memorandum sent to Johnson after the president had received Neustadt's letter concerning his son's Vietnam petition.

NOTES

Foreword

1. Frances Perkins, "The Roosevelt I Knew: The War Years," *Collier's*, September 21, 1946, p. 102.

Chapter One

1. Richard E. Neustadt and Ernest R. May, *Thinking in Time: Uses of History for Decision Makers* (New York: Free Press, 1986).

2. Ibid.

3. See William Strauss and Neil Howe, *Generations: The History of America's Future, 1524 to 2069* (New York: HarperPerennial, 1992). G.I., which originally stood for "government issue," became the generic label for personnel in the U.S. armed services in World War II.

4. Richard E. Neustadt and Harvey V. Fineberg, *The Epidemic That Never Was: Policy-Making and the Swine Flu Scare* (New York: Vintage Books, 1983).

5 . See Martha Joynt Kumar, "Richard Elliot Neustadt, 1919–2003: A Tribute," *Presidential Studies Quarterly* 34, no. 1 (March 2004): 14–25.

6. Neustadt and May, *Thinking in Time,* p. 102.

7. Richard E. Neustadt, *Presidential Power and the Modern Presidents: The Politics of Leadership,* rev. ed. (New York: Free Press, 1990).

Chapter Two

1. See Richard E. Neustadt, "Presidential Clearance of Legislation: Legislative Development, Review, and Coordination in the Executive Office of the Presidency" (Ph.D. dissertation, Harvard University, 1950); Neustadt, "Presidency and Legislation: The Growth of Central Clearance," *American Political Science Review* 48, no. 3 (September 1954): 641–71; and Neustadt, "Presidency and Legislation: Planning the President's Program," *American Political Science Review* 49, no. 4 (December 1955): 980–1021.

2. See Richard E. Neustadt, *Report to JFK: The Skybolt Crisis in Perspective* (Cornell University Press, 1999).

3. "The White House Staff: Later Period—Discussion," transcript of a discussion among several former Truman aides, in *The Truman White House: The Administration of the Presidency 1945–1953*, edited by Francis Howard Heller (Regents Press of Kansas, 1980), p. 165.

4. Charles O. Jones, "Richard E. Neustadt: Public Servant as Scholar," *Annual Review of Political Science* 6 (June 2003): 1.

5. Ibid., p. 3. The following biographical information draws primarily on Jones's article.

6. See, for example, the description of the BoB in this period provided by Roger Jones, oral history interview, August 14, 1969, Truman Library, pp. 8–15.

7. This was not the only bureaucratic rival with which the BoB dealt at this time; the Office of War Mobilization and Reconversion (OWMR), which had responsibility for dismantling the myriad wartime government agencies and settling military contracts, also impinged on the BoB's administrative management and budgetary responsibilities. It was the lineal descendant of the Office of War Mobilization, established in 1942 to coordinate all U.S. economic activities related to the war effort. In 1944 its powers were extended to problems of the reconversion to peace and it was consequently renamed Office of War Mobilization and Reconversion. However, the OWMR was terminated shortly after Truman became President.

8. Richard E. Neustadt, "Basic Questions and Assumptions Involved in the Prospective Workload," memo, December 12, 1946, Richard E. Neustadt Papers, Harry S. Truman Library (hereafter: Neustadt Papers, Truman Library).

9. Neustadt to Staats, February 27, 1947, Neustadt Papers, Truman Library.

10. Neustadt to Gross, November 27, 1946, Neustadt Papers, Truman Library.

11. Neustadt, "Kaiserling [*sic*] on the Council's External Relations," memorandum for the files, February 24, 1947, Neustadt Papers, Truman Library.

12. Neustadt to Staats and Carey, August 12, 1946, Neustadt Papers, Truman Library.

13. Charles O. Jones, "Richard E. Neustadt," p. 4.

14. Ken Hechler, oral history interview, November 29, 1985, p. 105, Truman Library.

15. James Webb (former Truman aide), in oral history interview with the Truman White House, February 20, 1980, p. 51, Truman Library.

16. Milton P. Kayle, oral history interview, November 9 and 10, 1982, p. 59, Truman Library.

17. Roger Jones, "The Executive Office Agencies," in Heller, *Truman White House*, p. 175.

18. Kayle, oral history interview, p. 68.

19. Neustadt to Roger Jones, August 25, 1946, Neustadt Papers, Truman Library.

20. Neustadt, "Tentative List of Legislative Items for Review prior to Convening of 81st Congress," August 20, 1948, Neustadt Papers, Truman Library.

21. Roger Jones, oral history interview, p. 176.

22. Neustadt to Charles Stauffacher, D. Bell, and J. Weldon Jones, "Departmental Reports to the President re State of the Union Message, Economic Report, and Legislative Program," November 4, 1948, Neustadt Papers, Truman Library.

23. Donald Macphail and Neustadt to Roger W. Jones, "Bureau Procedure for Utilizing Agency Legislative Programs Submitted under Sec. 86, 'Call for Estimates,'" September 6, 1949, in Record Group 51, Legislative Reference Division, Subject Files, 1939–70 (series 39.39), Box 4, Legislative Program, 81st Congress, 2nd session, National Archives II, College Park, Maryland.

24. Neustadt to R. Jones, "Weekly Reports on Anticipated Congressional Schedules," 15 May 1950, in Record Group 51, Legislative Reference Division, Subject Files, 1939–70, Box 4, Legislative Program—82nd Congress, 1st session, National Archives II, College Park, Maryland.

25. The National Security Resources Board was an eight-member agency created in 1947 to do long-range and continuous planning to prepare the United States for industrial and economic mobilization.

26. See Neustadt to Staats, "Legislative Clearance and Legislative Proposals Originating with the NSRB," October 27, 1948, Box 1, Chronological Files, May–December 1948, Neustadt Papers, Truman Library.

27. Neustadt to Staats, November 22, 1948, Box 1, Chronological Files, May–December 1948, Neustadt Papers, Truman Library.

28. Neustadt to Dean Payson S. Wild, May 5, 1948, Neustadt Papers, Box 1, Chronological Files, 1947–65, May–December 1948, Truman Library.

29. Ibid., 2.

30. Neustadt to Merle Fainsod, July 10, 1950, Neustadt Papers, Truman Library.

31. Ibid.

32. Neustadt to Herman Somers, August 4, 1949, Neustadt Papers Box 1, Chronological Files, 1947–65, 1949, January–September, Truman Library.

33. Philleo Nash, oral history interview, October 17, 1966, p. 280.

34. Stephen Spingarn, oral history interview, March 2, 1975, Truman Library, p. 395.

35. Charles Murphy, oral history interview, July 24, 1963, Truman Library.

36. Neustadt to Fainsod.

37. Spingarn, oral history interview, pp. 396–98.

38. Neustadt to Fainsod.

39. In addition to Neustadt, Murphy's aides included David Bell, George Elsey, Don Hansen, Ken Hechler, and David Lloyd, although not all served at the same time.

40. David Bell, oral history interview, September 12, 1968, Truman Library, p. 73. In subsequent years, the ranks of the titles have been reversed; special assistants are now viewed as senior to administrative assistants.

41. Kayle, oral history interview, p. 88.

42. The President's Committee on Administrative Management, more commonly known as the Brownlow Committee after its chair, Louis Brownlow, was appointed by President Franklin Roosevelt in 1936 to undertake a study of executive branch organization. Its report, issued in 1937, provided a partial blueprint for the creation of the Executive Office of the President, including the White House Office, in 1939.

43. Harold Enarson, oral history interview, August 5, 1996, Truman Library, p. 11.

44. Lincoln Gordon, oral history interview, July 17, 1975, Truman Library, p. 168. Averell Harriman joined Truman's White House staff as military consultant at the outbreak of the Korean War in 1951.

45. George Elsey, oral history interview, July 10, 1969, Truman Library, p. 181.

46. Ibid., p. 186.

47. Neustadt to Mrs. Pratt, March 19, 1951, Neustadt Papers, Truman Library.

48. Jones, "Richard E. Neustadt," p. 5.

49. Nash, oral history interview, Truman Library, 280-81.

50. Elsey, oral history interview, p. 128.

51. Joseph G. Feeney, oral history interview, September 20, 1966, Truman Library, 118; see also Theodore Tannenwald, oral history interview, July 14, 1969, Truman Library.

52. Neustadt, "The White House Staff: Later Period," in Heller, *Truman White House*, p. 101.

53. Elsey, oral history interview, p. 167.

54. Tannenwald, oral history interview (www.trumanlibrary.org/oralhist/tannen.htm#transcript [May 2007]).

55. Enarson, oral history interview, p. 11.

56. Ibid.

57. Information on attendance at White House meetings is drawn from President's Daily Appointment Records, accessible at the Truman Library website, www.trumanlibrary.org/ hstpaper/connellyhst.htm.

58. Similarly, Neustadt also served as a point of contact for politicians and others seeking to reach Murphy. John Barriere, who worked for the Democratic National Committee, remembers, "I would get calls from Murphy, and nearly always, if I picked up the phone and called Murphy I could get him, and if I couldn't get him would make sure that somebody like Neustadt particularly . . . somebody to whom I could relay [a] message with authority . . . I could get a hearing on it" (see John E. Barriere, oral history interview, December 20, 1966, pp. 40, 45).

59. Neustadt, "White House Staff: Later Period," p. 164.

60. Ibid., p. 114.

61. Ibid., pp. 164–65.

62. See Murphy, oral history interviews, July 24, 1963, and July 15, 1969.

63. Jones, "Richard E. Neustadt," p. 5.

64. James Sundquist, oral history interview, July 15, 1963, Truman Library, p. 19.

65. Ibid., pp. 30–31.

66. Available in its entirety at the Harry S. Truman Library website, http://trumanlibrary.org/calendar/viewpapers.php?pid=2059.

67. Bell, oral history interview, pp. 157, 168–69; see also Wesley McCune, oral history interviews, September 15 and 16, 1988, Truman Library, p. 137.

68. Bell, oral history interview, p. 193.

69. Conversation with author.

70. Spingarn, oral history interview, p. 396.

71. Bell, oral history interview, p. 206.

72. Neustadt, "White House Staff: Later Period," p. 115.

73. Nash, oral history interview, 281.

74. Neustadt, *Presidential Power and the Modern Presidents: The Politics of Leadership*, rev. ed. (New York: Free Press, 1990), p. 293.

75. Neustadt, interview with Harry Truman, December 28, 1955, notes, Richard E. Neustadt Papers, John F. Kennedy Library.

76. Charles O. Jones, "Richard E. Neustadt," p. 1.

Chapter Three

1. Richard E. Neustadt, "*Presidential Power* and the Research Agenda," *Presidential Studies Quarterly* 32, December 2002: 721.

2. Richard E. Neustadt, "A Preachment from Retirement," in *Presidential Power: Forging the Presidency for the Twenty-First Century*, edited by Robert Y. Shapiro, Martha Joynt Kumar, and Lawrence R. Jacobs (Columbia University Press, 2000), p. 466.

3. Richard E. Neustadt (REN), interview with the author, conducted at the Reform Club in London, November 1, 2001. Interviews and all referenced correspondence in possession of the author.

4. REN, correspondence to author, September 30, 2003.

5. *PS: Political Science and Politics* 37, January 2004: 125–27; 131–32.

6. REN, letter to Tom Mann, April 30, 1993.

7. *Passages to the Presidency: From Campaigning to Governing* (Washington, D.C.: Brookings Institution Press, 1998).

8. *Preparing to Be President: The Memos of Richard E. Neustadt* (Washington, D.C.: American Enterprise Institute Press, 2000).

9. *The Presidency in a Separated System* (Washington, D.C.: Brookings Institution Press, 1994).

10. REN, correspondence to Bruce MacLaury, president of Brookings Institution, July 16, 1993.

11. REN to author, September 4, 1997.

12. REN, interview with author, Cross Plains, Wisconsin, April 20, 2002.

13. REN to author, April 24, 2002.

14. "Richard E. Neustadt: Public Servant as Scholar," *Annual Review of Political Science*, vol. 6 (2003): 11.

15. These observations are based on conversations. Dick asked me not to quote from specific passages in his letters on this topic, and I have honored that request.

16. Norman Ornstein and Thomas Mann, eds., *The Permanent Campaign and Its Future* (Washington, D.C.: American Enterprise Institute and Brookings Institution, 2000), chapter 8.

17. See Dick Morris, *Behind the Oval Office* (New York: Random House, 1997), pp. 138–57.

18. The preceding three excerpts are from REN to author, January 30, 1997.

19. REN to author, March 26, 1997. As seen here, Dick insisted on capitalizing the word *President*. It irritated him considerably that editing rules accepted the capitalization of *Congress* but not *President*. Accordingly I made certain that Neustadt editing rules were followed in *Preparing to Be President*.

20. REN to author, January 13, 1998.

21. Charles O. Jones, *Clinton and Congress, 1993–1996: Risk, Restoration, and Reelection* (University of Oklahoma Press, 1999), pp. 168–69, and David R. Mayhew, *Divided We Govern*, 2nd ed. (Yale University Press, 2005), pp. 208–13.

22. Neustadt, *Presidential Power*, p. 55.

23. REN, interview with author, Reform Club, London, November 1, 2001.

24. REN, interview with author, Cross Plains, Wisconsin, April 20, 2002.

25. Ibid.

Chapter Four

1. Richard E. Neustadt, *Presidential Power and the Modern Presidents: The Politics of Leadership*, rev. ed. (New York: Free Press, 1990).

2. Ibid., p. 248.

3. Richard E. Neustadt, "Presidential Transitions: Are the Risks Rising?" *Miller Center Journal* 1, Spring 1994: 7.

4. Richard E. Neustadt, "Neustadt Advises the Advisers in 2000," in *Preparing to Be President: The Memos of Richard E. Neustadt*, edited by Charles O. Jones (Washington, D.C.: American Enterprise Institute Press, 2000), p. 143.

5. Neustadt, "Presidential Transitions," p. 3.

6. See Theodore C. Sorensen's "Richard E. Neustadt, Presidential Expert," in chapter 5 here.

7. Richard E. Neustadt, introductory remarks to speech by Theodore Sorensen at the twenty-fifth anniversary of the Harvard Institute of Politics, Cambridge,

Massachusetts, October, 1991. The memo Sorensen was reading was "Organizing the Transition," the first of three monographs on the transition Neustadt prepared for President-elect Kennedy.

8. Theodore Sorensen, *Kennedy* (New York: Harper & Row, 1965), p. 229.

9. The press view of Clinton's transition was more favorable, and polls in December 1992 showed 72 percent public approval of his transition. See Fred I. Greenstein, "The Presidential Leadership Style of Bill Clinton," *Miller Center Journal* 1, Spring 1994: 21.

10. Neustadt, *Presidential Power*, p. 239.

11. Carter's emphasis on government reorganization and regulatory reform is an exception that proves the rule. Political capital for management reform was quickly swept away by a hailstorm of domestic policy initiatives. See Neustadt, *Presidential Power*, p. 238

12. Sorensen, *Kennedy*, p. 228.

13. Jones, "Neustadt Advises the Advisers," p. 143.

14. Ibid., p. 169.

15. Martin Anderson, *Revolution* (San Diego: Harcourt Brace Jovanovich, 1988), pp. 56–57.

16. Steve Dougherty, *Hopes and Dreams: The Story of Barack Obama* (New York: Black Dog and Leventhal, 2007), p. 89.

17. Neustadt, *Presidential Power*, p. 241.

18. Neustadt, "Neustadt Advises the Advisers in 2000," in *Preparing to Be President*, p. 146.

19. Ibid., p. 168.

20. The first Presidential Transition Act was signed by President Johnson in 1964; it mandated modest funding of transitions. Funds sufficient to support much larger transition teams were provided in the 1976 amendments to the act.

21. Neustadt, "Presidential Transitions," p. 7.

22. Richard E. Neustadt, "Staffing the Presidency: Premature Notes on the New Administration," *Political Science Quarterly* 93, no. 1 (Spring 1978): 8.

23. Neustadt, *Presidential Power*, p. 243.

24. Martha Joynt Kumar, "The Contemporary Presidency: Communications Operations in the White House of President George W. Bush: Making News on His Terms," *Presidential Studies Quarterly* 33, n. 2 (June 2003): 387.

25. John P. Burke, *Becoming President: The Bush Transition, 2000–2003* (Denver: Lynne Rienner, 2004), p. 53.

26. Porter quoted in John H. Kessel, "The Political Environment of the White House," in *The White House World: Transitions, Organization, and Office Operations*, edited by Martha Joynt Kumar and Terry Sullivan (College Station: Texas A&M University Press, 2003), p. 64.

27. Burke, *Becoming President*, p. 56.

28. Dana Milbank, "Bush Names Last Three Cabinet Choices," *Washington Post*, January 3, 2001, p. 1; Burke, *Becoming President*, p. 56.

29. Burke, *Becoming President,* p. 52.

30. Jim Hoagland, "Cheney's Undimmed Role," *Washington Post,* February 10, 2005, p. A23.

31. Peter Baker, "Rove Is Promoted to Deputy Chief of Staff," *Washington Post,* February 9, 2005, p. A21.

32. Burke, *Becoming President,* p. 60.

33. Charles O. Jones, *Passages to the Presidency: From Campaigning to Governing* (Washington, D.C.: Brookings Institution Press, 1998), p. 82.

34. Ron Suskind, "Why Are These Men Laughing?" *Esquire,* January 2003.

35. Richard E. Neustadt, "Challenges Created by Contemporary Presidents," in *New Challenges for the American Presidency,* edited by George C. Edwards III and Philip John Davies (New York: Pearson Longman, 2004), p. 13.

36. Ibid.

37. Neustadt, Preface, *Presidential Power,* p. xviii.

Chapter Five

1. The Skybolt report was published in 1999 by the Cornell University Press as *Report to JFK: The Skybolt Crisis in Perspective.*

Chapter Six

1. The paper was originally delivered at the annual meeting of the American Political Science Association in Washington, D.C., September 8 to 11, 1965. It has subsequently been republished, sometimes in a slightly abridged form, in *The Public Interest* 2, Winter 1966, pp. 55–69; in Anthony King, ed., *The British Prime Minister,* 2nd ed. (Duke University Press, 1985), pp. 155–74; and Richard E. Neustadt, *Report to JFK: The Skybolt Crisis in Perspective* (Cornell University Press, 1999), pp. 139–54. Because the paper is quite short and because the pagination of the various versions differs widely, detailed page references have not been provided for the quotations here.

2. Neustadt, *Report to JFK,* pp. 26–27. The following two quotations are drawn from the chapter "British Refinements," written more than three decades later and published in the same volume, pp. 123 and 124.

3. Richard E. Neustadt, *Alliance Politics* (New York: Columbia University Press, 1970). The following two quotations can be found on pp. 61 and 67.

4. Neustadt, *Report to JFK,* p. 155.

Chapter Seven

1. All references to *Presidential Power* are from Richard E. Neustadt *Presidential Power and the Modern Presidents* (New York: Free Press, 1990).

2. Ibid., p. 153.

3. Ibid., p. 29. (Cater was a magazine editor who worked in Lyndon Johnson's administration as a special assistant from 1964 to 1968.)

4. Ibid., p. 262.

5. Ibid., p. 85.

6. Richard E. Neustadt, "Neustadt Advises the Advisers in 2000," in *Preparing to Be President: The Memos of Richard E. Neustadt,* edited by Charles O. Jones (Washington, D.C.: American Enterprise Institute Press, 2000), p. 153.

7. *Presidential Power,* p. 262.

8. Ibid., p. 275.

9. Ibid., p. 264.

10. Neustadt, *Preparing to Be President,* p. 153.

11. Michael Janeway, interview with the author, October 12, 2006.

12. David Broder, interview with the author, February 7, 2007.

13. Richard Tofel, interview with the author, October 5, 2006.

14. Richard E. Neustadt and Ernest R. May, *Thinking in Time: The Uses of History for Decisionmakers* (New York: Free Press, 1986).

15. See my "The Real Echoes of Vietnam," *Newsweek,* April 14, 2003.

16. Phil Bennett, interview with the author, December 7, 2006.

17. Ibid.

18. David Shribman, "Harvard Professor's Course Has Shaped Views of a Generation on the Power of the Presidency," *Wall Street Journal,* December 4, 1986, p. 68.

19. Newton Minow, interview with the author, October 10, 2006.

Chapter Nine

1. David Shribman, "Neustadt Left Us with Greater Understanding of Political Power," *National Perspective,* November 11, 2003, uexpress.com, www.uexpress.com/davidshribman/ index.html?uc_full_date=20031111.

2. Martha Joynt Kumar, "Richard Elliott Neustadt, 1919–2003: A Tribute," *Presidential Studies Quarterly* 34, no. 1 (March 2004): 14.

3. Richard E. Neustadt and Harvey V. Fineberg, *The Swine Flu Affair: Decision-Making on a Slippery Disease* (Washington, D.C.: U.S. Government Printing Office, 1978).

4. Richard E. Neustadt and Harvey V. Fineberg, *The Epidemic That Never Was: Policy Making and the Swine Flu Scare* (New York: Vintage Books, 1983).

Chapter Ten

1. Craig A. Lambert, "The Origins of the John F. Kennedy School of Government," Kennedy School of Government Case Program CR16-05-1784.0 (Cambridge, Mass.: Harvard University, 2005), p. 8.

2. Ibid., p. 8. See also John F. Kennedy School of Government, Institute of Politics, unpublished interview with Richard E. Neustadt, August 2003, transcript, pp. 15–16 (henceforth: August 2003 IOP interview).

3. August 2003 IOP interview, pp. 14, 16.

4. Alfred North Whitehead, *The Aims of Education and Other Essays* (New York: Free Press, 1929), p. 97.

5. *The John F. Kennedy School of Government: The First Fifty Years* (Cambridge, Mass.: Ballinger, 1986); Lambert, "Origins of the John F. Kennedy School of Government"; Institute of Politics website, "History," www.iop.harvard.edu/about_history.html; Graham Allison, "Emergence of Schools of Public Policy: Reflections by a Founding Dean," in *The Oxford Handbook of Public Policy*, edited by Michael Moran, Martin Rein, and Robert Goodin (New York: Oxford University Press, 2006), pp. 58–79.

6. Graham Allison, *Essence of Decision: Explaining the Cuban Missile Crisis* (New York: Little, Brown, 1971). *Essence of Decision* essentially made explicit the framework Neustadt had invented, especially in the development of a conceptual lens for analyzing the complexities of politics within a government in making foreign policy.

7. Richard E. Neustadt, *Presidential Power and the Modern Presidents: The Politics of Leadership from Roosevelt to Reagan* (New York: Free Press, 1990), p. xxi.

8. Institute of Politics, "History."

9. A brief chronology may be useful.

    1936: Faculty of Public Administration established

    1966: FPA renamed Kennedy School of Government, and Institute of Politics established

    1969: Public Policy Program created.

Neustadt was founding director of the Institute of Politics from 1966 to 1971 and associate dean of the Kennedy School from 1965 to 1975.

10. Institute of Politics website, "History."

11. August 2003 IOP interview, pp. 17–18.

12. Ibid., p. 17.

13. James Madison, *The Federalist Papers* (New York: Signet Classic, 2003), "No. 51," p. 317 (emphasis added).

14. Robert F. Kennedy, *Thirteen Days: A Memoir of the Cuban Missile Crisis* (New York: Norton, 1971), p. 91.

15. Xandra Bingley, Neustadt's assistant, personal communication, e-mail, November 3, 2006.

16. Institute of Politics website, "History."

17. August 2003 IOP interview, pp. 30–31.

18. Ibid., pp. 16, 20.

19. Lambert, "Origins of the John F. Kennedy School of Government," pp. 12–13.

20. Ibid., p. 8. See also August 2003 IOP interview, pp. 15–16.

21. Ira Jackson, personal communication, e-mail, October 3, 2006.

22. See John F. Kennedy Presidential Library and Museum website, "The President's Desk" (www.jfklibrary.org/Historical+Resources/Archives/Reference+Desk/The+Presidents+Desk+Page+2.htm).

23. Neustadt, *Presidential Power,* 208.

24. Ibid., p. 231. Roosevelt said in his May 22, 1932, speech at Oglethorpe University, "[T]he country demands bold, persistent experimentation. It is common sense to take a method and try it. If it fails, admit it frankly and try another. But above all, try something."

25. Ibid., p. 153 (including Holmes quote).

26. Ibid., p. 136.

27. Institute of Politics website, "History."

28. Michael D. Cohen, James G. March, and Johan P. Olsen, "A Garbage Can Model of Organizational Choice," *Administration Science Quarterly* 17, no. 1 (March 1972): 1.

29. ETOB is explained in Francis Bator and Graham Allison, "Harvard and Money," unpublished report to the University Committee on Governance, November 1970.

30. *John F. Kennedy School of Government,* p. 49.

31. Ibid., pp. 48–49.

32. Henry Rosovsky, *The University: An Owner's Manual* (New York: Norton, 1990), p. 242.

33. Vernon Jordan, personal communication, April 2007.

34. *John F. Kennedy School of Government,* p. 13.

35. Ibid., p. 5.

36. Lambert, "Origins of the John F. Kennedy School of Government," p. 3.

37. Quoted in Bruce Anderson, "The Parking Puzzle," *Stanford Magazine,* November–December 1996, available at www.stanfordalumni.org/news/magazine/1996/novdec/articles/parking.html.

38. F. M. Cornford, *Microcosmographia Academica: Being a Guide for the Young Academic Politician* (Cambridge: Metcalfe, 1908).

39. Neustadt, *Presidential Power,* p. 4.

40. Fred I. Greenstein, *The Hidden Hand Presidency: Eisenhower as Leader* (Johns Hopkins University Press, 1994), p. 5. Later, as dean, I often marveled at the workings of President Bok's hidden hand.

41. August 2003 IOP interview, p. 22.

42. Francis Bator, personal communication, e-mail, October 2, 2006.

43. Alva Myrdal won the Nobel Peace Prize in 1982 and Gunnar Myrdal shared the Nobel Prize for Economics with Friedrich Hayek in 1974.

44. Martha Joynt Kumar, "Richard Elliott Neustadt, 1919–2003: A Tribute," *Presidential Studies Quarterly,* 34, no. 1 (March 2004): 13.

45. *John F. Kennedy School of Government,* p. 57.

46. Ibid., p. 58

47. Mark Moore, personal communication (May 12, 2007).

48. Lambert, "Origins of the John F. Kennedy School of Government."

49. Milton Mayer, *Robert Maynard Hutchins: A Memoir* (University of California Press, 1993), p. 170.

50. The author expresses special appreciation to Minh Ly for his outstanding research in preparation of this chapter. The author is very grateful to Beth Neustadt, Shirley Williams, Francis Bator, Xandra Bingley, Derek Bok, Heather Campion, Al Carnesale, David Ellwood, Howard Husock, Ira Jackson, Vernon Jordan, Cathy McLaughlin, Jonathan Moore, Mark Moore, Tom Schelling, Edith Stokey, and Pete Zimmerman for contributing anecdotes about Dick Neustadt and for providing comments on earlier drafts. All errors of interpretation, however, are mine alone.

Chapter Eleven

1. Jo Sôares, *A Samba for Sherlock,* translated by Clifford E. Landers (New York: Pantheon, 1997).

2. Tony Smith, "Brazil Teeters; Will It Be Contagious?" *New York Times,* August 4, 2002, sec. 3, p. 1.

3. Helena Kerr do Amaral, "Notes from Richard Neustadt Lessons in June 2003," unpublished paper, ENAP, March 2004, p. 2, n. 1. Also present at this dinner was Francisco Gaetani, a former ENAP director who had studied with Barzelay at the London School of Economics and introduced Barzelay to Kerr in February 2003.

4. Helena Kerr, personal communication, October 24, 2006.

5. Elizabeth (Beth) Neustadt, personal communication, October 2006. As Barzelay wrote later, "[Neustadt] made the point that he would not go as a consultant because he thought ill of people who did that in places they knew nothing about (actually I think his language was more colorful than that)." Michael Barzelay, communication to Beth Neustadt, January 2007.

6. Kerr, "Notes from Richard Neustadt," p. 2.

7. Ibid., pp. 5–14.

8. Ibid., p. 3.

9. Barzelay, January 2007.

10. Ibid., p. 5.

11. Charles O. Jones, ed. *Preparing to Be President: The Memos of Richard E. Neustadt* (Washington, D.C.: AEI Press, 2000).

12. Kerr, "Notes from Richard Neustadt," p. 4, n. 8.

13. Ibid., p. 6.

14. "I will confine myself tonight to illustrations and conclusions from United States experience. I leave it to you to draw comparisons, if any, with Brazilian experience. I hope there are some useful ones for you. Otherwise I waste my time and yours by dwelling on these others tonight" (ibid., p. 6).

15. Ibid., p. 14.

16. Ibid., p. 4.

17. Helena Kerr, personal communication, October 2006.

18. Quotations reflect the author's transcription of English portions of the INTV interview of June 4, 2003, and may not be exact. According to Kerr, INTV is roughly analogous to the Public Broadcasting System (PBS) in the United States.

19. Quotations reflect the author's transcription of the INTV interview of June 6, 2003, and may not be exact. This interview includes English translations of questions put to Neustadt in Portuguese.

20. Anthony King, obituary of Richard E. Neustadt, *The Independent,* November 6, 2003.

21. Luiz Alberto Weber, "Bet on Lula and on Brazil," *Carta Capital,* June 18, 2003, p. 46. The translation relied on here was prepared by Emanuely Luna with assistance from Felix Gavi Luna, and adapted by the author.

22. King, obituary.

23. Beth Neustadt, personal communication, January 2004.

24. Charles O. Jones, "Richard E. Neustadt: Public Servant as Scholar," *Annual Review of Political Science* 6 (June 2003): 1–22.

25. Kerr, "Notes from Richard Neustadt," p. 3.

26. Ibid.

27. Kerr, personal communication, October 2006.

28. As Anthony King said, "He is not interested in process for its own sake, rather in how the substance of policy interacts with process. He doesn't see them as separate things at all" (quoted in Jones, "Richard E. Neustadt," p. 7).

29. See Jones, "Richard E. Neustadt"; Jones, *Preparing to Be President,* introduction; and King, obituary.

30. Jean-Jacques Rousseau, *Political Writings: Containing the Social Contract, Considerations on the Government of Poland, Constitutional Project for Corsica, Part I,* translated by Frederick Watkins (University of Wisconsin Press, 1986), p. xliv.

31. Kerr, personal communication, October 2006.

32. Jones, "Richard E. Neustadt," p. 3.

33. Beth Neustadt, personal communications, 2004 and 2006.

34. Kerr, "Notes from Richard Neustadt," p. 3.

35. For an excellent account of Lula's presidency in midterm, see Barry Bearak, "Poor Man's Burden," *New York Times Magazine,* June 27, 2004, p. 30.

36. See www.mds.gov.br for "Programme Family Grant."

37. "The Recent Decline in Inequality in Brasil," Technical Note, *Applied Economic Research Institute (IPEA),* July 21, 2006, p. 3.

38. Ibid., p. 2.

39. See, for example, Larry Rohter and Juan Forero, "Unending Graft Is Threatening Latin America," *New York Times,* July 30, 2005, p. 1.

40. Ibid.

41. Kerr, personal communication, October 2006.

Afterword

1. These Trumans, although to the best of my knowledge unrelated to the former President, also had a significant influence on us Neustadts. Dave, a senior colleague at Columbia, had recruited my father there, and no doubt had a hand in our eventual move to the lovely apartment overlooking Riverside Drive that was directly above theirs; Ellie was one of very few who succeeded in deciphering my father's longhand scrawl, and typed the entire manuscript of his first book; Ted, their son, became my favorite babysitter because he was *so* clever.

2. Dan Davidson to Beth Neustadt, personal communication, March 2007.

3. During this period all young men who were U.S. citizens were eligible to be conscripted into military service; like Rick, they would have had a student deferment, called a 2S, only while enrolled full-time in a recognized educational institution. Thereafter, the choices were all stark. Unless they could prove that they were conscientious objectors—that they were against all war in principle—their options were to burn their draft cards and go to jail; endeavor to leave the country, say, by crossing the border into Canada (with the prospect of never being able to come home, or of going to jail if they did return); pull strings, if they had any, for example having someone arrange for them to join the Navy as an officer in order to avoid combat duty in Vietnam (and then live with the guilt of having done so); deliberately engage in self-harm for the purpose of "flunking" the physical that was required of draftees; or report to the local draft board with the expectation of being sent into combat. Throughout their college years this set of options hung like a Damocles sword over the heads of young men who, like my brother, did not support or believe in the legitimacy of the Vietnam War. In a less direct but often equally disturbing way, their dilemma affected their girlfriends and sisters. The local draft board clearly was on its toes in Rick's case.

SELECT BIBLIOGRAPHY

This list is not intended to be exhaustive but rather to serve as a convenient compendium of the sources by and about Richard E. Neustadt, his works, and the historical context in which he wrote and served that are cited most often in this volume.

By Richard E. Neustadt (listed chronologically)

"Presidential Clearance of Legislation: Legislative Development, Review, and Coordination in the Executive Office of the Presidency." Ph.D. diss., Harvard University, 1950.

"Presidency and Legislation: The Growth of Central Clearance." *American Political Science Review* 48, no. 3 (September, 1954): 641–71.

"Presidency and Legislation: Planning the President's Program." *American Political Science Review* 49, no. 4 (December, 1955): 980–1021.

Presidential Power and the Modern Presidents: The Politics of Leadership, rev. ed. (New York: Free Press, 1990; originally published 1960). (Quotes in this volume are from this edition.)

"White House to Whitehall." *Public Interest* 2 (Winter, 1966): 55–69.

"Staffing the Presidency: Premature Notes on the New Administration." *Political Science Quarterly* 93, no. 1 (Spring, 1978): 1–9.

Alliance Politics (Columbia University Press, 1970).

With Harvey V. Fineberg. *The Swine Flu Affair: Decision-Making on a Slippery Disease* (Washington, D.C.: U.S. Government Printing Office, 1978).

With Harvey Fineberg. *The Epidemic That Never Was: Policy-Making and the Swine Flu Scare* (New York: Vintage Books, 1983).

With Ernest R. May. *Thinking in Time: Uses of History for Decision Makers* (New York: Free Press, 1986).

"Presidential Transitions: Are the Risks Rising?" *Miller Center Journal* 1 (Spring, 1994): 3–13.

Report to JFK: The Skybolt Crisis in Perspective (Cornell University Press, 1999).

"Neustadt Advises the Advisers in 2000." In *Preparing to Be President: The Memos of Richard E. Neustadt,* edited by Charles O. Jones (Washington, D.C.: American Enterprise Press, 2000).

"*Presidential Power* and the Research Agenda." *Presidential Studies Quarterly* 32 (December, 2002): 721.

"Challenges Created by Contemporary Presidents." In *New Challenges for the American Presidency,* edited by George C. Edwards III and Philip John Davies (New York: Pearson Longman, 2004).

About Richard E. Neustadt and the Presidency

Burke, John P. *Becoming President: The Bush Transition: 2000–2003* (Denver: Lynne Rienner, 2004).

John F. Kennedy School of Government. *The John F. Kennedy School of Government: The First Fifty Years* (Cambridge, Mass.: Ballinger, 1986).

Jones, Charles O. *The Presidency in a Separated System* (Washington, D.C.: Brookings Institution Press, 1994).

———. *Passages to the Presidency: From Campaigning to Governing* (Washington, D.C.: Brookings Institution Press, 1998).

———. *Preparing to Be President: The Memos of Richard E. Neustadt* (Washington, D.C.: American Enterprise Institute Press, 2000).

———. "Richard E. Neustadt: Public Servant as Scholar." *Annual Review of Political Science* 6 (June 2003): 1–22.

Kumar, Martha Joynt. "Richard Elliott Neustadt, 1919–2003: A Tribute." *Presidential Studies Quarterly* 34, no. 1 (March, 2004): 3–18.

Kumar, Martha Joynt, and Terry Sullivan, eds. 2003. *The White House World: Transitions, Organization, and Office Operation* (Texas A&M University Press, 2003).

Morris, Dick. *Behind the Oval Office* (New York: Random House, 1997).

Ornstein, Norman, and Thomas Mann. *The Permanent Campaign and Its Future* (Washington, D.C.: American Enterprise Institute and Brookings Institution, 2000).

Sorensen, Theodore. *Kennedy* (New York: Harper & Row, 1965).

Archival Sources

John F. Kennedy Museum and Library
Dorchester Massachusetts
   Neustadt Papers
   Neustadt Transition Memos

National Archives II
College Park, Maryland
   Record Group 51, Legislative Reference Division

Truman Presidential Museum and Library
Independence, Missouri
   Richard Neustadt Papers
   Oral Histories
   White House Staff 1945 to 1953

About the Contributors

GRAHAM ALLISON is the Director of the Belfer Center for Science and International Affairs and Douglas Dillon Professor of Government (a chair previously held by Richard E. Neustadt) at Harvard's John F. Kennedy School of Government.

JONATHAN ALTER has been a Senior Editor at Newsweek since 1991, where his beat includes the Presidency; he also writes the "Conventional Wisdom Watch." His book, *The Defining Moment: FDR's Hundred Days and the Triumph of Hope,* was published in 2006.

MATTHEW J. DICKINSON is Professor of Political Science at Middlebury College. Previously he taught at Harvard University, where he also received his Ph.D. under Richard E. Neustadt. He is the author of *Bitter Harvest: FDR, Presidential Power, and the Growth of the Presidential Branch* and has published numerous articles on the Presidency, presidential decisionmaking, and presidential advisers.

HARVEY V. FINEBERG is President of the Institute of Medicine of the National Academies. After serving for thirteen years as the Dean of the Harvard School of Health, he was Provost of Harvard University from 1997 to 2001. He is the recipient of several honorary degrees and the Joseph W. Mountin Prize from the U.S. Centers for Disease Control.

DORIS KEARNS GOODWIN, a former student and colleague of Richard E. Neustadt at Harvard University, is a Pulitzer Prize–winning historian who has written extensively about the American Presidency. Her most recent work is *Team of Rivals: The Political Genius of Abraham Lincoln.*

AL GORE is a former congressman and vice president of the United States, the author of several books, and the winner of an Academy Award for his film, *An Inconvenient Truth.* He is a Fellow of the American Academy of Arts and Sciences.

CHARLES O. JONES is Hawkins Professor of Political Science at the University of Wisconsin (Emeritus) and a Nonresident Senior Fellow in Governance Studies at the Brookings Institution. He has taught at Oxford University, the University of Virginia, and the University of Pittsburgh, and has served as president of the American Political Science Association.

ANTHONY KING, the Essex County Millennium Professor of British Government at the University of Essex, U.K., is coauthor of an ongoing series, *Britain at the Polls.* A Canadian by birth, he has served on the Royal Commission on the Reform of the House of Lords and has also studied and written extensively on the American political system.

ERNEST R. MAY is Charles Warren Professor of American History in Harvard's Faculty of Arts and Sciences and a Senior Research Associate at the Kennedy School's Belfer Center for Science and International Affairs, where he serves on the Board of Directors. A former Director of the Institute of Politics and consultant to various government agencies, he is currently a member of the Director of Central Intelligence's Intelligence Science Board and of the Board of Visitors of the Joint Military Intelligence College.

ELIZABETH A. NEUSTADT holds an MBA in public management from Boston University and a doctorate in psychology from University College London. She works as an organizational consultant and is currently Head of Consultancy and Professional Development at the Tavistock Institute of Human Relations in London

ERIC REDMAN has been a logger, longshoreman, Rhodes Scholar, and writing teacher, as well as a legislative aide to Senator Warren Magnuson of Washington. He is the author of *The Dance of Legislation,* for which Richard E. Neustadt wrote the foreword. Today he practices law in Seattle, specializing in public policy and energy law.

ARTHUR SCHLESINGER JR. was a historian and writer who taught history at Harvard and later at the City University of New York. He served as Special Assistant to John F. Kennedy and wrote a detailed account of the Kennedy administration, *A Thousand Days,* for which he won his second Pulitzer Prize. Writing about the Nixon administration and its influence on the institution of the Presidency, he popularized the term "the imperial presidency" in his book by that name. He died in Manhattan in February 2007.

THEODORE C. SORENSEN is best known as President John F. Kennedy's legendary speechwriter and Special Counsel and Adviser. His biography of JFK, *Kennedy,* published in 1965, became an international bestseller. He has had a prominent career as an international lawyer, advising governments and corporations.

HARRISON WELLFORD has over twenty years' experience managing presidential transitions, having made significant contributions during the Ford-Carter, Carter-Reagan, and Bush-Clinton transitions. In 2004 he chaired John Kerry's pre-election transition team. He is the author of numerous articles and two books and is a Fellow of the National Academy of Public Administration and of the Center for Excellence in Government.

INDEX